GHOSTS OF THE TSUNAMI

RICHARD LLOYD PARRY

JONATHAN CAPE

LONDON

1 3 5 7 9 10 8 6 4 2

Jonathan Cape, an imprint of Vintage Publishing,
20 Vauxhall Bridge Road,
London SW1V 2SA

Jonathan Cape is part of the Penguin Random House
group of companies whose addresses can be found
at global.penguinrandomhouse.com.

Penguin
Random House
UK

First published in the United Kingdom by Jonathan Cape in 2017

penguin.co.uk/vintage

A CIP catalogue record for this book is available from the British Library

ISBN (hardback) 9781911214175
ISBN (trade paperback) 9781911214182

Typeset in India by Integra Software Services Pvt Ltd, Pondicherry

Maps by Darren Bennett

Printed and bound in Great Britain by Clays Ltd, St Ives PLC

Penguin Random House is committed to a sustainable future for
our business, our readers and our planet. This book is made from
Forest Stewardship Council® certified paper.

MIX
Paper from
responsible sources
FSC
www.fsc.org   FSC® C018179

For Stella and Kit

On 11 March 2011 two catastrophes struck north-east Japan. The second began in the evening, when reactors at the Fukushima Dai-ichi nuclear power plant melted down, following the failure of their cooling systems. Explosions in three of the reactors scattered radioactive fallout across the countryside. More than 200,000 people fled their homes. But, thanks to a swift evacuation and a good deal of luck, nobody died as a result of the radiation. It is too soon to be sure about the long-term consequences of Fukushima – but it may turn out that nobody ever will.

The earthquake and tsunami that set off the nuclear disaster had a more immediate effect on human life. By the time the sea retreated, more than 18,500 people had been crushed, burned to death or drowned. It was the greatest single loss of life in Japan since the atomic bombing of Nagasaki in 1945.

This book is about the first disaster: the tsunami.

Contents

Maps

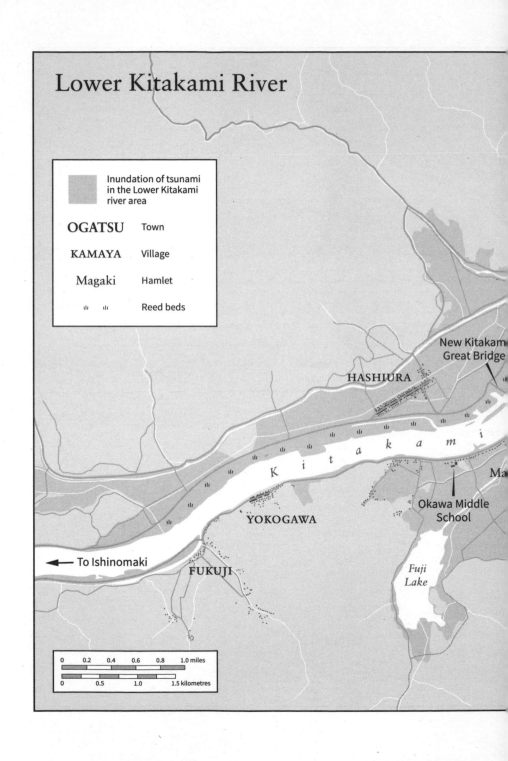

Lower Kitakami River

Inundation of tsunami in the Lower Kitakami river area

OGATSU Town

KAMAYA Village

Magaki Hamlet

Reed beds

New Kitakam
Great Bridge

HASHIURA

Kitakami

Ma

Okawa Middle
School

YOKOGAWA

← To Ishinomaki

FUKUJI

_Fuji
Lake_

| 0 | 0.2 | 0.4 | 0.6 | 0.8 | 1.0 miles |

| 0 | 0.5 | 1.0 | 1.5 kilometres |

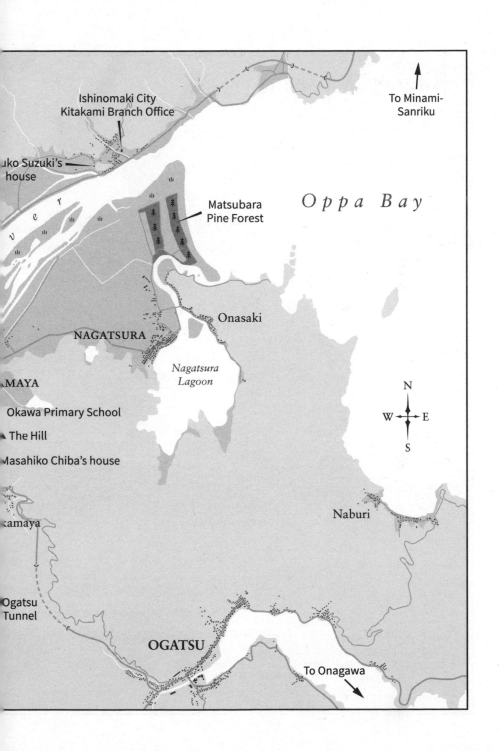

Ishinomaki City
Kitakami Branch Office

...uko Suzuki's
house

To Minami-
Sanriku

O p p a   B a y

Matsubara
Pine Forest

Onasaki

NAGATSURA

*Nagatsura
Lagoon*

...MAYA

Okawa Primary School

The Hill

...Masahiko Chiba's house

...amaya

Ogatsu
Tunnel

N
W — E
S

Naburi

OGATSU

To Onagawa

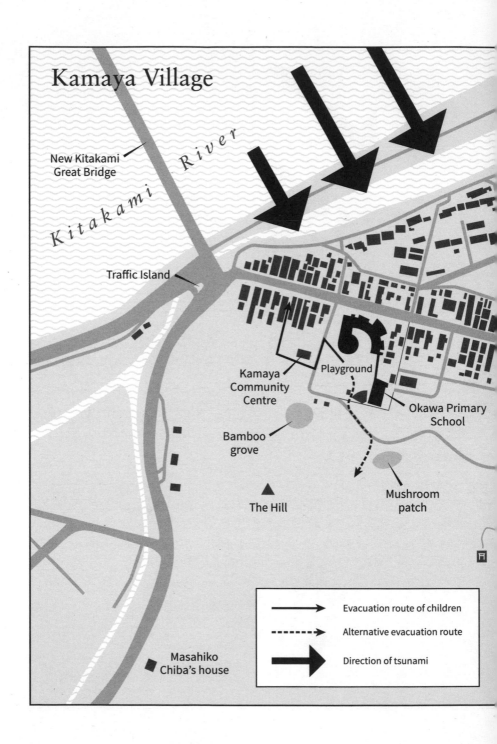

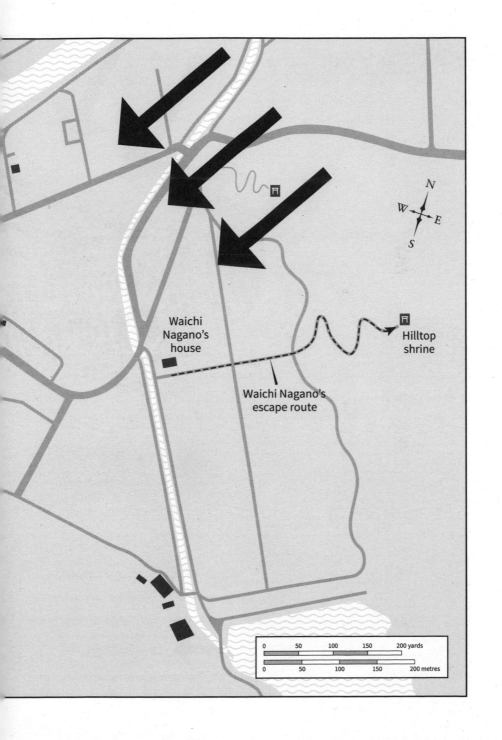

Waichi
Nagano's
house

Hilltop
shrine

Waichi Nagano's
escape route

N
W · E
S

0   50   100   150   200 yards

0   50   100   150   200 metres

Japan

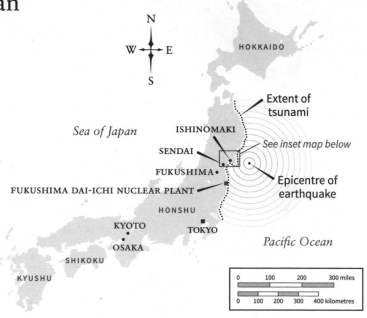

N
W E
S

HOKKAIDO

Sea of Japan

Extent of
tsunami

ISHINOMAKI

See inset map below

SENDAI

FUKUSHIMA

Epicentre of
earthquake

FUKUSHIMA DAI-ICHI NUCLEAR PLANT

HONSHU

KYOTO

TOKYO

OSAKA

Pacific Ocean

SHIKOKU

KYUSHU

| 0 | 100 | 200 | 300 miles |
| 0 | 100 | 200 | 300 | 400 kilometres |

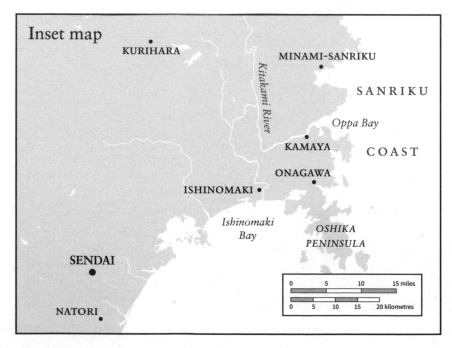

Inset map

KURIHARA

MINAMI-SANRIKU

Kitakami River

S A N R I K U

Oppa Bay

KAMAYA

C O A S T

ONAGAWA

ISHINOMAKI

*Ishinomaki
Bay*

*OSHIKA
PENINSULA*

SENDAI

NATORI

| 0 | 5 | 10 | 15 miles |
| 0 | 5 | 10 | 15 | 20 kilometres |

What is this flesh I purchased with my pains,
This fallen star my milk sustains,
This love that makes my heart's blood stop
Or strikes a sudden chill into my bones
And bids my hair stand up?

W. B. Yeats

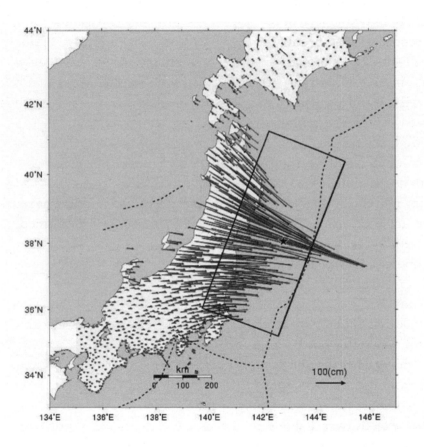

Prologue: Solid Vapour

The eleventh of March 2011 was a cold, sunny Friday, and it was the day I saw the face of my son for the first time. I was in a clinic in central Tokyo, peering at the images on a small screen. Beside me, F—— lay, exposed, on the examination bed. Her oval belly was smeared with transparent gel; against it, the doctor pressed a glowing wand of plastic. As the wand moved, the images on the screen shifted and jumped.

We knew what to look for, but it was still astonishing to see so much of the small creature: the familiar top-heavy outline; the heart, with its flickering chambers; brain, spine, individual fingers, and so much movement – paddling arms, bucking legs and nodding head. The angle of vision altered and revealed at once a well-formed, unearthly face, which gave a charming and very human yawn. Our second child – our boy, although we did not know this yet – was still in there, still patiently alive.

Outside the clinic it was chilly, gusty and bright, and the wide avenue was filling with midday shoppers and workers coming out of the offices for lunch. We pushed our toddler daughter to a café and showed her the murky photograph of her sibling-to-be, printed out from the scanner's screen.

Two hours later, I was sitting at my desk in a tenth-floor office. What exactly was I doing at the moment it began? Writing an email? Reading the newspaper? Looking out of the window? All that I remember of the hours before are those moments in front of the screen, which had already made the day unforgettable, and the sensation of looking into the face of my son, at the halfway point between his conception and his birth.

* * *

I had lived in Japan for sixteen years, and I knew, or believed that I knew, a good deal about earthquakes. I had certainly experienced enough of them – since 1995, when I settled in Tokyo, 17,257 tremors had been felt in the capital alone. A spate of them had occurred two days earlier. I had sat out the shaking, monitored the measurements of magnitude and intensity, and reported them online with a jauntiness that now makes me ashamed:

@dicklp
Wed Mar 09 2011 11:51:51
Earthquake!

Wed Mar 09 2011 11:53:14
Epicentre, Miyagi Prefecture. Tsunami warning in place on northern Pacific coast. In Tokyo, we are shaken, but not stirred.

Wed Mar 09 2011 12:01:04
More tremors …

Wed Mar 09 2011 12:16:56
@LiverpolitanNYC All fine here, thanks. Its wobble was worse than its bite.

Wed Mar 09 2011 16:09:39
Latest on today's Japan earthquake horror: 10cm tsunami reported in Iwate Prefecture. That's almost as deep as my washing-up water.

The following day there had been another strong tremor in the same zone of the Pacific Ocean off north-east Japan. This one, too, could be felt as far away as Tokyo, but even close to the epicentre it caused no injury or significant damage. 'The Thursday morning quake brought the number of quakes felt in Japan since Wednesday to more than thirty,' Kyodo news agency reported; and plenty of them were strong tremors, not the subterranean shivers detectable only by scientific instruments. The seismologists warned of the potential for a 'powerful aftershock' in the next week or so, although 'crustal activities' were expected to subside.

Clusters of proximate earthquakes are known as 'swarms', and they can be the precursor to larger tremors and even volcanic eruptions. But although many seismic disasters are preceded by such omens, the converse is not true; most swarms buzz past without any destructive crescendo. I had reported on this phenomenon a few years earlier, when a swarm of earthquakes hinted at a potential eruption of Mount Fuji. Nothing of the kind had happened then; clusters of lesser earthquakes continued to come and go; and there was no reason for particular attention or alarm this week.

Not that there was much else happening in Japan that day, certainly not of international interest. The prime minister was resisting half-hearted demands that he resign over a political funding scandal. The governor of Tokyo was expected to announce whether he would stand for another term. *Ibaraki Airport marks first anniversary*, noted one of the news agency's headlines. *Snack maker debuts on Tokyo Stock Exchange*, mumbled another. Then, at 2.48 p.m., came an urgent single-line bulletin: *BREAKING NEWS: Powerful quake rocks Japan.*

I had felt it about a minute earlier. It began mildly and familiarly enough with gentle, but unmistakable, vibrations, transmitted upwards through the floor of the office, followed by a side-to-side swaying. With the motion came a distinctive sound – the glassy tinkling of the window blinds as their vinyl ends buffeted against one another. The same thing had happened two days earlier and passed within moments. So even when the glass in the windows began to rattle, I stayed in my chair.

@dicklp
Fri Mar 11 2011 14:47:52
Another earthquake in Tokyo …

Fri Mar 11 2011 14:47:59
Strong one …

Fri Mar 11 2011 14:48:51
strongest I've ever known in 16 yers …

By the time the sliding drawers of the filing cabinets gaped open, my sangfroid, as well as my typing, was beginning to fail me. From the tenth-floor window I could see a striped red-and-white telecommunications mast on the roof of a building a hundred yards away. I told myself: 'When that mast starts to wobble, I'll move.' As the thought took form in my mind, I noticed that a much closer structure, an arm of the same building in which I was sitting, was flexing visibly. Very quickly indeed I bent myself into the narrow space beneath my desk.

Later I read that the vibrations had lasted for six minutes. But while they continued, time passed in an unfamiliar way. The chinking of the blinds, the buzzing of the glass and the deep rocking motion generated an atmosphere of dreamlike unreality; by the time I emerged from my funk hole, I had little sense of how long I had been there. It was not the shaking itself that was frightening, but the way it continued to become stronger, with no way of knowing when it would end. Now books were slumping on the shelves. Now a marker board fell off a partition. The building, a nondescript twelve-storey structure which had never seemed particularly old or new, sturdy or frail, was generating low groans from deep within its innards. It was a sound such as one hardly ever hears, a heart-sickening noise suggesting deep and mortal distress, like the death-sound of a dying monster. It went on long enough for me to form distinct images about what would happen in the next stage of the earthquake's intensification: the toppling of shelves and cabinets, the exploding of glass, the collapse of the ceiling onto the floor, the floor itself giving way, and the sensation both of falling and of being crushed.

At a point difficult to define, the tremors began to ease. The building's moans faded to muttering. My heartbeat slowed. My balance, I found, had been mildly upset and, like a passenger stepping off a boat, it was hard to tell whether motion had ceased completely. Five minutes later, the cords hanging from the blinds were still wagging feebly.

Over the internal loudspeakers, an announcement from the Disaster Counter-Measures Room – every big building in Tokyo has one – assured us that the structure was safe and that we should stay inside.

@dicklp
Fri Mar 11 14:59:44
I'm fine. A frighteningly strong quake. Aftershocks. Fires round Tokyo bay.

In Japan there is no excuse for not being prepared for earthquakes, and in my small office we had taken the recommended precautions. There were no heavy picture frames; the shelves and cabinets were bolted to the walls. Apart from a few fallen books and a general shifting of its contents, the room was in good order. Even the television, the most top-heavy object in the room, remained undisplaced. My Japanese colleague turned it on. Already, all channels were showing the same image: the map of Japan, its Pacific coastline banded with colours, red indicating an imminent danger of tsunami. The epicentre, marked by a cross, was upper right, off the north-east of the main island of Honshu. It was the same area that had been swarming these past days, the region of Japan known as Tohoku.*

---

* Pronounced 'Tour-Hock-oo', with the last syllable short and abrupt.

I was dialling and redialling F——'s number, without success. The problem was not that the infrastructure was damaged, but that everyone in eastern Japan was simultaneously using his or her mobile phone. I got through by landline to the lady who looked after our nineteen-month-old daughter; the two of them were wobbly but unhurt, and still sheltering beneath the dining-room table. F——, when I finally connected to her, was in her own office, brushing up the glass from a fallen picture frame. Our conversation was punctuated by pauses, as each of us in our distinct districts of the city experienced separately the aftershocks that had begun minutes after the mother quake.

The lifts were suspended, so I walked down nine flights of stairs to inspect the district of shops and offices immediately around the building. There was almost no visible damage. The stripy pole in front of an old-fashioned barber's shop lolled at an angle. I saw one crack in a window of plate glass, and a perforated gash in a wall of plaster. The streets were crowded with evacuated office workers, many of them wearing the white plastic helmets that Japanese companies provide for just such an occasion. Above the density of city buildings, a distant line of black smoke was visible in the east, where a petrol refinery had caught fire. Later, some accounts gave the impression that the earthquake had been a moment of hysteria in Tokyo, in which large numbers of people experienced the sensation of a close brush with death. They were exaggerations. Modern engineering and strict building laws, evolved out of centuries of seismic destruction, had passed the test. A fleeting spasm of alarm was followed by hours of disruption, inconvenience and boredom. But the prevailing emotion was bemused resignation rather than panic.

A man in an old-fashioned ceramics shop, where a vase sold for £5,000, had not lost a single plate. We talked to a group of elderly ladies in kimono who had been watching a play in the nearby kabuki theatre when the earthquake struck. 'They'd just started the last act, and people cried out,' one of them said. 'But the actors kept going – they didn't hesitate at all. I thought it would subside, but it went on and on, and everyone stood up and started flooding out of the door.' The star performers, the famous kabuki actors Kikugoro Onoe and Kichiemon Nakamura, bowed deeply to the audience as they fled, apologising for the interruption.

Fri Mar 11 16:26:40
Central Tokyo calm and undamaged. In 30 mins stroll in Ginza I saw one cracked window and a few walls.

Fri Mar 11 16:28:56
Seems to be just one fire in an oil facility in Chiba Prefecture.

Fri Mar 11 16:40:31
Eleven nuke power plants shut down in Japan. No problems reported after quakes.

Fri Mar 11 17:47:25
I've lost count of aftershocks. 15 or more. Latest one was from a different epicentre to 1st big quake, accdng to Jpn TV.

Fri Mar 11 18:20:10
To anyone struggling to get through to Tokyo – use Skype. Internet in Tokyo seems fine.

Back in the office, we turned to the television again. Already Japan's richly resourced broadcasters were mobilising aeroplanes, helicopters and manpower. The foreign channels, too, had given over their programming to rolling coverage of the situation, with that thinly disguised lust which appalling news excites in cable-news producers. I began to file reports for my newspaper's website, attempting to make sense of the packets of information that were arriving in the form of images, sounds and text, through cable,

satellite, internet, fax and telephone. But the facts were still frustrat-
ingly vague. An earthquake had come and gone, and the human
response to it was obvious enough: a disaster unit established at
the prime minister's office; airports, railways and highways shut
down. Yet what actual damage had been done so far? There were
patchy reports of fires, like the one at the oil refinery. But for
the first few hours the seismologists could not even agree on the
magnitude of the earthquake; and from the Tohoku coast itself
came only silence.

Casualty figures were especially elusive. At 6.30 p.m., the
television news was reporting twenty-three killed. By nine o'clock,
the figure had risen to sixty-one and, after midnight, the news
agencies were still speaking of sixty-four deaths. Clearly, these
numbers were going to increase as communications were restored.
But it also seemed obvious that in a situation such as this there
was a tendency to irrational pessimism and to embrace the very
worst imaginable possibility; and that probably, in the end, it
wouldn't be so bad as all that.

@dicklp
Fri Mar 11 17:58:43
No reports of deaths in Tokyo so far. My hunch is that there will
be scores, perhaps low hundreds in NE Japan, but no more. Not
megadeath.

* * *

There are several aerial films of the incoming tsunami, but the one
that plays and replays in my imagination was shot above the town
of Natori, south of the city of Sendai. It begins over land rather than
sea, with a view of dun winter paddy fields. Something is moving
across the landscape as if it is alive, a brown-snouted animal hungrily
bounding over the earth. Its head is a scum of splintered debris;
entire cars bob along on its back. It seems to steam and smoke as

it moves; its body looks less like water or mud than a kind of solid vapour. And then a large boat can be seen riding it inland, hundreds of yards from the sea, and – unbelievably – blue-tiled houses, still structurally intact, spinning across the inundated fields with orange flames dancing on their roofs. The creature turns a road into a river, then swallows it whole, and then it is raging over more fields and roads towards a village and a highway thick with cars. One driver is accelerating ahead of it, racing to escape – before the car and its occupants are gobbled up by the wave.

It was the biggest earthquake ever known to have struck Japan, and the fourth most powerful in the history of seismology. It knocked the Earth six and a half inches off its axis; it moved Japan thirteen feet closer to America. In the tsunami that followed, more than 18,000 people were killed. At its peak, the water was 120 feet high. Half a million people were driven out of their homes. Three reactors in the Fukushima Dai-ichi power station melted down, spilling their radioactivity across the countryside, the world's worst nuclear accident since Chernobyl. The earthquake and tsunami caused more than $210 billion of damage, making it the most costly natural disaster ever.

It was Japan's greatest crisis since the Second World War. It ended the career of one prime minister and contributed to the demise of another. The damage caused by the tsunami disrupted manufacturing by some of the world's biggest corporations. The nuclear disaster caused weeks of power cuts, affecting millions of people. As a result, Japan's remaining nuclear reactors – all fifty of them – were shut down. Hundreds of thousands of people took to the streets in anti-nuclear demonstrations; as a consequence of what happened in Fukushima, the governments of Germany, Italy, and Switzerland abandoned nuclear power altogether.

The earth around the nuclear plant will be contaminated for decades. The villages and towns destroyed by the tsunami may never be rebuilt. Pain and anxiety proliferated in ways that are still difficult to measure, among people remote from the destructive events. Farmers, suddenly unable to sell their produce, committed suicide. Blameless workers in electricity companies found themselves the object of abuse and discrimination. A generalised dread took hold, the fear of an invisible poison spread through air, through water – even, it was said, through a mother's milk. Among expatriates, it manifested itself as outright panic. Families, companies, embassies abandoned even Tokyo, 140 miles away.

Few of these facts were clear on that evening, as I sat in my office on the tenth floor. But they were becoming obvious the following morning. By then, I was driving from Tokyo towards the ruined coast. I would spend weeks in Tohoku, travelling up and down the strip of land, three miles deep in some places, which had been consumed by the water. I visited a hospital where the wards at night were lit by candles; a hundred yards away, to add to the atmosphere of apocalypse, burning industrial oil tanks sent columns of flame high into the air. I saw towns that had been first flooded, then incinerated; cars that had been lifted up and dropped onto the roofs of high buildings; and iron ocean-going ships deposited in city streets.

Cautiously I entered the ghostly exclusion zone around the nuclear plant, where cows were dying of thirst in the fields, and the abandoned villages were inhabited by packs of pet dogs, gradually turning wild; masked, gloved and hooded in a protective suit, I entered the broken plant myself. I interviewed survivors, evacuees, politicians and nuclear experts, and reported day by day on the feckless squirming of the Japanese authorities. I wrote scores of newspaper articles, hundreds of fizzy Tweets and was interviewed on radio and television. And yet the experience felt like a disordered dream.

Those who work in zones of war and disaster acquire after a time the knack of detachment. This is professional necessity: no doctor, aid worker or reporter can do his job if he is crushed by the spectacle of death and suffering. The trick is to preserve compassion, without bearing each individual tragedy as your own; and I had mastered this technique. I knew the facts of what had happened, and I knew they were appalling. But at my core, I was not appalled.

'All at once . . . something we could only have imagined was upon us – and we could still only imagine it,' wrote Philip Gourevitch. 'That is what fascinates me most in existence: the peculiar necessity of imagining what is, in fact, real.' The events that constituted the disaster were so diverse, and so vast in their implications, that I never felt that I was doing the story justice. It was like a huge and awkwardly shaped package without corners or handles: however many different ways I tried, it was impossible to hoist it off the ground. In the weeks afterwards, I felt wonder, pity and sadness. But for much of the time I experienced a numb detachment and the troubling sense of having completely missed the point.

It was quite late on, the summer after the tsunami, when I heard about a small community on the coast that had suffered an exceptional tragedy. Its name was Okawa; it lay in a forgotten fold of Japan, below hills and among rice fields, close to the mouth of a great river. I travelled to this obscure place, and spent days and weeks there. In the years which followed, I encountered many survivors and stories of the tsunami, but it was to Okawa that I returned time and again. And it was there, at the school, that I eventually became able to imagine.

PART 1

THE SCHOOL BENEATH THE WAVE

Having Gone, I Will Come

The first time I met her, in the big wooden house at the foot of the hills, Sayomi Shito recalled the night when her youngest daughter, Chisato, sat suddenly up in bed and cried out, 'The school has gone.'

'She was asleep,' her mother told me. 'And then she woke up in tears. I asked her, "Why? What do you mean 'gone'?" She said, "A big earthquake." She was really shouting. She used to sleepwalk occasionally, and she used to mutter odd things now and then. Sometimes she'd get up and walk around, not knowing what she was doing, and I had to guide her back to bed. But she had never had a fright like that before.'

It wasn't that Chisato, who was eleven, was particularly afraid of earthquakes. A few weeks after her nightmare, on 9 March 2011, there was a strong tremor, which shook the concrete walls of Okawa Primary School, where she was a pupil – the onset of the swarm that I also experienced 220 miles away in Tokyo. Chisato and the other children had crawled under their desks while the shaking continued, then put on their plastic helmets, followed their teachers out to the playground and stood in neat lines while their names were called out and ticked off. But rumbles large and small were common all over Japan, and at home that evening she had not even mentioned it.

Sayomi Shito was curly-haired, round-faced and bespectacled, an unabashed, confiding woman in her mid-forties. Japanese conventions of restraint and politesse sometimes made hard work of interviews, but Sayomi was an effusive talker, with a droll and gossipy sense of humour. I spent long mornings at her home, in a tide of jokes, cakes, biscuits and cups of tea. She could talk unprompted for an hour at a stretch, frowning, smiling and shaking her head as if taken aback by her own recollection. Some people are cast adrift by loss, and when Sayomi spoke of her grief, the pain was as intense as anyone's. But anger and indignation had kept her tethered, and bred in her a scathing self-confidence.

The Shitos (their name was pronounced 'Sh'tore', like a cross between 'shore' and 'store') were a very close family. Sayomi's older son and daughter, Kenya and Tomoka, were fifteen and thirteen, but the children all still slept on mattresses alongside their parents in the big room on the upper floor. That Friday, 11 March, Sayomi had risen as usual at quarter past six. It was the day of her son's graduation ceremony from middle school, and her thoughts were filled with mundane, practical matters. 'I used to wake Chisato after everyone else had got up,' she said. 'I'd sit her on my knee and pat her back, and hug her like a koala bear, and she'd lean into me. It was something I liked to do every morning. I'd hug her, and say, "Wakey, wakey" and we'd start the day. It was our secret moment. But that day she got up on her own.'

Chisato had been out of sorts that morning. It came out later that she had quarrelled, in trivial, childish fashion, with her older brother and sister. In the kitchen she prepared breakfast for herself; Sayomi still remembered hearing the *ting* of the grill when the toast was ready. The school bus reached the stop around the corner at 6.56, and Chisato always left the house exactly three minutes before. 'She walked past me with her bag on her shoulder, and I realised that I hadn't talked to her yet,' Sayomi remembered. 'So I said, "Chi, my love, wait a moment. What's up? Not so happy today?" She said, "It's nothing," but rather gloomily. Some days,

I used to give her a hug before she went out. That morning, to cheer her up, I gave her a high five. But she was looking at the ground when she walked away.'

In Japanese, domestic leave-taking follows an unvarying formula. The person departing says *itte kimasu*, which means literally, 'Having gone, I will come back.' Those who remain respond with *itte rasshai*, which means 'Having gone, be back.' *Sayonara*, the word that foreigners are taught is the Japanese for 'goodbye', is too final for most occasions, implying a prolonged or indefinite separation. *Itte kimasu* contains a different emotional charge: the promise of an intended return.

All along the lowest reach of the Kitakami River, from the lagoon in the east to the hills in the west, with varying degrees of alacrity and reluctance, young pupils of Okawa Primary School and their parents were conducting the same exchange.

– *Itte kimasu*.
– *Itte rasshai!*

Even before it began, Sayomi told me, Chisato's life had had about it something fated and magical. She had been conceived on Sayomi's thirty-third birthday; she was born on Christmas Eve 1999, a sentimental day even in Japan, where practising Christians are few. Sayomi went into labour in the afternoon; within an hour, she was back in her bed, eating Christmas cake. The following day, on Christmas morning, the ground was covered in immaculate snow; and a week later, the world celebrated the beginning of the third millennium. The infant Chisato was as undemanding in the world as she had been entering it. 'She was always with me,' Sayomi said. 'In the sling on my front. On my back, when I was cooking. Beside me, in the child seat in the car, or in my lap when I was sitting down. It was as if she was attached to my skin. And she always slept beside me, in the same room, at my right hand, up until that day.'

Fukuji was a gathering of hamlets around a triangular expanse of paddy fields. On two sides were low hills, forested densely with pine; the Shito family house stood on their lowest slope. On the third, northern side was the great Kitakami River, the longest and widest in northern Japan, flowing east towards the Pacific, six miles away. Within a few minutes of the Shitos' home, depending on the season, you could hike, toboggan, skate, hunt, fish and swim in fresh or salt water. Chisato played with dolls and drew pictures with her sister, but what she liked most was to run at large with her friends Mizuho and Aika, and the dog and cat that belonged to the old lady next door.

She had what her mother identified as a sixth sense. 'She used to do things for you before you said you wanted them,' Sayomi said. 'She had that gift of anticipation. For example, my husband is a joiner. The first time Chisato saw him do his carpentry at home she was standing watching him. And she'd know what tool or material he needed next. She'd say, "Here you are, Dad," and pass it to him. He'd say, "How much she understands! She's a remarkable girl."'

Her friends used to tease Chisato by calling her 'the security camera', because she was aware of things to which other eleven-year-olds were oblivious. She noticed, before the other girls, when a gang of boys in the class went into a sniggering cluster, plotting some prank. She knew who had a crush on whom, and whether the feeling was reciprocated. Okawa Primary School was a small place, with barely a hundred children; in Chisato's fifth-year class there were just fifteen. It was a warm, close, oppressively intimate arrangement, unforgiving of anyone who stood apart. Chisato hated it.

'There was no doubt about it,' said Sayomi. 'She hated the teachers. She used to say that school is where teachers tell you lies. But she never refused to go. She said, "If I miss school, it's you who'll get into trouble." She knew that she had to do something she didn't want to do.'

Sayomi said, 'I feel very bad now about letting her go to school with such a feeling. But I didn't want to be the mother who stops her child's education. It wasn't that she was bullied, or anything like that. But perhaps there are children who are better off staying at home, who love their mum more than being with their friends. Everyone you talk to says, "At least when it happened my child was at the school she loved, with the friends she loved, and the teachers she loved." Of course, parents want to believe that. But if they asked their kids, "Do you really like that school? Do you really love those teachers?" then not all of them would say yes.'

Many people spoke of it as just another day, but Sayomi Shito remembered a strangeness about that Friday.

After breakfast, she had driven to the local middle school for her son Kenya's graduation ceremony. She took the narrow road across the fields, turned right onto the highway along the river, and passed through the larger village of Yokogawa. Just beyond the village shrine, a small hill bulged out, forcing the road hard up against the water and blocking the view of its lower reaches. Beyond it a wide and magnificent vista opened up, of the broad river with its deep reed beds and stubbled brown paddies on both sides, and huge blue skies above green hills. In the distance was the low line of the New Kitakami Great Bridge, 600 yards across, connecting Okawa in the south with the Kitakami district on the northern bank.

After the ceremony, Sayomi and Kenya drove further down the river to the next village, where a modest celebration was being held for the middle-school graduates. This was Kamaya, where Okawa Primary School was also situated. Twenty or thirty teenagers and their mothers were gathering in a hall, virtually across the road from Chisato's classroom. Friends who might not see one another again said their goodbyes and exchanged gifts; there was a table of comforting home-cooked foods. Sayomi expected the event to go on until the mid-afternoon, but soon after two o'clock people began to drift away. Kenya wanted to go home. But first there was the question of what to do about Chisato.

Lessons at Okawa Primary School finished at 2.30, but it was always another ten or fifteen minutes before anyone began to leave, as the children gathered up their things, and the teachers handed out notices or made announcements. Should they linger in wait for Chisato, for what might be another half-hour? Or should they go home now, and leave her to take the bus as usual? Sayomi stood by her car in front of the school, considering this small dilemma. And, as she remembered it later, a powerful sense of the uncanny overcame her, in this, the last hour of the old world. 'It had been a clear, fine day until noon,' she said. 'By the time the party came to an end, it was already becoming cloudy, but there was no wind. Not a single leaf was moving on the trees. I couldn't sense any life at all. It was as if a film had stopped, as if time had stopped. It was an uncomfortable atmosphere, not the atmosphere of an ordinary day. I didn't like the fact that I couldn't hear the children in the school – even when they were in their lessons, you could always hear the voices of the little ones. Normally, I might have walked in and said, "I popped in to pick up my daughter." But the school felt . . . isolated.'

I asked Sayomi what explained this curious atmosphere. She said, 'Living here in this countryside, people coexist with nature. With animals, with plants, with all of this environment. When the wind blows, I hear the sound of the trees, and I know from that sound the condition of the wind. When it's about to snow, I sense the snow in the air. I feel by instinct the character of the atmosphere surrounding me. That air and that atmosphere are important, almost more important than people. I think Chisato was a girl who also had those instincts.

'But then Kenya said, "Shall we go?" And I thought that it was time to go home. Perhaps it was some kind of intuition that I had to leave. Perhaps that was it. But what I said to myself was: "If we go home now, he will have more time to see his friends." So we went home.'

Sayomi was upstairs changing when the shock struck. Her older daughter, Tomoka, had been at home when they returned and had had no lunch. Sayomi set a pan of noodles on the flame, and went to her room. As soon as the shaking began, at 2.46 p.m., she shouted down to the children to turn off the stove and to get outside. Her keenest anxiety was not for them, but for her elderly parents, who lived with the family on the ground floor. Sayomi's mother was frail and slow; her father was both mildly confused and very stubborn. She ran downstairs to find him attempting to gather up the polished black funeral tablets of the family's dead ancestors, which were tumbling from the household Buddhist altar. Sayomi gave up trying to reason with him and stumbled outside, to the big tree where the rest of the family had gathered.

'The shaking was so strong, I couldn't stand up,' she said. 'Even outside, crouching down, we were almost falling over. I looked at the metal shutters on the garage – they had ripples going through them. The electricity lines and poles were swaying. It was as if the whole world was collapsing – it was like the special effects in a film about the end of the world. I was amazed that the house didn't fall down. I tried to get the kids into the car, but I couldn't even get the door open. Even holding on to the car, I was afraid that it was going to roll over. So I told the children, "Stay away from the car," and then all that that we could do was crouch on the ground.'

She remembered being conscious of sounds, and of their absence. Despite the proximity of the forest, there was no birdsong, or any sign of birds on the wing. But the next-door neighbour's dog, a placid animal and a favourite of Chisato, was barking raucously, while the cat pelted into the hills and out of sight. 'It felt as if it continued for a long time, perhaps five minutes,' Sayomi said. 'And the feeling of being shaken carried on, even after the shaking had stopped. The electricity poles and wires were still wobbling, so it was difficult to know whether the earth was still moving or whether it was the trembling in myself. The children were upset. Kenya was looking round and shouting, "Grandpa! What happened to Grandpa?"'

The old man finally tottered from the house, without his ancestors.

But now the poles and wires and shutters were vibrating again, in the first of a long succession of aftershocks. Sayomi herded her parents and the children into the car, and drove down the lane to a spot in the rice fields where much of the population of Fukuji was already converging. Chairs and mattresses were being laid out for children and old people, and neighbours were exclaiming to one another over what had happened. But from this vantage point, it was clear that any physical damage had been remarkably slight. Apart from the displacement of a few roof tiles, none of the houses in the area, as far as Sayomi could tell, had collapsed or suffered serious damage. There was wonder, and a residue of alarm, but no one was panicking or hysterical. Like the reflection of the sky in rippling water, normality seemed steadily to be reasserting itself.

Sayomi sent a text message to her husband, reporting on the family's situation, and received one in return. The building site where Takahiro was working had been thrown into disarray by the shaking, but he was unhurt. She looked around, at friends and neighbours performing acts of kindness, a community spontaneously organising itself to help the old, young and weak. It occurred to her then that the returning bus, which would bring Chisato home from school, was due at any moment. After settling her parents and children among their neighbours, she drove the few hundred yards to the river to meet it.

* * *

Half a dozen cars had pulled up on the main road along the river; their drivers stood beside them, discussing the situation. Wood from a timber yard was said to have spilled onto the road up ahead, making the way hazardous. None of the drivers had seen the obstruction for himself. But none made any move to investigate. People were calm; none gave any sign of impatience or trepidation. But in the inertness of the scene, Sayomi intuited anxiety and strain. She tried to text her husband again. Immediately after the earthquake, messages had gone through without difficulty, although voice calls were impossible. But now the network had shut down.

Over the next hour, Sayomi drove backwards and forwards between the road, where she waited for the appearance of the school bus, and the rice field, where she checked on the well-being of her family. As she shuttled to and fro, the soothing sense of normality winning out over disaster drained rapidly away.

Sayomi's attention was drawn to one of the channels that connected with the great river, part of a network of slack creeks that irrigated the paddies. Its level rose and fell with the cycles of the rice crop, but it was never completely dry. Now, though, the water in it had almost entirely disappeared; the muddy bottom was visible, glistening greyly. The next time she looked, the situation had reversed: the stream was engorged with surging water from the river, and pieces of dark unidentifiable debris were racing along its churning surface. Soon, the adjoining fields were flooded with water. The spectacle was remarkable enough for Sayomi to make a film of it on her mobile phone. The brief clip recorded the time, 3.58 p.m., and a snatch of news from the car radio: '. . . as a result of the tsunami which hit Onagawa, houses are reported to have been inundated up to their roofs and vehicles have been washed away. Maintain strict vigilance . . .'

The word 'tsunami' was well known to Sayomi, of course; stronger earthquakes, if they occurred under the sea, were commonly followed by a tsunami warning. The size of the waves would be reported on the television as they came in: thirty inches, fifteen inches, four inches – phenomena scarcely visible to the untrained eye, often measurable only by harbour gauges. But the radio was speaking of Ō-*tsunami* – a 'super-tsunami', twenty feet high – and all of this in Onagawa, a fishing port just an hour's drive to the south. 'I knew that twenty feet was big, although knowing it is different from feeling it,' Sayomi said. 'But to hear that it was capable of washing away cars, that brought it home. I tried to stay calm. There was nothing else I could do.'

Sayomi went back to the main road and waited for her daughter, as dusk swallowed up the day.

She had been standing in front of Okawa Primary School an hour and a half ago; it should have been the most natural thing in the world to drive back down the road along the river to collect Chisato. It was only four miles downstream, but there were no cars at all coming from that direction. The drivers loitering at the lock said that the way was dangerous, although no one seemed willing to explain exactly why. Wet, sleety snow had begun to fall. The river was behaving as if it was possessed. The surface of the water was bulging and flexing like the muscles beneath the skin of an athlete; large, irregularly shaped objects were dimly visible on its surface. Sayomi lingered by the river, watching the road, until after it was dark.

At home, she found her house intact, but littered with fallen and broken objects, and without electricity, gas or water. She improvised a meal out of leftovers, and forced herself not to worry about Chisato. Plenty of families in Fukuji were waiting for children who had not come back from the primary school, and none showed excessive concern. Chisato's teachers were trained to deal with emergencies. The concrete school was built more strongly than the wooden houses of Fukuji, all of which had ridden out the earthquake. Most reassuring to Sayomi, who had attended the school herself, was its position immediately in front of a 700-foot hill. A track, rising from the back of the playground, ascended quickly to a point beyond the reach of even a 'super-tsunami'. Without electricity, people in Fukuji had no access to television or the Internet; none had yet seen the images of the devouring wave, which were being played over and again across the world. Instead, they listened to the local radio station, which was retailing the cautious, official casualty figures: scores confirmed dead, hundreds more likely. Then came an unambiguous report, which everyone waiting up that evening remembered: 200 people, locals and children, were sheltering in Okawa Primary School, cut off and awaiting rescue.

Sayomi's relief at hearing this was a measure of the anxiety that she had been reluctant to admit even to herself. 'One of the other mums was saying that they were probably staying in the upper gallery of the gym, and enjoying a pyjama party,' Sayomi remembered. 'We said to one another, "Poor old Chisato. She's going to be hungry and cold." We were no more worried than that.'

But when Takahiro finally reached home that night, after an exhausting journey along cracked and congested roads, the first thing she said to him was, 'Chisato's not back.'

The family spent the night in the car, as a precaution against aftershocks. Squeezed side by side in the upright seats, no one slept much. Sayomi was kept awake by a single phrase, which sounded over and over in her head: 'Chisato's not here, Chisato's not here, Chisato's not here.'

It was bitterly cold, and the darkness was overwhelming. Everyone who lived through that night was amazed by the intense clarity of the sky overhead and the brightness of the stars. They found themselves in a land without power, television, telephones, a place suddenly plucked up and folded into a pocket of time, disconnected from the twenty-first century.

Sayomi got up at dawn, stiff and cold. Gas and water had been restored, so that she could at least make tea and cook. Then came news that spread excitedly among the mothers of Okawa Primary School. A helicopter was flying there to pick up the trapped children and to lift them out. Takahiro and the other men of the village were preparing a place for it to land. Chisato was coming home at last.

Where Are the Children?

Daisuke Konno was a stalwart of the judo team and captain of the sixth-year class, but he was a gentle, soft-hearted boy and that day he didn't want to go to school, either. There was barely a week to go until graduation; his mother, Hitomi, pushed him out of the door. It was a cold morning in the unreliable period between winter and spring. But there was nothing ominous about it, and neither mother nor son was the kind to be troubled by supernatural intimations of disaster. Photographs of Daisuke show a cheery round face with a self-deprecating smile. 'He loved judo,' Hitomi said. 'And to his friends he put on a tough face. But to me, back at home, he used to complain about the pain of being thrown. And at school it seems that a group of the boys had been told off by the teacher. That was the only reason he didn't want to go.'

– *Itte kimasu*, said the reluctant Daisuke.

– *Itte rasshai*, Hitomi responded.

The Konno family lived in the village of Magaki, three miles downstream of Sayomi's home in Fukuji. The bus passed through here, but Okawa Primary School was close enough that the children of Magaki made the journey by foot. Daisuke (his name was pronounced 'Dice-keh') walked along the river's edge with a slouching gang of classmates. The river bank at this point was hardly elevated at all; the breadth of the road was all that separated the houses from the lapping water.

Hitomi's husband had already gone to work. She followed soon after her son, leaving behind her parents-in-law and two teenage daughters. She drove south, away from the river and up a road that ascended into the hills through hairpin bends and entered a mile-long tunnel, to emerge above the fishing port of Ogatsu. By eight o'clock she was seated at her keyboard in the small doctor's surgery where she worked as a receptionist, awaiting the arrival of the first patient of the day.

It was an unexceptional morning. Hitomi ate a packed lunch at her desk. She was a warm, calm woman of forty, with a core of firm-minded common sense beneath an exterior of kindly humility, well suited to dealing with the clinic's mostly elderly, and frequently confused, patients. Apart from handling appointments, processing payments and keeping the accounts, she supervised the operation of an elaborate apparatus which used an electrical current to massage the muscles. She had just plugged two old ladies into the current when the earthquake began its violent shaking.

She tried to rise, but couldn't. The patients in the waiting room were crying out in alarm. Behind Hitomi were tall flasks in which metal instruments were being sterilised. The boiling water inside them was slopping noisily over the sides, to form steaming pools on the floor.

When the motion had subsided, Hitomi removed the electrodes from the old ladies and handed back the insurance cards as the patients hurried out.

She sent a text message to her oldest daughter, Mari, who was at home in Magaki. The reply quickly came back: *We're all fine. Don't worry.*

Hitomi mopped up the water from the sterilising flasks and discussed with the doctor what to do. Ogatsu was on the sea, at the head of a narrow bay. After the strong, but lesser, earthquake two days ago, many people had evacuated the town; but no tsunami had come. As they were recalling this, a man entered the clinic, a sales rep for a pharmaceutical company, with the news that an evacuation warning had been issued and that everyone should retreat to higher ground. Hitomi picked up her jacket and bag and walked to her car. 'I remember that the whole town was incredibly quiet,' she said. 'I could hear a tap dripping at the back of the clinic, the kind of sound that you would never normally notice.' Later, she realised this was that ghostly moment in the advent of a tsunami when the water withdraws, exposing seabed and harbour-floor, before surging back in with full force. It was the absence of the familiar shush and slap of the sea that made tiny, domestic noises unnaturally noticeable.

She drove back up the hill; even inside the moving car, she could feel the aftershocks. Without thinking, she entered the tunnel, and then immediately began to worry about the solidity of its ceiling, and the unimaginable volumes of stone and earth above it. On the far side, she pulled into a lay-by where other evacuees were waiting, and sat for a while, considering what to do next. She started off down the road again and passed a local man she knew, who waved her to a stop.

'I wouldn't go down there, if I were you,' the man said, pointing in the direction of Hitomi's home in Magaki.

'Why not?' Hitomi asked. But the man just mumbled something she couldn't hear.

It had begun snowing. 'It wasn't late, still not yet four clock,' Hitomi remembered. 'I was sending text messages and trying to phone home, but now nothing connected. It was very dark, unusually dark overhead. I started driving down again, but someone else I knew stopped me and said, "Don't go on."'

A few hundred yards down the road was a vantage point from which Magaki and the country around it could be seen clearly. The man gave no explanation for his warning, and Hitomi did not press him for one. Instead, she retreated to the lay-by and spent a cold and uncomfortable night in the car.

She drove down the road again as it started to become light, and soon reached the point where the hills fell away on the left, revealing the broad Kitakami river valley below, the view Hitomi saw every afternoon when she drove back from work. On both of its banks, a wide margin of level fields rose suddenly into forested hills. On the nearside was Hitomi's home village of Magaki, and then an expanse of paddies stretching to the Fuji lake; the polished blue and red roofs of other hamlets glittered at the edges of the hills. It was an archetypal view of the Japanese countryside: abundant nature, tamed and cultivated by man. But now she struggled to make sense of what she saw.

Everything up to and in between the hills was water. There was only water: buildings and fields had gone. The water was black in the early light; floating on it were continents and trailing archipelagos of dark scummy rubble, brown in colour and composed of broken tree trunks. Every patch of land that was not elevated had been absorbed by the river, which had been annexed in turn by the sea. In this new geography, the Fuji lake was no longer a lake, but the inner reach of an open-mouthed bay; the river was not a river, but a wide maritime inlet. Okawa Primary School was invisible, hidden from view by the great shoulder of hills from which Hitomi looked down. But the road, the houses and Magaki, where Hitomi's home and family had been, were washed from the earth.

Upstream in Fukuji, the news about the helicopter set off a clatter of collective activity. Sayomi's husband, Takahiro, spent the early morning helping to mark off a space where the rescued children could land safely. Sayomi and the other mothers made heaps of rice balls, and brought them to the local community centre where the evacuees were to be taken to recover from their ordeal. She kept two of the rice balls back and put them in her pocket so that, even if she was one of the last to arrive, Chisato would not go hungry.

The helicopter was expected at 11 a.m. Families converged on Fukuji from along the river: brothers, sisters, parents and grandparents, dressed against the cold in fleeces and puffer jackets, and carrying bags and rucksacks with hot drinks and bars of chocolate, and more warm clothes for their returning sons and daughters.

They stood looking up at the sky. There was almost no conversation between them. Helicopters came and went all morning. The blue ones were from the police. One or two might have been military aircraft of the Japan Self-Defence Forces. None of them landed at Fukuji.

'We waited for four hours,' Sayomi said. 'There weren't just a few helicopters, there were a lot. We waited and waited. None of them even came close to us. A very desperate feeling was growing in me.'

The men of the village conferred once again, and decided to send a team downriver to go to the school and find out for themselves what was going on.

They drove past the spilled planks from the timber yard and through the village of Yokogawa, where everything appeared normal: a Shinto shrine, Buddhist temple, and two rows of houses facing one another across the road, none of them visibly damaged. Then they reached the rise that jutted out and concealed the view of the last stretch of the great river. It became obvious only as they crossed it that this unremarkable barrier marked the threshold dividing life from death.

Physically, Yokogawa had been untouched by the disaster. A high embankment and the bend in the river had shielded it from the water. But beyond the hill, the tsunami had surged upstream, overwhelmed the embankment, and risen with deadly force. The men looked out to see what Hitomi, from her opposite vantage point, also saw: the highway and embankment overwhelmed, the bridge broken, and the land turned to sea.

Hitomi drove down in the dawn light, through perfect stillness and hush. Hers was the only car on the road; it was as if the world was newly formed and she was the first to enter it. The surface of the great expanse of water flashed black and silver with the changing angle of the sun. But at the foot of the hill, Hitomi discovered that not all of the land had been overwhelmed.

In the innermost reaches of the valley, a hamlet called Irikamaya had been spared. The village hall had become a refuge centre. Hitomi could see human figures milling around it. The roofs were covered in snow. The people were wrapped in coats and fleeces against the morning chill. She stumbled out of her car, calling out her children's names and reeling from face to face in search of one that she knew. But everyone seemed to be looking for somebody, and none was from Magaki. Then, with a jolt of recognition and relief, she saw a boy whom she knew from Okawa Primary School – Tetsuya Tadano, a younger member of Daisuke's judo team. His clothes were filthy. His right eye was bruised and swollen shut.

'Tetsuya! Oh, Tetsuya, are you OK? What happened, Tetsuya? What happened to Daisuke?'

'We were running away,' said Tetsuya. 'When we were running, Dai fell over. I tried to pull him up by his collar, but he couldn't get up.'

'So what happened to him? What happened to him, Tetsuya?'

The boy shook his head.

Then Hitomi noticed another fifth-year boy, Kohei Takahashi, similarly ragged and begrimed.

'Kohei, where's Daisuke?'

'Dai was with me,' he said. 'He was behind me, running. We were in the water together. He was just behind me.'

'So what happened to him, Kohei?'

'He was floating.'

Outside she found a third face from the primary school: a teacher named Junji Endo, a man who, surely, could provide some answers.

'Mr Endo! Mr Endo, it's Hitomi Konno, Daisuke's mother. What happened? What happened at the school?'

The teacher was sitting alone, hugging his knees with both hands. Hitomi leaned down to him and repeated herself. He hardly looked up.

'Mr Endo? What happened at the school, Mr Endo?'

He appeared to be in a state of deep abstraction. To Hitomi, it was as if his emotions had drained out of him.

'No idea,' he mumbled eventually. 'No idea what's going on.'

Hitomi struggled to assemble these fragments of information. The primary school was on the other side of the hill from where she now stood. The boys and their teacher must have climbed up and over it in just the last few hours. If they had escaped, then others, including Daisuke, must have done the same; he might be up there still, on that hill. Hitomi walked away from the community centre and back down the road, wading in places, and began to climb the hill herself, calling her son's name.

'Dai! Daisuke! Has anyone seen Daisuke Konno?'

But there was no one there. The area was so large, and paths branched in all directions, separated from one another by a density of pines. She descended the hill and stopped. Then she turned towards the river and waded further up the road to the place where her home had been.

'It was just a lake,' Hitomi remembered. 'I couldn't even see the foundations of the houses. I was walking all around, and getting very wet, calling the names of each member of my family. I wasn't really conscious of what I was doing. I thought that if I kept calling their names, someone would reply. People tried to stop me. They were looking at me as if I was mad. But I couldn't think what else to do.'

Sayomi's husband, Takahiro, did not accompany his neighbours on their mission downriver. For reasons that were not discussed, it had been decided that men with children at Okawa Primary School should be excluded from the party. But Takahiro heard from them on their return. They had eventually got a lift by boat to a spot on the embankment close to Magaki. One group of men had gone to Irikamaya. The rest had picked their way through the rubble to the school itself.

Going about the village, Sayomi crossed paths with the wife of one of the men in the party. 'The woman was weeping,' she remembered. 'She refused to look me in the eye.' But Sayomi insisted that she didn't feel hopeless. She said, 'I strongly believed that, although they might not be coming back by helicopter, the children were fine. There were no phones or electricity. They might have been taken to the big sports centre in town, and just not been able to get in touch with us.'

She was at home when Takahiro came back from the briefing by the search party. Japanese parents address one another as *otō-san* and *okaa-san* – Father and Mother – particularly when family matters are being discussed, and this was how Takahiro began.

'He came in and called to me, "Mother . . . "' Sayomi remembered. 'And I thought it might be good news.'

'Mother, there's no hope,' Takahiro said. 'There's no hope.'

'What?' said Sayomi. 'No hope for what?'

'The school is done for,' he said. 'There is no hope.'

'I just seized his shirt,' Sayomi told me. 'I grabbed his chest. "I don't understand," I said. Then I couldn't stand up any more.'

Takahiro recounted what he been told: that the bodies of two children from the school had been recovered so far, with many more certain to be found, and that only a handful had survived, including two pupils from the fifth year.

'One of them must be Chisato,' Sayomi said.

'They are both boys,' said Takahiro.

'Who?'

'One of them is Kohei.'

To Sayomi, leaning backwards over the brink, this name was like a harness buckled around her waist; a smile came to her mouth as she recalled the moment. For in the fifth-year class Chisato and Kohei were the keenest rivals, and had been since they were small. 'After sports day, Chisato would say, "I was faster than Kohei" or "I easily beat Kohei,"' Sayomi told me. If Kohei had survived, then it was impossible that Chisato was not alive too.

Jigoku

Hitomi Konno finally reached the school early the following morning. It was the 13 March 2011, the Sunday.

In a different time, the walk from Irikamaya would have taken twenty minutes, but Hitomi spent more than an hour picking her way along the road beneath the hill, over an obstacle course of water and debris. The rubble included large sections of houses which had been picked up and then dropped by the wave, cars and vans, upended and crushed, and the smallest household items: shoes, sodden garments, cooking pots, tea pots, spoons. Broken pine trees made up an inexplicably large volume of the mess; their resinous scent competed with the corrupt stink of the black mud, which coated everything that was not submerged in water. Of the houses that had once been here, not one in twenty survived even as a ruin.

Finally Hitomi reached the point where the inland road met the highway along the river, beside the New Kitakami Great Bridge. The northernmost third of the bridge, a span of 200 yards, had collapsed and disappeared into the water, exposing bare concrete piles. From here the road had angled down into Kamaya, a typic-ally jumbled Japanese village of low concrete buildings alongside traditional wooden houses with tiled roofs. Until two days ago, all but the top of Okawa Primary School had been obscured by them, and by the cherry trees planted around it.

Today, though, the school was the first thing Hitomi saw, or its outline. It was cocooned in a spiky, angular mesh of interlocking fragments, large and small – tree trunks, the joists of houses, boats, beds, bicycles, sheds and refrigerators. A buckled car protruded from the window of one of the upper classrooms. A hundred yards beyond, a single concrete structure – the village clinic – was still standing, and in the middle distance a filament-thin steel communications mast. But the buildings in the main street of houses, the lanes that led off it and the houses and shops arrayed along them — all had ceased to exist.

Beyond Kamaya had been a succession of hamlets, and beyond them fields, low hills, the swaying curve of the river and finally the Pacific Ocean. At the river's distant mouth there was a beach, popular with surfers and swimmers, and a dense forest of pines, which had been planted as a windbreak and a place of recreation. It was those pine trunks, 20,000 of them, that had been ripped out and transported three miles inland, distributing their distinctive smell. The village, the hamlets, the fields and everything else between here and the sea had gone.

No photograph could describe the spectacle. Even television images failed to encompass the panoramic quality of the disaster, the sense within the plane of destruction of being surrounded by it on all sides, sometimes as far as the eye could see. 'It was hell,' Hitomi said. 'Everything had disappeared. It was as if an atomic bomb had fallen.' This comparison, for which many people reached, was not an exaggeration. Only two forces can inflict greater damage than a tsunami: collision with an asteroid, or nuclear explosion. The scenes along 400 miles of coast that morning resembled those of Hiroshima and Nagasaki in August 1945, but with water substituted for fire, mud for ash, the stink of fish and ooze for scorched wood and smoke.

Even the most intense aerial bombing leaves the walls and foundations of burned-out buildings, as well as parks and woods, roads and tracks, fields and cemeteries. The tsunami spared nothing, and achieved feats of surreal juxtaposition that no explosion could match. It plucked forests up by their roots and scattered them miles inland. It peeled the macadam off the roads, and cast it hither and thither in buckled ribbons. It stripped houses to their foundations, and lifted cars, lorries, ships and corpses onto the top of tall buildings.

A man named Ryosuke Abe reached Kamaya at about the same time as Hitomi. His house, his wife, his daughter, his son-in-law and his two grandchildren had been in the village at the time of the tsunami. Abe himself worked on a building site in the city, and his way home had been blocked by the flooded road and broken bridge. By the time he got to the village, two policemen had taken up positions in front of it. To his amazement and indignation, they diffidently tried to bar his way. He began to argue, then gave up and simply walked straight past them.

Abe, Hitomi and everyone describing the scene in the first days after the tsunami used the same word. *Jigoku*: hell. The image they had in mind was not the conventional landscape of lurid demons and extravagant, fiery tortures. There are other hells in Japanese iconography – hells of ice and water, mud and excrement, in which naked figures, stripped of all dignity, lie scattered across a broken plain.

'What stays in my memory,' Abe said, 'is pine trees, and the legs and arms of children sticking out from under the mud and the rubbish.'

Abe was a village leader, a construction boss, an active, practical-minded man in his early sixties. He began to pull bodies out and to lay them out on the roadside. At first he used his bare hands. Then he waded back to his car and returned with his tools. In some places a shovel was useless, because the bodies of the children were so thickly heaped on top of one another, where they had been laid by the retreating wave.

By the afternoon, a handful of people had gathered to join the effort. It was dangerous, precarious work, because there was so little solid ground. Even where the waters had receded, they had left layered decks of rubble that slid or collapsed underfoot, all of it broken, much of it razor-sharp and covered with foul, squelching mud. Stepping uncertainly among the jutting spines and raw edges, the men in the group hauled up tree trunks and broken spars of wood, bent back sheets of corrugated aluminium and prised open the doors of crushed cars. When they found bodies, they carried them to a traffic island opposite the bridge where the women, among them Hitomi Konno, laid them out and washed them in murky water hauled by bucket out of the river. 'Of course there was nothing to cover the bodies with,' Hitomi said. 'We pulled mattresses out of the rubble and laid them out on those, and covered them up with sheets, clothes, anything we could find.' Almost as carefully as the bodies, they retrieved and set aside the distinctive square rucksacks, carefully labelled with name and class, which all Japanese primary schoolchildren carry.

There was no panic, or even much sense of urgency. Without anyone saying as much, it was understood that there was no question of finding anyone alive. 'No one was just looking for his own friends or grandchildren,' Mr Abe said. 'We were pulling everyone out, whoever they were. Every man was weeping as he worked.'

Friends, rivals, neighbours, schoolmates, nodding acquaintances, blood relatives, old sweethearts – all came out of the undiscriminating muck.

By the end of the first day, Abe had dug out ten children. Most of them had lost their clothes and their name badges. But he recognised many of the faces.

That afternoon, someone told Abe that they had seen his wife, Fumiko. He hurried to Irikamaya and there she was, with his daughter, both of them uninjured. 'It was more than a matter of being relieved,' he said. 'I couldn't believe that they were alive.' But his son-in-law and two granddaughters were still missing.

He would spend three months in the village, picking through mud in the search for bodies. One day, the women called him over to the place where the bodies were laid out for washing. Among them was his own ten-year-old granddaughter, Nao. Abe had lifted her out himself. She had been so covered with mud that he had not recognised her.

Nao's nine-year-old younger sister, Mai, was found a week later, and their father a week after that. 'The older girl was just the way she had always been,' Abe told me. 'She was perfect. It was just as if she was asleep. But a week later – well, seven days in those conditions makes a big difference.' And he wept.

Nine miles inland, beyond the reach of the wave, was an indoor sports centre, which had become a centre for emergency relief. Entire families were sleeping in the basketball court on borrowed blankets and squares of folded cardboard. Sayomi Shito's eldest sister, Takami, a brisk and formidable woman whose own family lived safely inland, took upon herself the job of going there to find her niece and bring her home. The confusion caused by the disaster was extreme, but people did not simply disappear. How difficult could it be?

Okawa Primary School.

Fifth Year.

Chisato Shito.

But after joining the throng inside the sports centre, Takami's confidence fell away. She found herself one among hundreds, moving anxiously from one desk and dormitory and noticeboard to another.

After several fruitless hours, someone suggested a different kind of place where such a girl might be. Takami's heart quailed at the thought; she didn't have the strength to go alone. She picked up her other sister and drove with her to the place, where they consulted a much shorter list of names. But only immediate family members were allowed inside.

She went to Chisato's father, Takahiro, and told him what she had found.

Soon after, Takahiro came to Sayomi. She was in the kitchen again, preparing the latest batch of rice balls. Takahiro said, 'Mother, it's time to prepare yourself. We've found Chisato.'

Sayomi told me, 'When I heard that, I started to leave at once. But then I realised that I'd need food for her to eat, and clothes for her to wear, and all kinds of things, so I went about getting them all together.'

Takahiro said, 'You don't need any of that. Just come.'

It was two years later when Sayomi told me the story. As she remembered it, she got into the car without knowing where she was being taken, but in the calm belief that she was about to be reunited with her daughter.

To Sayomi's surprise, they drove past the sports centre where the refugees were sheltering and up the hill to a place she knew intimately – the high school where Sayomi and her sisters had all been pupils, and where Chisato would eventually go. 'There was a kind of reception desk which they'd set up there,' she said. 'Takahiro and my brother-in-law stood by it, going through some sort of documents. They told me to stay in the car.'

Sayomi slipped out and ran into the school. She found herself inside its gymnasium.

'It was the first time I'd been there in thirty years,' she said. 'There were tables and chairs. They'd divided off part of the gym with plastic sheets. So I looked in, and there were blue tarpaulins on the floor and shapes laid out on them, covered with blankets.'

A man was approaching Sayomi, holding out a pair of shoes. 'He was saying, "Is there any mistake?" There wasn't a mistake. They were Chisato's shoes. I saw her name inside them, in my handwriting.'

Now Takahiro was in the gymnasium. He was gathering one of the shapes up in his arms and lifting the blanket.

'Don't come yet,' he said to Sayomi.

'But I could see,' she told me.

She went on: 'He lifted up one of the blankets. And then he was nodding, and saying something to the man who was in charge there. When I saw that, I thought, "What are you nodding for? Don't nod. Don't nod." They were telling me not to come in, but I rushed in. Chisato was there. She was covered in mud. She was naked. She looked very calm, just as if she was asleep. I held her and lifted her up, and called her name over and over, but she didn't answer. I tried to massage her, to restore her breathing. But it had no effect. I rubbed the mud from her cheeks, and wiped it out of her mouth. It was in her nose too, and it was in her ears. But we had only two small towels. I wiped and wiped the mud, and soon the towels were black. I had nothing else, so I used my clothes to wipe off the mud. Her eyes were half open – and that was the way she used to sleep, the way she was when she was in a very deep sleep. But there was muck in her eyes, and there were no towels and no water, and so I licked Chisato's eyes with my tongue to wash off the muck, but I couldn't get them clean, and the muck kept coming out.'

Hitomi Konno and her husband, Hiroyuki, found one another the following week. It was at that moment that she gave up hope. She had been spending mornings at the school, where she washed and identified bodies, and the afternoons in Irikamaya village hall, where she cooked and cleaned for her fellow refugees. It was difficult to know what else to do, for she was still looking for her children, Mari, Rika and Daisuke, and her mother- and father-in-law. Hitomi had no illusions about what had happened; she understood what the worst was, for it was all around her. But she was sustained, like many in her situation, by the simple instinct that, whatever was happening to other people, it was impossible – in fact, it would be ridiculous – for her own family to be extinct. Insupportable, soul-crushing, unfathomable – but also just silly. *We're all fine. Don't worry*, Mari had written in those first moments after the earthquake. 'I thought, "They must be alive. They must be alive,"' Hitomi said. 'I couldn't give up. When the phones came back on, I sent text messages, I tried calling over and over again.'

Hitomi took a boat to the big sports centre, and found Hiroyuki there.

It is conventional to picture such reunions as joyful moments of emotional release. But the emotions are too big, and too mixed with despair. Over the past few days, Hiroyuki had arrived at the belief that he had lost his parents, two daughters, son and wife. When he saw Hitomi, he adjusted his understanding: as it turned out, he had lost his mother, father and three children. 'Of course we were glad to see one another,' Hitomi said. 'But we were so preoccupied with thoughts of the children. Until I found them, I couldn't feel any relief.'

Hitomi's head-shaking refusal to take death seriously was not shared by her husband. Hiroyuki joined the search for bodies, in Kamaya, and in the area of the Fuji lake, where many of the component parts of their home village, Magaki, had fetched up. One day they found the top part of their house – the upper floor and roof, virtually intact, tossed by the wave onto a shore of the lake. A team was grimly assembled to break through the tiles. The Konnos expected the fulfilment of all their fears, the trapped corpses of their family. Inside, the tatami mats were still in place, but there was little else there. They found Rika's pink Hello Kitty purse and what came to be very precious: an old album filled with photographs of the children when they were small.

Daisuke was the first to be recovered, a week after the wave, followed by Hiroyuki's father. Rika, who had died four days before her seventeenth birthday, was found at the end of the month. Old Mrs Konno and eighteen-year-old Mari were found in early April.

Daisuke was at the bottom of the hill behind the school, not far from the traffic island, in one of several small heaps of children. The girls and their grandparents lay in different places, but there were clues that suggested what had happened to them. Old Mr Konno had his car keys in his pocket. His wife was carrying bags of clothes, and the girls had snacks and charger cables for their mobile phones. They were preparing a departure; they might have been about to get into the car when the tsunami struck. Perhaps they were worried about Daisuke, or about Hitomi. Perhaps they were waiting for one or both of them to return before making their escape.

Hitomi went to see Daisuke at the high-school gymnasium, and found him uninjured. 'He looked as if he was sleeping,' she said. 'He looked as if he would wake up if I called his name. I still remember his face as it was then.' But when she came back the next day, a jolting change had taken place. Drops of blood had issued from Daisuke's eyes, like tears. She wiped them away, but overnight, and every night after that, Daisuke shed more tears of blood. Hitomi understood that this was because of changes that were taking place inside the container of her son's body. But she couldn't help also seeing it as a symbol of the pain of his hovering spirit, and of how desperately he had wanted to live.

It had been difficult even to find coffins. Every crematorium within reach of the coast was backed up for several days. People were driving for hundreds of miles to hold a funeral. What Hitomi and Hiroyuki most urgently needed now was a supply of dry ice, first for one, then for two and eventually for five sets of remains. An undertaker explained that each body needed four pieces of ice – two to go under the arms and two under the legs. As the spring warmth came on, each piece lasted only a few days. Hiroyuki would drive around for hours and finally locate ice in a neighbouring town – but the next time he went there, its supply would be gone. In the month it took for all five bodies to be recovered and cremated, Hitomi and Hiroyuki's lives were dominated by the daily struggle to protect their children and parents from decay.

Apart from their family, the Konnos had also lost their home and everything in it. While they were organising ice and funerals, Hitomi and Hiroyuki stayed first with his elderly grandmother, and then moved to a vacant house owned by an aunt and uncle. For them, as for many of the parents from the school, those early weeks were a time of numb frenzy rather than supine grief, a losing struggle to remain on top of a hundred pressing practical matters.

It was about a month after the disaster that Hitomi had a phone call from Kazutaka Sato, a man she knew as Yuki's dad.

Yuki Sato was Daisuke's best friend and confrère in mischief. The two boys walked to school together, practised judo together and fished together in the Kitakami River. Yuki had also died on 11 March.

By this stage, the scale of the tragedy at Okawa Primary School had become clear. The school had 108 children. Of the seventy-eight who were there at the moment of the tsunami, seventy-four, and ten out of eleven teachers, had died. But a handful of parents had gone to the school after the earthquake, picked up their children and taken them to safety. One of the girls who had been saved in this way, Amane Ukitsu, had been in the sixth-year class with Daisuke and Yuki. Mr Sato had recently talked to Amane, and now he was telephoning, full of emotion, to share with Hitomi the story that he had heard from their sons' surviving classmate.

Sato had asked Amane about the moments before her mother took her away from the school, the period after the earthquake and before the tsunami. His beloved son had died at the age of twelve; now he wanted to know everything that it was possible to know about Yuki in the last minutes of his life. How had he appeared? What had he spoken of? Had he been afraid?

Amane described how the building shook violently, but suffered no serious damage, and how the children and teachers evacuated the building, just as they had for the lesser tremor two days earlier. The pupils had lined up by class. Amane stood with Yuki, Daisuke and the rest of the sixth year.

The names were quickly checked off, and the children were told to remain where they stood. Soon, sirens and announcements could be heard, urging evacuation to higher ground. It was cold in the playground. But there was no move to go back inside, or anywhere else. Chilled by the wind, the children became restless. And now there was a loudspeaker van driving around, broadcasting warning of a 'super-tsunami' coming in from the sea.

Amane recounted how Daisuke, the class captain, and Yuki, his sidekick, addressed their class teacher, a man named Takashi Sasaki.

Sir, let's go up the hill.

We should climb the hill, sir.

If we stay here, the ground might split open and swallow us up. We'll die if we stay here!

The teacher shushed them, and told them to remain where they were.

Soon afterwards Amane's mother arrived and hurriedly drove her away. The family lost their house, but she was one of only five children left alive from the sixth-year class.

Mr Sato's telephone call left Hitomi trembling. She had had no time or energy left over to contemplate them before – but this story lit up like a floodlight questions that had been flickering dimly in her grief-darkened mind. What, after all, had been going on at the school in the period between the earthquake and the wave? Why had everyone not evacuated to the hill behind it, as her own son had apparently suggested? If he had been able to see the sense of this, why had not his teachers? Why had they, and Daisuke, and everyone else, had to die?

PART 2

AREA OF SEARCH

Abundant Nature

The territory of the Okawa Primary School appears on globes and atlases as an unlabelled blank. The two great plains surrounding Tokyo and Osaka, the mega-cities at Japan's core, are a density of roads, railways and place names, which dwindle and fade to the north of the main island of Honshu. Even before disaster struck its coast, nowhere in Japan was closer to the world of the dead.

In ancient times, the region known as Tohoku was a notorious frontier realm of barbarians, goblins and bitter cold. Even today, it remains a remote, marginal, faintly melancholy place, the symbol of a rural tradition that, for city dwellers, is no more than a folk memory.

The seventeenth-century *haiku* poet Basho wrote about Tohoku in his famous travel sketch *The Narrow Road to the Deep North*, in which it figures as an emblem of loneliness and isolation. Even after Japan's rapid modernisation in the late nineteenth century, Tohoku was poorer, hungrier and more backward than anywhere else. Northern men, tough and uncomplaining, filled the imperial armies. The fields were rich in grain and fruit, but their produce was consumed in the richer south, and a bad harvest often left Tohoku in famine. There were three commodities, it used to be said, which the north supplied to Tokyo: rice, fighting men and whores.

Today, Tohoku makes up one-third of the area of Honshu, but one-tenth of its population. It is associated with an impenetrable regional dialect, a quality of eeriness and an archaic spirituality that are exotic even to modern Japanese. In the north, there are secret Buddhist cults, and old temples where the corpses of former priests are displayed as leering mummies. There is a sisterhood of blind shamanesses who gather once a year at a volcano called Mount Fear, the traditional entrance to the underworld. Tohoku has bullet trains and Wi-Fi, and the rest of the twenty-first century conveniences. But the mobile network gives out in the remoter hills and bays and, beneath the glaze of affluence, something lingers of the old stereotype of Tohoku people as brooding, incomprehensible and a little spooky.

I knew the region's largest city, Sendai, which was as blandly pleasant as most of Japan's prefectural capitals. But the other names reeled off by the television news on the night of 11 March – Otsuchi, Ofunato, Rikuzen-Takata, Kesennuma – were as obscure to many Japanese as they were to foreigners. And between Kesennuma and the fishing port of Ishinomaki, an intricately spiky coastline, indented with deep and narrow bays, the atlas displayed no place names at all.

A larger-scale map revealed the name of this obscure zone: the Sanriku Coast. Three physical features distinguished it: two obvious and spectacular, the other stealthy and invisible. The first was the Kitakami, Tohoku's greatest river, which rose in the mountains and flowed south to empty itself through two distinct mouths, one in Ishinomaki, one at a thinly populated place called Oppa Bay. The second was those sharp, fjord-like bays, called rias, formed by river valleys which over the millennia had been drowned by the rising sea. The third was the meeting point, deep beneath the ocean, of the Pacific and North American tectonic plates, titanic segments of the Earth's crust, from whose grating friction earthquakes and tsunamis are born.

On this jagged coast, close to Oppa Bay, was Okawa Primary School. I travelled there for the first time in September 2011. Half a year had passed since the disaster, and in that time I had made repeated journeys to the tsunami zone. At first it had been accessible only by car, along roads strewn with rubble, after hours of queuing for a single jerrycan of rationed fuel. In time, petrol supplies resumed and, after anxious checks on the safety of its tracks, the *shinkansen*, or bullet train, restarted its northbound service. Early September is high summer in Japan; the air was hot and full, and the sky was a cloudless, fine-grained blue. The *shinkansen* raced smoothly and effortlessly north, slurping up the distance so quickly that the ninety-minute journey felt closer to commuting than to travel. But to come to Tohoku was always to experience a transformation. In spring, the snow in the north-east lingered longer and deeper on the ground. Plum and cherry blossoms flowered and fell later; summer here was less harsh, less sticky and gave way sooner to the chill of autumn. Arrival from Tokyo brought a palpable shift in the air and its qualities, a sense of transition experienced on the skin and in the back of the throat.

Sendai station, where my companions and I alighted, displayed no visible signs of the disaster. Our hire car manoeuvred north, through a city centre of silver office buildings and department stores, and mounted the overhead expressway, also recently reopened after months of structural checks. After an hour, the city of Ishinomaki came into view on the coastal plain ahead: hangar-like factories and shopping malls, and billows of white smoke out of aluminium chimneys.

No city suffered more in the tsunami than Ishinomaki. Most of its centre had been inundated; one-fifth of those who died in the disaster died here, in a town of 160,000 people. The fishing port had been entirely destroyed by the wave, along with the shipyard and an immense paper mill. But three-quarters of the Ishinomaki municipality was another world altogether, a hinterland of steep hills and forests, penetrated by the broad agricultural plain of the Kitakami River; and fishing villages at the head of the deep ria bays, separated from one another by elaborately ramifying peninsulas, which extended talon-like fingers into the ocean.

Beyond the town, we descended from the expressway and entered a realm of bright fields bordered by dark hills. Some of them contained heavy-stalked rice, ripe for harvest; others held greenhouses of tomatoes and fruit. The houses along the road were built of wood with stately tiled roofs. The sky, which was already huge overhead, gaped wider as the hills fell away and we turned east along the bank of the Kitakami.

Most Japanese rivers are a wretched sight, even outside the big cities. Upstream dams drain them of power and volume. Towns and factories suck off their waters and pump back effluent, human and chemical. The Kitakami, by contrast, is wide, full, clean and alive. Its single dam is in the upper northern reaches, leaving the salmon free to swarm every autumn to their spawning grounds. Its breadth – hundreds of yards across, even deep inland – opens up vistas of sky and mountains in the built-up towns through which it passes. Herons, swans and teal live among the dense beds of reeds that grow along its banks; every year the reeds are harvested to furnish thatch for temples and shrines. The river's southern outlet, where it meets the sea at Ishinomaki, is a tumult of wharves, cranes and containers. But its other mouth, at Oppa Bay, is that rare thing in a populous industrialised country – a great river estuary left to sand, eagles, rocks and currents.

This was the prospect revealed to us as we drove along the Kitakami into Okawa that morning: the arching sky; the green hills divided from one another by valleys packed with rice; villages at the edge of the fields; and, in the hazy distance, lagoon and sea. It was an ideal, an archetypal scene: farm and forest, fresh and salt water, nature and humanity in balance. Trees covered the mountains, and the sea dashed the rocks, but both were welcoming to the hunter and fisherman. The river was wide and powerful, but tamed by bridge and embankment. The tiled houses were small and few, but the fields, hills and water paid tribute to them. Human civilisation was the pivot about which the natural world turned.

On the Sanriku Coast you experienced the sensation of entering an altered world. It was a subtle change – for all the jokes about spooky Tohoku yokels, there was nothing unsophisticated about northerners. But there was a shagginess about them, compared to the lacquered neatness of Tokyo people – a robust, tousled quality suggestive of bracing weather, and an indifference to indulgences such as indoor heating. Everyone had strong boots and thick socks; in the colder months, they all wore nylon fleeces, often two, even inside. The hair of both men and women stuck up in tufts, as if it had just been tugged through several layers of thick sweaters and incompletely patted down. Certain surnames – Konno, Sato, Sasaki – cropped up again and again, as if there was a limited supply of them, as in a society composed of clans. People in Sanriku had clear, pale complexions, and the transition from bitter wind to warm interior flushed their cheeks rosy and bright. Everyone talked about the beauty of nature, and his or her relationship with it. Everyone seemed to have deep family roots in the area, reaching decades and centuries into the past.

I met an old man named Sadayoshi Kumagai whose memory went back before the Second World War. His ancestors had been samurai riflemen; the family had lived in the area for 300 years. Old Mr Kumagai was a master thatcher who had travelled the country constructing temple roofs out of the fine Kitakami reeds. 'It was a while before I understood,' he said. 'But there's no doubting it. I've been everywhere in this country, from Hokkaido to Okinawa. And nowhere else has the abundance of nature we have here: mountains, river, marsh, sea. People who never leave the area don't understand how lucky they are. There's no place like this.'

He grew up in Hashiura, a village opposite Okawa Primary School on the north bank of the river. It was an isolated, even backward community of horse-drawn carts and unmade roads. But for a young boy it was a place of wonder and adventure. In the summer, the village children swam in the river and the sea. In autumn, they followed the trails into the hills and gathered nuts and chocolate vine. A little way off the road was the site of a Neolithic village: classmates of Kumagai used to come to school bearing fragments of 4,000-year-old pots. Kumagai's grandfather taught him to shoot – there were duck and pheasant in the hills above the river and, in Oshika to the south, wild deer. 'We didn't hunt for fun, but for a living,' he said. 'When we took game, we sold it.' Once, in a moment of opportunistic mischief, the young Kumagai shot and slayed a swan. 'I was so proud of myself, and I told everyone what I'd done. Well, the police heard about it, and they came round and gave me a good telling off.'

On their hunting expeditions, Kumagai's grandfather told the boy about the wonder and horror of the tsunami. The old man had lived through two of them in his own lifetime, and the historical record went back much further than that. 'The province of Mutsu' – eastern Tohoku – 'trembled and greatly shook,' recorded a chronicle of AD 869, the eleventh year of the Jogan Era:

> People cried and screamed, and could not stand. Some died beneath the weight of their fallen houses; some were buried alive in earth and sand when the ground sheared open beneath them . . . Great walls, gates, warehouses and embankments were destroyed. The mouth of the sea roared like thunder, and violent waves rose up, surging through the rivers, until, in the blink of an eye, they reached the wall of Taga Castle. The flood extended for so many *ri* that you could not tell where the sea ended and the land began. Fields and roads were transformed into ocean. There was no time to board boats or to climb the hills; a thousand people drowned.

Geologists found layers of fine sand across the sedimentary layers of the Sendai plain – the wash of immense tsunamis that had recurred at intervals of 800 to 1,000 years. Lesser waves were more frequent. Among many other years, they struck the Sanriku Coast in 1585, 1611, 1677, 1687, 1689, 1716, 1793, 1868 and 1894. Their effects were especially devastating when they encountered the long, narrow ria bays, which concentrated the waves and channelled them like funnels onto the fishing villages within. The most destructive of modern times was the Meiji Sanriku Tsunami of 1896, when 22,000 died after what had felt – because it occurred far out at sea – like a mild and inconsequential earthquake. In 1933, the year before Sadayoshi Kumagai was born, another moderate tremor generated waves as high as 100 feet, which killed 3,000 people. 'My grandfather lived through both of those, and he talked about them,' he said. 'I was always told that when an earthquake strikes we must be prepared for a tsunami.' There were even 'tsunami stones' marking the extent of previous inundations, engraved by earlier generations with solemn warnings not to build dwellings below them. The fishermen on the Pacific coast to the east, whose homes faced directly onto the ocean, were brought up to know instinctively what to do after the earth shook: ascend without hesitation to high ground, and stay there. But the people of Kitakami lived on a river, not the sea. And what if there was no shaking at all?

On 22 May 1960, a 9.5-magnitude earthquake, still the most powerful ever recorded, struck the seabed off the west coast of Chile. Waves eighty feet high inundated the city of Valdivia, killing a thousand people along the coast. Twenty-two hours after the earthquake, the tsunami struck Japan, having traversed 10,500 miles of sea. It was the morning of 24 May; none but a handful of seismologists in Tokyo knew what had happened in Chile, and even they never imagined the effect it would have one day later on the far side of the Pacific. The Sanriku Coast saw the worst of it; in places, the water was more than twenty feet high. One hundred and forty-two people were killed that day, because of an occurrence in the depths of the ocean bed literally half a world away.

In Hashiura, Sadayoshi Kumagai saw the tsunami from Chile surging up the Kitakami River. 'It was this mass of black,' he said. 'Huge stones were rolling over and over upstream. It wasn't just one wave, but one after another. The water rose so high – it came halfway up the bank. I had never seen that happen before. I thought at the time what a strange and powerful thing it was. But I never imagined that it could ever come up *over* the bank.'

When the earthquake struck on 11 March 2011, Kumagai recognised immediately that a tsunami could follow, and what a menace it would be to anyone on the river. With a prickling of alarm, he remembered that eight of his employees were gathering reeds on an island close to the mouth of the Kitakami. He rushed down to the bank and supervised their evacuation by boat. Filled with relief that his people had been brought to safety, he drove back to Hashiura.

He was in the open when the tsunami arrived. He watched the black shape breach the bank and tumble towards him. He leaped into his car and reached the road into the hills seconds ahead of the water. From there, he looked down as the second tsunami of his life destroyed Okawa and Hashiura, including his own house and office. 'It was like a black mountain coming over,' he said. 'It was incredible that the mountain was moving. I saw a car with its tail lights on going under the water. There must have been somebody inside. Another few seconds and I would have been in the water too.'

Much of the beauty of Okawa derived from the many things that were not there – those everyday uglinesses unthinkingly accepted by city dwellers. Even as we drove in on that September afternoon, I was conscious of their absence. Between the outskirts of Ishinomaki and the sea, there were few traffic lights, road signs, vending machines or telegraph poles. There were no strip-lit restaurants or twenty-four-hour convenience stores, no advertising hoardings or cash dispensers. Most transforming of all was the character of local sound: the song of birds and cicadas in the trees, the low noise of the river, the slap of waves and a subtle, pervasive, barely audible susurration, which took me days to identify – that of air passing through the reeds.

Ryosuke Abe, who spent those weeks searching through its remains after the disaster, was the headman of Kamaya; no one I met talked more passionately about the life of the village. The home he described, and the childhood he remembered, was that of the archetypal *furusato*, the Japanese Arcadia, the village of the imagination, with its forested hills, paddies cut by a meandering river, a small local school and family-run shops.

There was Aizawa the tobacconist and, across the road, Mogami the sake-seller, with its distinctive green-and-orange awning. Suzuki the tofu-seller was further down the road, next to the Takahashi Beauty Parlour. Kamaya had its own *koban*, or police box, manned by a single officer, and the Kamaya Clinic run by the well-regarded Dr Suzuki. And dominating the centre of the village, fronted by a row of cherry trees, was the school.

'Kamaya was a place of abundant nature,' Abe said. 'The natural world was so rich. These days, when kids go for a picnic, they get on a bus. They don't really know their way round their own area. But we roamed far and wide – Nagatsura, Onosaki, Fukuji. We'd play baseball on the beach – each hamlet had a little team. We played in the river – you could swim anywhere. We spent the whole summer outside.'

Most families had more than one source of income: a job, or at least part-time work, in Ishinomaki, supplemented by a small household farm and gleanings from the forest and river. The hills produced their own harvest of mushrooms, berries and chestnuts. The local rice variety was called Love-at-First-Sight. The briny mingling of the fresh water and the salt had intriguing effects on natural life. It made the reeds thin, but very strong. It nurtured unlikely fish, such as the spiky-finned, bull-headed sculpions, and *shijimi* clams, which were sold across Japan as a delicious ingredient for soup. 'We had so much from the river,' Ryosuke Abe said. 'We used to make a trap out of an oak branch and leaves. You put it on the river bed, and when you pulled it up onto the boat with a landing net, it was full of eels – big fat eels.'

Three hundred and ninety-three people lived in Kamaya at the time of the tsunami. More than half of them – 197 people – died, and every one of their houses was destroyed. Virtually all who survived did so because they were away from the village at the time, at work or school. Of those who were present in Kamaya that afternoon, only about twenty had not drowned by the time the sun went down. And these numbers did not include the teachers and children who died at the school. It was easy, often too easy, to reach for superlatives in describing the tragedy of the tsunami. But in all the disaster zone, I reflected as I drove in that September afternoon, I knew of no single community that had lost so much of itself.

The road, which had been fully repaired, at first gave no clues about what had happened six months earlier. The vegetation along the riverside had begun to grow back, and the rubble had been tidied away. But the fields, which a mile back had the glow of ripe rice, were muddy and unplanted, and here and there were discreet relics of destruction: a buckled pickup truck among long grass; a windowless, roofless building alone in the mud. My eye was drawn to the screen of our car's satellite navigation system. Kamaya was visible upon it as a mesh of lines and rectangles, with each block of houses distinct, the school, the police station and the community centre individually marked. We reached the turning to the New Kitakami Great Bridge, which was teeming with repair workers in yellow vests. On the satnav screen, the moving dot representing our car paused on the threshold of the glowing village. But in the real world there was nothing there.

I knew what had happened at Okawa. Everyone knew. It was the worst of the tsunami, the story hardest among all the stories to hear. I was always conscious, on reaching the school, of a faint dizziness, a quailing of the heart at the idea of the place. And yet the site itself possessed an air of quiet, even tranquillity: a two-storey block beneath an angled red roof, with concrete arms enclosing what would once have been the playground. The buildings were windowless and battered, their surfaces abraded by impacts, with walls warped and toppled in places, but still sound on their steel frame. Above was a steep and thickly wooded hill, buttressed at its foot by a concrete wall.

At the front was a weather-beaten table bearing a jumble of objects that identified it as a makeshift shrine. There were vases of flowers, incense holders and wooden funeral tablets bearing characters brushed in ink. There were bottles of juice and sweets, soft toys and a framed photograph of the village in sunshine, with the river, hills and summer sky magnificent in the background.

Standing in front of the shrine, tidying a vase of flowers, was a figure in boots and a heavy coat, her hair tied up in a ponytail. Her name was Naomi Hiratsuka. She lived upriver; her daughter, Koharu, had been a pupil at the school. She was the woman I had come here to find.

The Mud

Naomi lived in a big house in the village of Yokogawa, with four generations of her husband's family. Its oldest occupant, his grandmother, was in her late nineties; Naomi's younger daughter, Sae, was two and a half. Naomi had been in her bedroom at the moment of the earthquake, lulling the small girl to sleep. The fast, vertical motion was 'like being inside a cocktail shaker'. By the time the shocks had dissipated, the house was an obstacle course of books, furniture and broken glass. Her six-year-old son Toma was trapped in another room, its door blocked by fallen objects. It took Naomi half an hour to free him, as the walls and floor flexed and wobbled in the aftershocks.

Nobody in the family had been physically hurt, but downstairs the house was in even greater disarray. Naomi's mother-in-law was tending to the distraught great-grandmother; her father-in-law, who held high office in the local neighbourhood association, was taking stock of the situation outside.

He was an uncommunicative man; 'traditional' would have been the polite way of describing his conception of family and the appropriate behaviour of its members. When he returned from his reconnoitring, Naomi was preparing to go to Okawa Primary School to collect her twelve-year-old daughter, Koharu. 'I had no doubt that the school was OK,' she said. 'But it had been such a strong quake, I thought I ought to pick her up.' Mr Hiratsuka Senior resisted this idea, for reasons that were obscure. 'He said, "This is not the moment,"' Naomi remembered. 'I didn't know exactly what he meant.' The old man had walked round the village; Naomi realised later that he must have looked over the bank and observed the condition of the river. But he was a man who rarely felt the need to explain his decisions, certainly not to a daughter-in-law. 'I think that he himself was in a panic, although he didn't show it,' she said. 'We didn't have much conversation. He's the kind who keeps his thoughts to himself.'

Naomi had sent a text message to her husband, but received no reply before the network went down. There was no electricity and therefore no television. Even the municipal loudspeakers, which broadcast information in times of emergency, were silent; and it was snowing. 'I remember thinking about Koharu stuck at the school, and I thought that it must be so cold there,' Naomi said. 'I was glad that I'd told her to put on an extra layer of underwear. I thought that as long as they wrapped up well, they'd be OK.' In the absence of any news – good or bad – about the state of the wider world, all she could think of was to stay inside and tend to those members of the family who were safe at home.

This course of action coincided exactly with her father-in-law's view of the role and duties of a young woman and mother.

Shortly before dusk, old Mr Hiratsuka announced that he was going out again. His intention was to walk downriver and retrieve a radio from the hut at his nearby allotment. It was still light when he left. He returned in darkness an hour later, gasping and reeling, drenched in water, plastered with mud and leaves and lucky to be alive.

Physically, Yokogawa was untouched by the disaster that was taking place. The high embankment and the bend in the river had shielded it from the water, to the extent that Naomi still had no idea there had been a tsunami. But on the far side of the jutting hill, five and a half miles from the sea, Mr Hiratsuka found himself on a road rinsed by the ocean. As he walked along it, a new surge broke the river's edge and quickly covered the asphalt.

It tugged at his feet, and then at his ankles and knees, and before he understood what was happening he had lost his footing and was flailing in currents of black water. They were dragging him back towards the river, where he would certainly have drowned, when he became painfully, but securely, entangled in a tree, which held him fast while the water drained away.

He staggered back home past the bend in the river, without his radio. 'He said later that he nearly died,' Naomi remembered. 'He was upset. He didn't say so, but perhaps that was the moment when he understood what had happened.'

The following morning, Naomi persuaded her father-in-law to make an effort at reaching the school. Immediately beyond Yokogawa the water had receded, and they were able to drive to the point where the road disappeared into the water. A group of people had gathered there; some of them seemed to be crying. Mr Hiratsuka told Naomi to stay in the car, and strode over to investigate. He came back a few minutes later; the terseness of his replies suggested that he hadn't found out very much. Naomi was not especially worried. Like everyone else, she had heard the report that 200 children and local people were cut off by water at Okawa Primary School, awaiting rescue. Like the other mothers, she had turned up that morning to meet the helicopter that never came. But mostly she was preoccupied with the burden of feeding and cleaning a household in which she was expected to be the source of nurture for both young and old. 'The children were scared by the aftershocks,' she said. 'And the old people were all in a dither. I was on maternity leave – I was supposed to be looking after my child. But for the next few days, all I can remember was cooking. When the time came to go out and find food, my mother- and father-in-law did that. I was at home taking care of the children, and cooking and cooking again, morning, noon and night.'

On Sunday morning, two of Naomi's friends, the mother and father of two children at Okawa Primary School, called by to say that they were going to make another attempt at getting through. Would Naomi like to come? She badly wanted to go with them – but who would look after the other two children in her absence? Her father-in-law had a solution: she would stay at home, and he would go instead.

He returned at lunchtime.

'What happened?' asked Naomi.

'We got to the school,' he said.

'How was it?' asked Naomi.

'I saw Arika's body there.' Arika was a twelve-year-old classmate of Koharu. 'There were several other bodies of children there. But not Koharu. I could not find Koharu. I heard that a few of the children survived and went to Irikamaya. But Koharu was not there. So I think it is hopeless. You need to give up.'

Naomi found herself unable to speak. 'I wanted to ask so much more, I wanted to know the details,' she said. 'But there was something about the way he said, "Give up."'

Then Mr Hiratsuka said, 'We have to accept this. You need to give up hope. The important thing now is to look after the children who are still alive.' With that, the conversation was over.

Naomi told me: 'He had said it – and so I realised there really was no hope. That was the moment when I knew that Koharu was not alive. But I couldn't show my grief. Mr Hiratsuka is . . . Mr Hiratsuka is a very strict, controlled person. He is not the kind of man who allows his natural feelings to show. He had lost his granddaughter. I know that he may have felt very sad, but he contains his feelings. Nonetheless, if he found me in a state of sadness, he should have refrained from saying words that would hurt me. But he did not refrain.'

Naomi's mother-in-law had heard the exchange and stood nearby, weeping. Mr Hiratsuka spoke scoldingly to his wife and ordered her to quell her tears.

Naomi's husband, Shinichiro, reached home the following day. Like his wife he was a teacher at a high school in Ishinomaki, which had become the refuge for a thousand people made homeless by the tsunami. His presence diluted the authority of his father and made acceptable Naomi's absence from the house. With Shinichiro, she drove down the road as far as the waters allowed. There she met the mother of another girl from Okawa Primary School, who told them that she had just identified her own daughter at the school gymnasium upriver. She thought she might have seen Koharu's body there too.

The Hiratsukas drove inland to the gymnasium mortuary. More and more bodies were coming in, and the place was in the grip of bureaucratic confusion. There were papers to be filed, and incoming bodies had to be examined by a doctor and formally logged, a process that sometimes took days. Naomi and Shinichiro had young children and needy old people back at home; they couldn't wait. They filled out the necessary documents and left.

The following day, Shinichiro said goodbye to his family and went back to his school in the city to help with the care of the refugees there. His wife did not question the decision; none in his family regarded it as bizarre or remarkable, any more than it was bizarre to expect a mother newly grieving for her young daughter to cook, wash and clean. None of his colleagues would have reproached Shinichiro if he had walked away from his school to look for his child's body. But no self-respecting Japanese teacher could have done so with an easy conscience. It was just one example of the dutifulness routinely expected of a public servant.

Shinichiro came home whenever he felt able. When he did, he and Naomi went to the school gymnasium. There were 200 bodies there by the end of the week. 'They were laid out on blue tarpaulins,' she said. 'A lot of them were people I knew. There were parents of pupils of mine. There were classmates of Koharu. I was able to say, "I know him, and I know him, and I know her." But none of them was Koharu.'

After ten days they decided to go to Okawa Primary School to see what was happening there. The water had receded to the point where they could drive and wade to Kamaya. Rough paths had been cleared by the volunteer firemen, who were using a digger to part the debris. But rubble still overwhelmed the school buildings, and on top of the clagging mud was a thin layer of snow. Next to the traffic island at the entrance to the village there were blue vinyl sheets, on which bodies were laid out to be washed before being taken to the mortuary. Half a dozen mothers lingered there, waiting for their children to be lifted out.

Naomi looked at the faces of the people on the blue sheets, hoping all the time to recognise Koharu. She was a tall girl with unruly, shoulder-length hair and a plump, humorous face. Naomi thought about the last moments they had spent together. As her mother tended to Koharu's little brother and sister, as her septuagenarian grandfather prepared breakfast for her grandmother, and the grandmother fussed over her near-centenarian great-grandmother, Koharu had quietly dressed, eaten and left for the school bus. She was about to enter her last week of primary school; she and Naomi had discussed what she would wear for the graduation ceremony. Most of the other girls favoured jackets and tartan skirts, in emulation of the starlets of a toothsome pop band. But Koharu had chosen a *hakama*, an elegantly formal traditional skirt of high pleats worn over a kimono. The skirt had been Naomi's, but Koharu was almost as tall as her mother, and it required little alteration.

Naomi came back to the school whenever she could. Time, as she experienced it, was passing in an unfamiliar way. There was so much to do for the family at home, and doing it was such an effort. She would spend hours queuing for petrol and food, drive home, drop off her supplies and then drive to the mortuary, or wade through black water to the school to scrutinise the dead. One day she found one of Koharu's shoes, and later her school backpack. These finds were heartbreaking and consoling at the same time. Naomi harboured no false hopes. Bodies were still coming out of the debris at the rate of several a day. She knew it was only a matter of time before her daughter came out too.

At the beginning of April, the nurseries and kindergartens reopened. With the two youngest children off her hands during the day, Naomi was able to devote herself to the search for Koharu.

She found herself one of a dwindling group of parents, loitering by the traffic island at the entrance to Kamaya. There was a shy, quiet man named Masaru Naganuma who was looking for his seven-year-old son, Koto; as a qualified heavy-vehicle operator, Masaru sometimes drove the digger that scooped and divided the mud. Naomi became especially close to a woman named Miho Suzuki, who had buried her twelve-year-old son, Kento, but was still searching for her nine-year-old daughter, Hana.

Masaru, in particular, was unswerving in his determination to find his son. Each morning Naomi would come to the school and watch him out in the black mud, turning it over and over with the arm of the yellow digger. As spring came on, rich colour returned to the hills and the river – the dark green of the pines, the lighter shades of the deciduous trees, and the fluffy yellow of bamboo. But at the heart of the landscape of leaf and water was darkness: this pit of mud, which had sucked down everything precious and refused to give it up. How deep was that mud? It seemed bottomless. It stuck to Naomi's clothes and boots, and followed her home in her car. Liquid mud dripped off the caterpillar tracks on Masaru's digger, as he rode it out every morning to look for his little boy.

'Just look around this place,' Naomi said. 'What parent could rest, having left the body of their child under this earth and rubble, or floating out there in the sea?'

Naomi was a teacher of English. She spoke it well, when she tried, with a clear American accent. But she lacked all confidence, and in our conversations she used Japanese. Describing the events following the disaster, she talked fast and fluently, with sharp, emphatic gestures. But when I asked her about herself, she became hesitant and ill at ease.

She had grown up in Sendai, but studied at a university in Okinawa, the chain of beautiful, subtropical islands far south of the Japanese mainland, where her father had been born. She had gone there filled with excitement and aspiration, but came away disappointed. 'I have Okinawan blood, but I had never lived there,' she said. 'I wanted to study the old Okinawan language and learn Okinawan dance. But I accomplished less than half of what I wanted.' After graduation, she left the sunny south and returned to the cold northern territory of her birth.

Of all the Okawa mothers I met, Naomi was the clearest-sighted, even in the intensity of grief. For many of those who experienced it, the tragedy of the tsunami was formless, black and ineffable, an immense and overwhelming monster that blocked out the sun. But to Naomi, no less stricken than the others, it was glittering and sharp and appallingly bright. This harshly illuminated clarity was the opposite of consoling. It pierced, rather than smothered, and left nowhere to hide.

In all the time I spent with Naomi, I never went to her home. Her father-in-law did not care for journalists, and she didn't want to upset him unnecessarily. We would meet at the school and drive back up the road towards Ishinomaki to talk in a road-side restaurant. At the beginning, she told me, the search for the missing children had been performed by local people, who cleared away what rubble they could, and by the police, who supervised the processing of the dead. Then came soldiers of the Japan Self-Defence Forces. At first this had been a cause for optimism, as the mesh of rubble encasing the school was removed piece by piece. But the longer the search for the children went on, the more the scale of the task was exposed.

In the early days, children had been found all around, thrown up against the hollows of the hill – thirty-four of them in one soft heap. Then they began to come out in smaller groups of one or two; and then the flow diminished to a trickle. By late March, some thirty of the seventy-four missing children had still not been found; a fortnight later, there were just ten missing. At the end of April, four children were recovered in quick succession from a pond that had supplied water to the rice fields of Kamaya. Some of them were five feet below the water and mud, beyond the reach of the rescuers' probing poles. It had become obvious that to search the area fully, the whole area would first have to be drained. So mechanical pumps were acquired, and a generator that had to be fuelled around the clock. Then bodies began to turn up in the Fuji lake, two miles away, on the far side of the hill.

Rather than comprising a single wave, the tsunami had consisted of repeated pulses of water, washing in and washing out again, weaving over, under and across one another. Some of the objects that fell into its embrace had been lifted and deposited close to their point of origin; but many had been sucked under and thrown up, pulled back and dashed forward again, in an irretrievably complex operation of internal currents and eddies. The obvious places had all been searched; nowadays, new sets of remains were being found far from the school; and whenever this happened, the potential area of search expanded once again.

In May, a doctor took swabs from the mouths of Naomi, Shinichiro and their children, in order to isolate Koharu's DNA. At the end of that month, parts of a small body washed up in

Naburi, a fishing village on the Pacific coast, four miles from the school, across lagoon and mountains. The condition of the remains made it impossible to identify them by sight; it took three months for the laboratory to establish that they belonged not to Koharu, but to another missing girl.

The soldiers extended their search upriver to Magaki and towards the Fuji lake, and downriver to the villages around the Nagatsura lagoon. New units rotated in and out from all over the country; Naomi met so many different commanders that, with their short hair and identical uniforms, she found it hard to tell them apart. Then, three months after the tsunami, the Self-Defence Forces withdrew.

The search operation, which formerly consisted of ten earth-movers and hundreds of men, shrank to a single team of policemen, and Masaru Naganuma in his digger. Naomi and Miho still came to the school every day. By this stage, there wasn't much they could usefully do. When Masaru's steel arm uncovered something, they would wade out and examine it. They found mattresses and motorcycles and wardrobes, but no more remains. They tidied the shrine in front of the school, and threw away the dead flowers. Sometimes a second digger would work in tandem with the first one. As they moved side by side, their long yellow limbs waving and plunging, it was almost as if they were dancing.

An idea was taking form in Naomi's mind. She consulted Masaru about it. 'Why not try?' he said. In late June, she participated in a week-long course at a training centre near Sendai. All the other participants were men. They showed no curiosity about Naomi, and she felt no urge to explain herself. At the end of the week she came away with a licence to operate earth-moving equipment, one of the few women in Japan to possess such a qualification. She went immediately to work, borrowing a digger of her own and sifting the mud in search of Koharu.

Her father-in-law strongly opposed this development. He argued that operating heavy machinery was dangerous for a woman, and that her place was at home, looking after her children, husband and in-laws. Naomi listened patiently to what he had to say and paid it no attention.

The Old and the Young

When I heard the news, two weeks afterwards, the surprise was not that Takashi Shimokawara was dead, but that he had lived this long. I was driving back to Tokyo late in March 2011 when a friend called and read out the small, down-page headline in the Japanese newspaper: *Noted Athlete Dies in Tsunami*. For the past fortnight, as I travelled among the ruined coastal towns of northeast Japan, I had found myself thinking about Mr Shimokawara and the afternoon that I had spent with him two and a half years earlier.

I had never heard of Kamaishi, the town where he lived; the train that took us there was slow and trundling, and stopped at stations that were no more than platforms beside a deserted road. It was a freezing December afternoon in one of the coldest parts of the country, but Mr Shimokawara's house was cosy and warm. His daughter-in-law served green tea and biscuits as he showed us his world-record certificates, and later we drove to the recreation ground where he trained, and photographed him as he stretched and jogged and made practice throws of his javelin and shot.

After more tea, we said our goodbyes, and took the slow train home again. One fact alone had elevated this from an interesting to an unforgettable experience: Mr Shimokawara was 102 years old.

Even to lift a javelin would be an achievement for most such men, but Mr Shimokawara threw it further than anyone his age.

He competed in the class known as M-100, for athletes in their eleventh decade of life. His record throw – of 12.75 metres, at the Japan Masters Athletics championship in 2008 – broke the world centenarian javelin record, formerly held by an American. Often, after our brief meeting, I would find myself thinking of Mr Shimokawara and wondering how he was.

Far from having merely clung on to life, he had flourished. The previous year, he had turned 104. The article recording his death reported that at the Japan Masters in 2010 he had narrowly failed to beat his own world records. Eighteen thousand five hundred people died in the disaster, and each of them was a tragedy. But to have survived to such a great age triumphantly fit and alert, to have lived through two World Wars, only to be felled by something as capricious and random as a tsunami, was unbearably bitter and ironic.

A month later, I went back to Kamaishi to look for traces of one of the disaster's oldest victims. I found them in the home where I had talked to him two and half years before, a stout two-storey house, still standing 400 yards from the sea. Mr Shimokawara's middle-aged grandson, Minoru, was sorting through what remained, with a team of helpers and friends. There was his grandfather's white tracksuit, and the postcard confirming his most recent achievements – 3.79 metres in the shot and 7.31 metres in the discus. And there were photograph albums, sodden but intact, the colours of the prints bulging and dissolving before our eyes.

They contained pictures of Mr Shimokawara holding his medals, standing alongside his wife and at a school reunion. All of them showed a cheerful elderly man, not all that much fitter or healthier than the one I had met – and plenty of these photographs were more than forty years old.

This is the most dizzying, and at the same time the most banal, thing about the situation of centenarians – just how very, very old they are. Takashi Shimokawara was born eight years before the First World War, and outlived all of his contemporaries and two of his six children. The youngest of his eight great-grandchildren was younger than him by more than a century. And yet there had been nothing about Mr Shimokawara to suggest that he would live to such an age.

Both his parents died in their fifties. He led an active life as a high-school PE teacher, but he had his share of illness, including tuberculosis and gallstones. He admitted to me that as a young man he used to drink and smoke heavily, and that he still enjoyed a glass of sake with meals.

'When did you give up smoking?' I asked.

'When I was eighty,' he said.

I recounted this to his grandson, who smiled and said, 'He lied. When I went drinking with him he had much more than a glass, and he used to cadge my cigarettes.'

All his life Mr Shimokawara was active in the community, as a teacher, local councillor and in later years as a local celebrity. But despite being surrounded by people, I recognised something painful: that he was intensely, unquenchably lonely. He had been a widower for thirty-five years. Many of the children he taught as a schoolmaster had long ago died of old age. 'All my brothers and sisters are dead,' he said. 'I'm the last. My oldest friends are twenty years younger than me. My situation is fearful, in a way. So many have died around me – I have been to so many funerals. I don't cry about it, but this is my biggest sadness, this loneliness.'

The second painful thing dawned on me a little later: that, at the age of 102, Mr Shimokawara had a lively fear of death.

Lulled by clichés about 'serene' old people, I had assumed that attachment to life diminishes with age. But here was an extreme example of the opposite: an ancient man fending off death with javelin and discus. It was this – the urge to stay on his feet at all costs – that drove his athletic achievements. 'The most important thing of all is to stay supple and flexible,' he said. 'The moment you will be most stiff is when you die – you never get stiffer than that. So you've got to sleep well, eat well and keep moving.' And all of this made the facts of his eventual death all the more pitiful.

Because Mr Shimokawara's son and daughter-in-law died with him, his friends and family had to work out for themselves the puzzle of the family car. It was found a few days after the disaster, carefully parked on a hill, safely beyond the reach of the tsunami. This discovery immediately inspired hope – for repeated searches of the area around the family home had turned up no trace of the Shimokawaras. Then eight days later, the three bodies were recovered from a public hall a few hundred yards from the house – and it was this that unlocked the sad truth.

In Kamaishi, as elsewhere, the earthquake itself caused little serious damage, and tsunami warnings were immediately broadcast through loudspeakers across the town. Mr Shimokawara's seventy-three-year-old son had plenty of time to help his father and wife into the car and to drive them to the single-storey public hall. It was only a few hundred yards from the sea, and scarcely more elevated than the family house. But by the time this became obvious, it would have been much too late.

The wave surged around Mr Shimokawara's house, although its upper floor was spared. But it overwhelmed the public hall and drowned those who had retreated there. Three minutes' walking distance further up the road, the water petered out against a steadily rising slope. 'If they had stayed with the car, or walked up the road, or even just stayed at home and climbed the stairs, they would have made it,' said Keizo Tada, an old friend. Instead, as a good citizen obediently following the drill, Mr Shimokawara's son drove to safety, parked his car and calmly and obliviously walked back down the hill to his death.

Takashi Shimokawara had lived through the 1933 tsunami, the Chile tsunami in 1960, and countless minor waves and false alarms. When his old friend Tada last spoke to him, he had talked of the forthcoming athletics championship when he would compete in the over-105 age group. Without question, he would have set new world records – he would, literally, have been in a class of his own.

The funeral of such an old man would not normally be an occasion of intense grief and tragedy, but this one was. 'To be honest, I still don't feel as if they are dead,' said Minoru, who buried his mother, father and grandfather on the same day. 'Of course, I have identified the bodies, signed the documents, and organised the cremation. But it's as if I'm in the middle of a nightmare, and the real pain is still coming towards me.'

The tsunami was a disaster visited above all upon the old. Fifty-four per cent of those who perished were 65 or older, and the older you were, the worse your chances. But the converse of this was even more striking. The younger you were, the more likely you were to survive – and the number of children who were killed was astonishingly small.

In the Indian Ocean tsunami that struck Indonesia, Sri Lanka and Thailand in 2004, children died disproportionately because they were less physically capable of swimming and dragging themselves to safety. In Japan, the opposite was true. Out of the 18,500 dead and missing, only 351 – fewer than one in fifty – were schoolchildren. Four out of five of them died somewhere other than school: because they were off sick that afternoon or had been quickly picked up by anxious parents. It was much more dangerous, in other words, to be reunited with your family than to remain with your teachers.

If you are ever exposed to a violent earthquake, the safest place you could hope to be is Japan; and the best spot of all is inside a Japanese school.* Decades of technological experiment have bred the most resilient and strictly regulated construction in the world. Even against the immensity of the tsunami, Japan's sea walls, warning systems and evacuation drills saved an uncountable number of lives: however great the catastrophe of 2011, the damage caused would have been many times worse if it had happened in any other country. And nowhere are precautions against natural disaster more robust than in state schools.

They are built on iron frames out of reinforced concrete. They are often situated on hills and elevations, and all of them are required to have detailed disaster plans and to practise them regularly. On that afternoon, Japanese architecture and bureaucracy did an almost perfect job of protecting the young.

No school collapsed or suffered serious physical damage in the earthquake. Nine of them were completely overwhelmed by the tsunami, and at one of them, in the town of Minami-Sanriku, a boy of thirteen was drowned as his class hurried to higher ground. But with one exception, every other school got all its children to safety.

On 11 March 2011, seventy-five children in Japan died in the care of their teachers. Seventy-four of them were at Okawa Primary School. Later, many of their parents were tormented by self-reproach for not rushing there to collect them. But far from being neglectful or lazy, they had followed the course of action which, in every other circumstance, would have been most likely to secure their safety and survival.

* * *

* One of the worst places, of course, is anywhere near a nuclear reactor, such as those inside the Fukushima Dai-ichi nuclear power plant. But the fact of that man-made disaster, set off by the naturally occurring earthquake and tsunami, does not contradict what I have to say here about the resilience of Japanese construction in general.

'I was hardly conscious of what I was doing,' said Katsura Sato. 'There were so many feelings. All I could do was to deal with life one piece at a time. We had lost Mizuho, my dearest girl. But we hadn't lost anything else. My other two children were fine. Our house was untouched. People on the coast lost their families, their houses and their community. There were people who were still looking for their loved ones. They were much worse off than us. Once water and electricity returned, we got back to some kind of ordinary life.'

Katsura was an art teacher at a high school in Ishinomaki and lived with her husband, parents-in-law and three children in Fukuji, a few hundred yards from Sayomi Shito and her family. Katsura and Sayomi's daughters, Mizuho and Chisato, were best friends at Okawa Primary School. They were cremated on the same day. 'Until then,' Katsura said, 'that was all I could concentrate on. After the cremation – well, I'm usually healthy, but I became ill. I couldn't get up. I stayed in bed for three days. And I started thinking and thinking, and I became very suspicious about the circumstances in which we lost our daughter. I knew that this was a great natural disaster, and I assumed at the beginning that there must have been many other cases like this, other schools where the same thing happened. But why did I never hear of them?'

In the villages along the river, as they began to catch their breath in the weeks following the disaster, other parents were asking the same question.

Much of their suspicion focused on the actions of two men. The first of them was Junji Endo, the only teacher to have survived the tsunami, whom Hitomi Konno had seen, stunned and almost speechless, in Irikamaya in the early morning after the disaster. The second was the headmaster of the school, a man named Teruyuki Kashiba. By chance, Kashiba had been off work that Friday afternoon and was attending the graduation ceremony of his own daughter at another school miles inland. Whatever had gone wrong at Okawa, the testimony of these two – the only surviving adult witness to the events at the school, and its head, the man responsible for all its safety procedures – was clearly crucial. But since that first morning of dread and confusion, no one seemed to have seen or heard from Endo; and even the headmaster had been strangely elusive.

The searchers picking through the mud were surprised not to see Kashiba at the ruins of the school. He eventually put in an appearance, six days after the tsunami, followed by a train of journalists and cameramen. Two weeks later, Katsura Sato was startled to see Kashiba's face on the local television news, and even more amazed by the subject of the report – a ceremony at Okawa Primary School. The thirty surviving children were marking the start of the new school year, which in Japan begins in April. Okawa Primary had been reconstituted in a classroom at another school in the area. Katsura remembered clearly the words that the headmaster used in addressing the children: 'Let's forge a common effort to rebuild a school full of smiles, for the sake of our friends who died.'

'At first the children were a bit nervous,' Kashiba told the television interviewer. 'But when I said these words to them, they nodded firmly.'

School ceremonies, even for young children, are a matter of great importance in Japan, occasions of pleasure and pride for an entire family. Fifty-four families had lost children at the school; none had received notification of a ceremony in which their dead sons and daughters should have been participants. The intention was clear enough – to make some attempt at resuming normal life, and to create a place where the survivors could pick up again the business of simply being schoolchildren. But it was experienced by many of the grieving families as a punch to the stomach.

'The invitations were sent out to the parents of the kids who survived,' Katsura said. 'I thought, "Our kids are gone, but aren't we still Okawa parents?" We had had no explanation – no word from the school at all. This headmaster, Kashiba, turned up at the school once or twice, without even getting his hands dirty. And then we see him on television, talking about "smiles".'

Katsura went on, 'It was as if they were abandoning us before the kids were even buried. That night I couldn't sleep for anger. I said to my husband, "How can we let this happen?" And I wondered: was it just me who thought like that?'

Explanations

Four weeks after the tsunami, the Ishinomaki City Board of Education, supervisory authority of Okawa Primary School, convened an 'explanatory meeting' for families of the children who had died there. The meeting gave the impression of having been arranged hastily, in chastened response to the fusillade of anger that had been directed against the board after the mishandled opening ceremony. It was held on a Saturday evening at the inland school to which the surviving children of Okawa Primary had been relocated. Journalists were not admitted, but one of the parents made a video recording of the proceedings. It shows Kashiba, the headmaster, and five representatives of the education board seated on a row of chairs in the blue overalls which arc the uniform of Japanese public officials. Opposite, with only their backs visible to the video camera, sit the parents and other relatives, ninety-seven of them all told. The room was unheated; in the film, everyone is swaddled in coats, hats and scarves.

The meeting opened conventionally enough, with introductions by a Mr Konno, head of the secretariat of the board of education. He began with an apology: he had lost his voice, and would therefore deliver only brief opening remarks. 'Good evening to you all,' he croaked. 'I extend my sincerest sympathies to those who fell victim to this disaster. In particular, I offer sincere prayers for those who died. This month, the children should have welcomed spring, their breasts swelling with hope. However, on the eleventh of March, the day of that huge disaster, a great tsunami snatched away in a moment the smallest pleasures of daily life. Having lost the irreplaceable, precious lives of many children and teachers, we face an unhappy spring.'

Public meetings in Japan are blandly formulaic occasions, by and large, replete with stock phrases, and characterised by an absence of confrontation or verbal fireworks. But then Konno gave the floor to Kashiba, the headmaster, and it quickly became clear that this was not going to be an ordinary meeting.

Grief and anger threatened the reputations of everyone connected to the school; for many people, it became impossible to look objectively on the character of Teruyuki Kashiba. He was a short, plump, grey-haired man in his late fifties, with oval spectacles and a habit of sucking in his lips at moments of stress or reflection. After a decade as deputy head in other schools, he had been appointed to Okawa the previous April. Even before the disaster, no one seemed sure quite what to make of Kashiba. After a year, not all the parents knew who he was.

It was not his fault that he had been away from the school that afternoon; his horror and distress can only be imagined. But he made a grave error of judgement, first in taking so long to go to the site after the disaster, and then by his conduct when he did show his face. He was never forgiven for his failure to make any effort, even a token one, to help with the search for bodies. On his first visit, he answered questions from the media and took a lot of photographs with an expensive camera. On another occasion, he was seen expending anxious effort in a hunt for the school safe.

By the time of the meeting in the school, the rage and misery of the parents had been gathering for a month. That evening they found their object in Kashiba.

'Until the afternoon of the eleventh of March,' he mumbled, when his turn came to speak, 'there were smiles on the faces of the children, and laughter in the voices of the children, but, truly, seventy-four children, ten teachers were lost. I apologise sincerely.'

'Can't hear you!' called a voice from the audience.

'Don't you have a mike?' said someone else.

Kashiba continued. 'At the school, when I stood in front of the building, I could imagine the faces of the children. It was terrible.'

'When did you go to the school?' someone interrupted.

'Yeah, when did you go?' called another.

'What day did I go?' asked the ruffled headmaster. 'It was the seventeenth of March.'

'Our daughter died on the eleventh.'

Kashiba bowed his head. 'I apologise,' he said. 'The delay in responding, the failures – there were so many – I am truly sorry.'

At that moment, a frisson passed through the gathered parents, as people in the room became aware of an unexpected presence – a man sitting at the far left, dressed in black. His head and shoulders were slumped forward, to the extent that it was difficult to see his face at all.

'Well, well, well,' someone called out. 'If it isn't Junji Endo.'

Even those who later harboured the greatest distrust towards him admitted that, before the disaster, Endo had been a successful and popular teacher. He was a self-deprecating, bespectacled man in his late forties, third in the hierarchy of the school's small staff. As head of teaching, he had no classroom of his own, but moved between the different year groups teaching nature and science. 'The children were very close to him,' Hitomi Konno told me. 'Daisuke was a member of the nature club, and Mr Endo used to show them deer horns, and how to make fish hooks, and tell them all kinds of stories about crocodiles and piranhas. They thought he was amazing.'

He had previously taught in the fishing village of Aikawa, seven miles up the coast. Among his responsibilities at Aikawa Primary

School had been disaster preparedness. Plenty of teachers would have treated this as a routine matter, demanding nothing more than the organisation of evacuation drills and the updating of parents' telephone numbers. But Endo went much further. The emergency manual at Aikawa stated that, in the case of a tsunami warning, pupils and staff should evacuate to the flat roof of the three-storey building. Endo judged this to be inadequate. He rewrote the plan to require escape up a steep hill to the Shinto shrine behind the school.

Aikawa Primary had been built on flat ground virtually at sea level, just 200 yards from the water. When the tsunami struck here, it was more than fifty feet high and it overwhelmed the school completely. The roof was covered by the waves: anyone who had retreated there would have died. But, following the revised procedure, the teachers and children had quickly climbed the hill, and not a single one was hurt. At his old school, Junji Endo could rightly claim to have saved scores of lives.

In different circumstances, he might have been an object of sympathy and admiration. But since the morning after the disaster, no one seemed to have heard from him. His whereabouts, and the story he had to tell, had become matters of intense speculation – and now here he was.

'He saved his own life,' someone called from the audience. '*He*'s still alive. So let him talk to us.'

A board of education official named Shigemi Kato spoke. 'Mr Endo himself has injuries – he suffered a dislocation and frostbite and had to go to hospital. He's presently suffering from a serious psychological illness. Please keep this in mind as you listen to him.'

'No fucking kidding,' someone said. 'Well, we parents are ill too.'

With an appearance of great difficulty and distress, Endo began to speak. His head and upper body were bent almost parallel to the ground. He frequently became choked with emotion; sometimes he appeared to be on the verge of collapse.

'I'm sorry,' he said. 'I couldn't help. I'm so truly sorry for that.' The heckling ceased.

'Allow me to describe what happened on that day,' he said. 'There may be gaps in my memory. Please forgive me if there are.'

'It was a Friday,' Endo began, 'and lessons had just finished for the day when the shaking began. It must have been the time when the children were getting ready to go home, and they were with their teachers for the class meeting. The electricity was cut off and the tannoy didn't work, so I ran up to the classrooms on the second floor and said to each class, 'Get under your desks, and hold on to them.' The children seemed scared, but the class teachers were telling them that it would all be OK. After the tremors subsided, I went back to each class in turn and told them to come out and evacuate.'

Endo remained behind, and checked the classrooms and toilets for stragglers. By the time he emerged, the register had been taken and the children were sitting in the playground. 'Some of them were vomiting from panic,' Endo said, 'and some could not stop crying. The teachers were trying to calm them down. It had begun to snow, and some of the children had escaped in bare feet. I went back in and brought jumpers and shoes, and had them put them on.'

By now, local people from Kamaya were turning up at the school. They had fled their homes during the shaking, and asked to be allowed to shelter in the school gym. Endo explained that the broken glass there made it unsuitable. 'While I was doing that,' he said, 'parents began arriving to pick up their children, and it was the deputy head, mainly, who checked off the names and handed them over.'

A voice cried out from the audience of bereaved parents, 'Why did you do that? If you'd just put everyone in cars and driven up a hill, they would all have been saved.'

Endo continued without replying. 'After that, I learned that a tsunami was on its way. Of course, one alternative was the hill. But because the shocks were so strong and it was shaking continuously, I . . .'

He trailed off, then began again. It is difficult to translate what came next: the sentences were rambling and ungrammatical; the sequence of events was confused. 'So when the tsunami hit,' he said, 'because we never imagined such a big tsunami coming, we discussed whether we should evacuate to the safest part of the school, the upper gallery of the gym or the second floor of the school building, and I – because the damage to the school building was so bad – I went into the school building to have a look. Various things had fallen over, but I thought that we could go back in there. I returned to the playground, but by then a move had begun to evacuate immediately.'

The destination was the traffic island near the bridge, 400 yards away and around the corner on the main road. The children formed a column, which threaded out of the back of the school and through the car park of the Kamaya Village Hall. Endo brought up the rear.

As he was passing through the car park, he became aware of a powerful rush of air.

He said, 'It was a tremendous gust of wind, and a noise like I'd never heard before. I didn't know what was happening at first, but when I looked at the road in front of the school in the direction of the Kamaya high street, I could see an immense tsunami. It was coming down the road.' The column of children was advancing directly into the coming wave. Endo immediately shouted, 'The hill! The hill! This way!' and urged the children in the opposite direction, towards the rear of the school. 'But when I reached the hill,' he said, 'I was slipping on the snow and couldn't climb, and there were children all around me.

'Just as I reached the hill, two cedars collapsed. They struck me on my right arm and left shoulder, and I became trapped. I felt the tsunami wash over me, and I thought that was it, but the tree was lifted off me, perhaps by the water, and when I looked up the slope I saw a boy from the third year calling for help. I'd lost my glasses and my shoes, but I knew I had to do everything to save this child. "Go, go up!" I called. "Climb for your life!" . . . The noise of the water was getting closer. "Up, up!" I shouted, as I pushed him.'

By now it had begun to snow. The boy had swallowed a lot of water, and both his clothes and the teacher's were soaking wet. 'I realised that it was impossible to go down,' Endo said, 'and that I would have to spend the night on the hill with this child.' They found a hollow at the foot of a tree, and sat shoulder to shoulder on a heap of pine needles. 'But the noise of the water was still getting closer,' Endo said. 'And then – I don't know if it was just a feeling – it seemed that with every aftershock there was a crunch of trees falling down. The boy said, "It's coming! It's still coming closer! I'm scared, I'm scared! Let's go, let's go higher."'

At the top of the hill, the ground was covered with thickening snow. Endo found that he was unable to move his arm, the one that had been struck by the tree. Propped against his teacher's shoulder, the child nodded off, and Endo began to worry about the small sleeping body in its wet clothes. 'It was getting dark and it was terribly cold,' he said. 'I thought if we stayed as we were, the child might freeze to death.'

In the blacknesss, he could see little without his spectacles. But he supposed that, if they walked down the other side of the hill, they would eventually encounter cars and motorists on the Ogatsu road. 'I asked the boy to be my eyes,' Endo said, 'and to tell me whether it was safe to go down. As we walked down step by step, I could make out headlamps on the road. We headed in that direction. We walked towards the light. And then there were people at a house, and we said, "Please help," and they helped us.'

They ended up at Irikamaya, where Hitomi found them. The next day, Endo was helped to the hospital in Ishinomaki; and from there he went home.

Endo said, 'There are moments that have slipped from my mind, but this is more or less how it was on that day.'

He said, 'Every single day I dream about the children playing happily in the schoolyard. I dream about the teachers and the deputy head, who were preparing so hard for the graduation ceremony which was coming up. I'm so sorry.'

With that, his head and upper body slumped; at one point, it appeared that Endo was going to collapse onto the floor, and the members of the board of education jumped to their feet to support him. His naked distress, as raw as a wound, must have seemed to them to supply everything that they could not, with their formal politeness and their flowery clichés about swelling breasts. Who could question the abject pain of Mr Endo, and the agony of his survival? Konno, Kashiba, and the other suited officials might have hoped that this would be the end of the meeting, perhaps the beginning of the end of the whole dreadful business. There was a silence, as those present adjusted to the fact that Endo's account was over. The meeting was poised at a moment of pivot: it might have turned either way. Then a man in the audience got to his feet.

His name was Toshimitsu Sasaki. His seven-year-old boy, Tetsuma, and his nine-year-old daughter, Nagomi, had died at the school. 'Teachers, headmaster, members of the board of education,' he said – and the formality of this address must have raised the hope that matters would continue hereafter on a stable and predictable footing. Then he continued.

'Why didn't you come quickly to the school the next day?' he asked Kashiba. 'Why didn't you come until the seventeenth? Do you know how many children are still missing now? Can you name them? Can you name the children who died? The families left behind – all of us have been going mad. There are ten of them still missing out there. *Do you understand?* Imagine how we feel, those parents who are still searching every day. Every day in dirty clothes. And if we don't go there to search, we go mad.'

Sasaki stood up in front of the table behind which the officials sat, their eyes on the ground. He was wearing a blue windcheater and brandishing something in his hand, which he waved in their downturned faces.

'Just this shoe,' he said, his voice rising. 'That's all we've found. All ruined, like this. My daughter – is this it?' He slammed the shoe down on the table, and Konno flinched. 'My daughter!' he screamed. 'Is she a shoe?'

The meeting went on for two and a half hours. In all that time, Kashiba and the others spoke in total for no more than a few minutes. Now and then, a request for information would be formulated, and a faltering and incomplete answer given – about what tsunami warnings had been given and received, and what Kashiba had done and failed to do, and when. But most of the time was taken up by the parents, one after another, shouting, snarling, pleading, whispering and crying, with an anger directed almost exclusively towards the figure of the headmaster. On the video, he sits with his eyes on the ground. The faces of his accusers are invisible; their backs tremble as they denounce him:

– Tricky old bastard.
– Fuck off, you sod!
– I will devote my whole life to this, you bastard. I will spend my whole life avenging those children. I won't let you hide anywhere.

People almost never speak like this in Japan – not in public, not to teachers and government officials. It is difficult to exaggerate the violence of these interventions, and the intensity of emotion that they betrayed.

One woman said: 'We believed that they would come back the next day. Everyone believed that. Everyone had faith in the school. Everyone believed they must be safe, because they were at school.'

A man said: 'Every day I hear our son and daughter crying, screaming, "Dad, help me!" They are crying out in my dreams. They never leave my dreams.'

Much of the torrent of words took the form of questions. 'Did you see those swollen faces?' a father asked. 'They had changed so much after one month. A rotten thing. That was a human being, you know. A person. Humped up onto a truck, covered with a rag. Come and talk to us after you find your own child like that, you bastard.'

Another asked: 'Do you know the number of missing children in each class, Headmaster? *Without* looking at that piece of paper. You don't, do you? You have to look at your piece of paper. Our kids – are they just a piece of paper? You don't remember any of their faces, do you?'

Their grief was unquenchable, but what they were seeking was not mysterious – and a group of more sensitive men, less oppressed by protocol and panic, could have transformed the atmosphere in the room. All the parents wanted was a reflection of their own grief, a glimmer of recognition of their loss, a sense that they were facing not a government department, but fellow human beings. As their passion rose, they abandoned the indirectness of standard Japanese and expressed themselves ever more bluntly in the slurring dialect of Tohoku. And rather than emerging to meet them, the bureaucrats retreated in the opposite direction, into ever fussier and more bloodless speech.

Asked about the search for the missing, Konno said: 'At present, personnel from the Japan Self-Defence Forces, central government and the police are making their best efforts to recover remains of those regrettably not found yet. Hereafter, we will continue the search beneath the detritus, and the like.'

Pressed on a proposal to hold a joint funeral for the children, Kashiba, the head, responded: 'By consulting with members of the board of education, and talking to bereaved family members, I suppose I think that I want to decide whether we will do this or not.'

'Don't patronise us, like bumpkins,' someone shouted.

'Is it because we are in the country that you treat us like this?' asked another.

'If we were in the city, this wouldn't happen,' said a third voice. The words came, and kept coming:

– Headmaster, have you ever thought about the feelings of the children during that hour that they were waiting? How scared they must have been – have you thought about that? How cold they were, and their screaming for their mums and dads. And there was a hill, a hill right there!

– You people who came to the school after the road was cleared – you don't know anything. I was there when it was just trees, pine trees scattered all around. We didn't know where to start. Walking through the water in boots, with that sound, *squelch-squelch*. You'll never understand what it was like to walk through that water, with the squelching, and the mud getting into your boots. Even when they found their own children, mums and dads came back to look for the others. What did you look for? Fuck you. You looked for the school safe.

– Will you come to the school, Headmaster? Will you search?
– We'll lend you a shovel, if you don't have one.
– If you haven't got the boots, we can give you as many as you want.
– You've only got nice leather shoes, haven't you?
– And he's got a nice camera.

– It took us four years to have a child . . .
– Us too. We managed only after long years. And now he's gone.
– Can't you do something?
– Please return our child to us.
– Every night, I . . . What . . . ? What can we do?
– They were our future.
– Please, please, return him.
– Yes!
– Release him!

It was after nine o'clock by the time the meeting broke up. Kashiba looked dazed. There were plenty of people present who had not spoken, but who felt sympathy for the headmaster and had been mortified by the shouting. Now their minds were racing. Much remained unresolved – but they had, at least, finally heard from the wretched Endo, and received an account of the missing time in the playground, on which everyone had been so unbearably fixated. His account made it clear that there had been tsunami warnings, that they had been received by the teachers and acted on – even if much too late.

The nine-year-old boy who had been with Endo on the mountain, whom he had huddled against in an effort to save him from the cold, was called Seina Yamamoto. His mother was present at the meeting and went to the teacher to thank him. While they were talking, another mother, whose son had died, also approached. She wanted to ask Endo if he remembered anything about her own boy; like many of the parents, she was avid for a last glimpse of him, just the memory of a word or two, or the look on his face. But the education officials told her that Endo was 'unwell', and prevented her from speaking to him. Quickly, it would become clear that much of what he had said that evening was not true at all. And after that evening, he vanished from sight.

Ghosts

I met a priest in northern Japan who exorcised the spirits of people who had drowned in the tsunami. The ghosts did not appear in large numbers until autumn of that year, but Reverend Kaneta's first case of possession came to him after less than a fortnight. He was chief priest at a Zen temple in the inland town of Kurihara. The earthquake on 11 March was the most violent that he, or anyone he knew, had ever experienced. The great wooden beams of the temple's halls had flexed and groaned with the strain. Power, water and telephone lines were fractured for days; deprived of electricity, people in Kurihara, thirty miles from the coast, had a dimmer idea of what was going on there than television viewers on the other side of the world. But it became clear enough when first a handful of families, and then a mass of them, began arriving at Reverend Kaneta's temple with corpses to bury.

More than 18,000 people had died at a stroke. In the space of a month, Reverend Kaneta performed funeral services for 200 of them. More appalling than the scale of death was the spectacle of the bereaved survivors. 'They didn't cry,' Kaneta said. 'There was no emotion at all. The loss was so profound, and death had come so suddenly. They understood the facts of their situation individually – that they had lost their homes, lost their livelihoods and lost their families. They understood each piece, but they couldn't see it as a whole, and they couldn't understand what they should do, or sometimes even where they were. I couldn't really talk to them, to be honest. All I could do was stay with them, and read the sutras and conduct the ceremonies. That was the thing I could do.'

Amid this numbness and horror, Reverend Kaneta received a visit from a man he knew, a local builder whom I will call Takeshi Ono.

Ono was ashamed of what had happened, and didn't want his real name to be published. It was difficult at first to understand the reason for this shame. He was a strong, stocky man in his late thirties, the kind of man most comfortable in blue overalls, with a head of youthfully dense and tousled hair. 'He's such an innocent person,' Reverend Kaneta said to me. 'He takes everything at face value. You're from England, aren't you? He's like your Mr Bean.' I wouldn't have gone so far, because there was nothing ridiculous about Ono. But there was a dreamy ingenuousness about him, which made the story he told all the more believable.

He had been at work on a house when the earthquake struck. He clung to the ground for as long as it lasted; even his lorry shook as if it was about to topple over. The drive home, along roads without traffic lights, was alarming, but the physical damage was remarkably slight: a few telegraph poles lolling at an angle, toppled garden walls. As the owner of a small building firm, he was perfectly equipped to deal with the practical inconveniences inflicted by the earthquake. Ono spent the next few days busying himself with camping stoves, generators and jerrycans, and paying little attention to the news.

But once television was restored, it was impossible to be unaware of what had happened. Ono watched the endlessly replayed image of the explosive plume above the nuclear reactor, and the mobile-phone films of the black wave crunching up ports, houses, shopping centres, cars and human figures. These were places he had known all his life, fishing towns and beaches just over the hills, an hour's drive away. And the spectacle of their destruction produced in Ono a sensation of glassy detachment, a feeling common at that time, even among those most directly stricken by displacement and bereavement.

'My life had returned to normal,' he told me. 'I had petrol, I had an electricity generator, no one I knew was dead or hurt. I hadn't seen the tsunami myself, not with my own eyes, so I felt as if I was in a kind of dream.'

Ten days after the disaster, Ono, his wife and his widowed mother drove over the mountains to see for themselves.

They left in the morning in good spirits, stopped on the way to go shopping and reached the coast in time for lunch. For most of the way, the scene was familiar: brown rice fields, villages of wood and tile, bridges over wide, slow rivers. Once they had climbed into the hills, they passed more and more emergency vehicles, not only those of the police and fire services, but green lorries of the Self-Defence Forces. As the road descended towards the coast, their jaunty mood began to evaporate. Suddenly, before they understood where they were, they had entered the tsunami zone.

There was no advance warning, no marginal area of incremental damage. The wave had come in with full force, spent itself and stopped at a point as clearly defined as the reach of a high tide. Above it, nothing had been touched; below it, everything was changed.

This was the point at which shame entered Ono's narrative, and he became reluctant to describe in detail what he did or where he went. 'I saw the rubble, I saw the sea,' he said. 'I saw buildings damaged by the tsunami. It wasn't just the things themselves, but the atmosphere. It was a place I used to go so often. It was such a shock to see it. And all the police and soldiers there. It's difficult to describe. It felt dangerous. My first thought was that this is terrible. My next feeling was, "Is it real?"'

Ono, his wife and his mother sat down for dinner as usual that evening. He remembered that he drank two small cans of beer with the meal. Afterwards, and for no obvious reason, he began calling friends on his mobile phone. 'I'd just ring and say, "Hi, how are you?" – that kind of thing,' he told me. 'It wasn't that I had much to say. I don't know why, but I was starting to feel very lonely.'

His wife had already left the house when he woke the next morning. Ono had no particular work of his own, and passed an idle day at home. His mother bustled in and out, but she seemed mysteriously upset, even angry. When his wife returned from her office, she was similarly tense.

'Is something wrong?' Ono asked.

'I'm divorcing you!' she replied.

'Divorce? But why? Why?'

And so his wife and mother described the events of the night before, after the round of needy phone calls. How Ono had jumped down onto all fours and begun licking the tatami mats and futon, and squirmed on them like a beast. How at first they had nervously laughed at his tomfoolery, but had been silenced when he began snarling, 'You must die. You must die. Everyone must die. Everything must die and be lost.' In front of the house was an unsown field, and Ono had run out into it and rolled over and over in the mud, as if he was being tumbled by a wave, shouting, 'There, over there! They're all over there – look!' Then he had stood up and walked out into the field, calling, 'I'm coming to you. I'm coming over to that side', before his wife physically wrestled him back into the house. The writhing and bellowing went on all night until, around five in the morning, Ono cried out, 'There's something on top of me', collapsed and fell asleep.

'My wife and my mother were so anxious and upset,' he said. 'Of course, I told them how sorry I was. But I had no memory of what I did or why.'

It went on for three nights.

The next evening, as darkness fell, he saw figures walking past the house: parents and children, a group of young friends, a grandfather and a child. 'The people were covered in mud,' he said. 'They were no more than twenty feet away, and they stared at me, but I wasn't afraid. I just thought, "Why are they in those muddy things? Why don't they change their clothes? Perhaps their washing machine's broken." They were like people I might have known once, or seen before somewhere. The scene was flickering, like a film. But I felt perfectly normal, and I thought that they were just ordinary people.'

The next day, Ono was lethargic and inert. At night, he would lie down, sleep heavily for ten minutes, then wake up as lively and refreshed as if eight hours had passed. He staggered when he walked, glared at his wife and mother and even waved a knife. 'Drop dead!' he would snarl. 'Everyone else is dead, so die!'

After three days of pleading by his family, he went to Reverend Kaneta at the temple. 'His eyes were dull,' Kaneta said. 'Like a person with depression after taking their medication. I knew at a glance that something was wrong.' Ono recounted the visit to the coast, and his wife and mother described his behaviour in the days since. 'The Reverend was looking hard at me as I spoke,' Ono said, 'and in part of my mind I was saying, "Don't look at me like that, you bastard. I hate your guts! Why are you looking at me?"'

Kaneta took Ono by the hand and led him, tottering, into the main hall of the temple. 'He told me to sit down. I was not myself. I still remember that strong feeling of resistance. But part of me was also relieved – I wanted to be helped, and to believe in the priest. The part of me that was still me wanted to be saved.'

Kaneta beat the temple drum as he chanted the Heart Sutra:

There are no eyes, no ears, no nose, no tongue,
no body, mind; no colour, sound, or smell;
no taste, no touch, no thing; no realm of sight,

no realm of thoughts; no ignorance, no end
to ignorance; no old age and no death;
no end to age and death; no suffering,
nor any cause of suffering, nor end
to suffering, no path, no wisdom
                            and no fulfilment.

Ono's wife told him later how he pressed his hands together in prayer and how, as the priest's recitation continued, they rose high above his head as if being pulled from above.

gone gone gone beyond
gone altogether beyond
O what an awakening
– all hail!

The priest splashed him with holy water, and then abruptly Ono returned to his senses and found himself with wet hair and shirt, filled with a sensation of tranquillity and release. 'My head was light,' he said. 'In a moment, the thing that had been there had gone. I felt fine physically, but my nose was blocked as if I'd come down with a heavy cold.'

Kaneta spoke sternly to him; both of them understood what had happened. 'Ono told me that he'd walked along the beach in that devastated area, eating an ice cream,' the priest said. 'He even put up a sign in the car in the windscreen saying DISASTER RELIEF, so that no one would stop him. He went there flippantly, without giving it any thought at all. I told him, "You fool. If you go to a place like that where many people have died, you must go with a feeling of respect. That's common sense. You have suffered a kind of punishment for what you did. Something got hold of you, perhaps the dead who cannot accept yet that they are dead. They have been trying to express their regret and their resentment through you."' Kaneta suddenly smiled as he remembered it.

'Mr Bean!' he said indulgently. 'He's so innocent and open. That's another reason why they were able to possess him.'

Ono recognised all of this, and more. It was not just the spirits of men and women that had possessed him, he saw now, but also animals – cats and dogs and other beasts which had drowned with their masters.

He thanked the priest, and drove home. His nose was streaming as if with catarrh, but what came out was not mucus, but a pink jelly like nothing he had seen before.

The wave penetrated no more than a few miles inland, but over the hills in Kurihara it transformed the life of Reverend Taio Kaneta. He had inherited the temple from his father, and the task of dealing with the survivors of the tsunami tested him in ways for which he was unprepared. It had been the greatest disaster of post-war Japan. And yet the pain did not announce itself; it dug underground and burrowed deep. Once the immediate emergency had abated, once the bodies were cremated, the memorial services held and the homeless sheltered, Reverend Kaneta set about trying to gain entry into the dungeon of silence in which he saw so many of the survivors languishing.

He began travelling around the coast with a group of fellow priests, organising a mobile event which he called 'Café de Monku' – a bilingual pun. As well as being the Japanese pronunciation of the English word 'monk', *monku* means complaint. 'We think it will take a long time to get back to a calm, quiet, ordinary life,' read the flyer that he distributed. 'Why don't you come and join us – take a break and have a little moan? The monks will listen to your complaint – and have a *monku* of their own too.'

Under this pretext – a casual cup of tea and a friendly chat – people came to the temples and community centres where Café de Monku was held. Many were living in 'temporary residences', the grim prefabricated huts, freezing in winter and sweltering in summer, where those who could afford nothing better ended up. The priests listened sympathetically, and made a point of not asking too many questions. 'People don't like to cry,' said Kaneta. 'They see it as selfish. Among those who are living in the temporary homes, there's hardly anyone who has not lost a member of their family. Everyone's in the same boat, so they don't like to seem self-indulgent. But when they start talking, and when you listen to them, and sense their gritted teeth and their suffering, all the suffering they can't and won't express, in time the tears come, and they flow without end.'

Haltingly, apologetically, then with increasing fluency, the survivors spoke of the terror of the wave, the pain of bereavement and their fears for the future. They also talked about encounters with the supernatural.

They described sightings of ghostly strangers, friends and neighbours, and dead loved ones. They reported hauntings at home, at work, in offices and public places, on the beaches and in the ruined towns. The experiences ranged from eerie dreams and feelings of vague unease to cases, like that of Takeshi Ono, of outright possession.

A young man complained of pressure on his chest at night, as if some creature was straddling him as he slept. A teenage girl spoke of a fearful figure who squatted in her house. A middle-aged man hated to go out in the rain, because of the eyes of the dead, which stared out at him from puddles.

A civil servant in Soma visited a devastated stretch of coast and saw a solitary woman in a scarlet dress far from the nearest road or house, with no means of transport in sight. When he looked for her again, she had disappeared.

A fire station in Tagajo received calls to places where all the houses had been destroyed by the tsunami. The crews went out to the ruins anyway, prayed for the spirits of those who had died – and the ghostly calls ceased.

A taxi in the city of Sendai picked up a sad-faced man who asked to be taken to an address that no long existed. Halfway through the journey, the driver looked into his mirror to see that the rear seat was empty. He drove on anyway, stopped in front of the levelled foundations of a destroyed house and politely opened the door to allow the invisible passenger out at his former home.

At a refugee community in Onagawa, an old neighbour would appear in the living rooms of the temporary houses and sit down for a cup of tea with their startled occupants. No one had the heart to tell her that she was dead; the cushion on which she had sat was wet with seawater.

Such stories came from all over the devastated area. Priests – Christian and Shinto, as well as Buddhist – found themselves called on repeatedly to quell unhappy spirits. A Buddhist monk wrote an article in a learned journal about 'the ghost problem', and academics at Tohoku University began to catalogue the stories. In Kyoto, the matter was debated at a scholarly symposium.

'Religious people all argue about whether these are really the spirits of the dead,' Kaneta told me. 'I don't get into it, because what matters is that people are seeing them, and in these circumstances, after this disaster, it is perfectly natural. So many died, and all at once. At home, at work, at school – the wave came in and they were gone. The dead had no time to prepare themselves. The people left behind had no time to say goodbye. Those who lost their families, and those who died – they have strong feelings of attachment. The dead are attached to the living, and those who have lost them are attached to the dead. It's inevitable that there are ghosts.'

He said: 'So many people are having these experiences. It's impossible to identify who and where they all are. But there are countless such people, and their number is going to increase. And all we do is treat the symptoms.'

* * *

When opinion polls put the question 'How religious are you?', Japanese rank among the most ungodly people in the world. It took a catastrophe for me to understand how misleading this self-assessment is. It is true that the organised religions, Buddhism and Shinto, have little influence on private or national life. But over the centuries both have been pressed into the service of the true faith of Japan: the cult of the ancestors.

I knew about the household altars, or *butsudan*, which are still seen in most homes and on which the memorial tablets of dead ancestors – the *ihai* – are displayed. The *butsudan* are cabinets of lacquer and gilt, with openwork carvings of flowers and trees; the *ihai* are upright tablets of black lacquered wood, vertically inscribed in gold. Offerings of flowers, incense, food, fruit and drinks are placed before them; at the summer Festival of the Dead, families light lanterns to welcome home the ancestral spirits. I had taken these picturesque practices to be matters of symbolism and custom, attended to in the same way that people in the West will partici-pate in a Christian funeral without any literal belief in the words of the service. But in Japan spiritual beliefs are regarded less as expressions of faith than as simple common sense, so lightly and casually worn that it is easy to miss them altogether. 'The dead are not as dead there as they are in our own society,' wrote the religious scholar Herman Ooms. 'It has always made perfect sense in Japan as far back as history goes to treat the dead as more alive than we do . . . even to the extent that death becomes a variant, not a negation of life.'

At the heart of ancestor worship is a contract. The food, drink, prayers and rituals offered by their descendants gratify the dead, who in turn bestow good fortune on the living. Families vary in how seriously they take these ceremonies, but even for the unobservant, the dead play a continuing part in domestic life. For much of the time, their status is something like that of beloved, deaf and slightly batty old folk who cannot expect to be at the centre of the family, but who are made to feel included on important occasions. Young people who have passed important entrance examinations, got a job or made a good marriage kneel before the *butsudan* to report their success. Victory or defeat in an important legal case, for example, is shared with the ancestors in the same way.

When grief is raw, the presence of the deceased is overwhelming. In households that had lost children in the tsunami, it became routine, after half an hour of tea and chat, to be asked if I would like to 'meet' the dead sons and daughters. I would be led to a shrine covered with framed photographs, with toys, favourite drinks and snacks, letters, drawings and school exercise books. One mother commissioned carefully Photoshopped portraits of her children, showing them as they would have been had they lived – a boy who died in primary school smiling proudly in high-school uniform, an eighteen-year-old girl as she should have looked in kimono at her coming-of-age ceremony. Another decked the altar with make-up and acrylic fingernails that her daughter would have worn if she had lived to become a teenager. Here, every morning, they began the day by talking to their dead children, weeping love and apology, as unselfconsciously as if they were speaking over a long-distance telephone line.

The tsunami did appalling violence to the religion of the ancestors.

Along with walls, roofs and people, the water carried away household altars, memorial tablets and family photographs. Cemetery vaults were ripped open by the wave, and the bones of the dead scattered. Temples were destroyed, along with memorial books, listing the names of ancestors over generations. 'The memorial tablets – it's difficult to exaggerate their importance,' Yozo Taniyama, a priest friend of Kaneta, told me. 'When there's a fire or an earthquake, the *ihai* are the first thing that many people will save, before money or documents. I think that people died in the tsunami because they went home for the *ihai*. It's life, the life of the ancestors. It's like saving your late father's life.'

When people die violently or prematurely, in anger or anguish, they are at risk of becoming *gaki*: 'hungry ghosts', who wander between worlds, propagating curses and mischief. There are rituals for placating unhappy spirits, but in the aftermath of the disaster, few families were in a position to perform these. And then there were those ancestors who lost all their living descendants to the wave. Their well-being in the afterlife depended entirely on the reverence of living families, which was permanently and irrevocably cut off: their situation was as helpless as that of orphaned children.

Tsunamis anywhere destroy property and kill the living, but in Japan they inflict a third kind of injury, unique and invisible, on the dead. At a stroke, thousands of spirits had passed from life to death; countless others were cut loose from their moorings in the afterlife. How could they all be cared for? Who was to honour the compact between the living and the dead? In such circumstances, how could there fail to be a swarm of ghosts?

It was in the summer after the tsunami that Naomi Hiratsuka began to speak to her dead daughter, Koharu. At first, and unlike most people she knew, she had hesitated. Shamanism, and varieties of mediumship, were deeply established in Tohoku, and many of the bereaved were turning to those who practised them. Naomi had her doubts about the existence of such gifts, but above all she detested the way in which some people, especially in the media, treated the subject, in an effort to squeeze spooky entertainment out of tragedy. She had been especially sickened by an article in a Japanese magazine about teenagers daring one another to make night-time visits to the site of Okawa Primary School, in the hope of encountering its ghosts.

But the search for Koharu and the other missing children was going so badly, bogged down both in the literal mud and in a morass of bureaucratic complication. Naomi was in close touch with the police unit, which was carrying out its own search, and got to know its commanders. One day, they made a suggestion that surprised her – that, if she knew of any mediums or psychics who had advice to offer, particularly about specific places to direct the search, she should pass it on.

A friend introduced her to a young man in his twenties who was known to have the ability to see and hear the dead. Recently, people said, he had heard a voice in a dense bamboo thicket by the Fuji lake – and when it was searched, bones were indeed found, and identified as the remains of a missing woman. Naomi arranged to meet the young psychic late one evening at the ruin of the school. It was the summer festival of Tanabata, the star festival, when people hang trees with handwritten poems and prayers, and with delicate paper decorations: streamers, purses, birds, dolls. They walked side by side in the humid darkness, between the shell of the school and the hill behind it. At a small shrine on the hill, Naomi tied decorations of her own around the bamboo and prayed for Koharu's return. It was a hot, windless night, but the coloured paper danced and shivered strangely in the motionless air. 'It is the children who are moving the decorations,' the psychic said. 'They are delighted with them.'

They walked past a long line of rubble, roughly heaped into great mounds. Hundreds of people had died in this small area. It was possible that bodies were still contained within the heaps. The psychic said, 'I can hear a voice. I think it is the voice of a woman, not a child.' And Naomi, straining, also heard it, although too faintly for the words to be distinguishable. 'It was just an ordinary voice,' she said. 'It sounded as if she was having an ordinary conversation. But when I looked around, there was nobody there.'

Naomi said, 'I didn't use to believe in such things, and I'd never had an experience like that before. But having lived through the disaster, having been through what I had, perhaps it's quite natural that I would hear such a voice.'

She spent a lot of time with the young man. They walked together for hours through the wide environs of the school – around the Fuji lake, and as far in the other direction as the Nagatsura lagoon. He gave Naomi a crystal on a length of cord, which she would hold suspended over a large-scale map in the hope of divining Koharu's whereabouts. She told the police about the voice she had heard at the rubble mounds, and they were thoroughly sifted. But no human remains were found.

During their long walks, the young psychic would describe to Naomi the invisible scene surrounding them. One might have expected a consoling picture of life after death, but the vision he described was appalling. Naomi compared it to a famous Japanese horror film, *Sadako*, which itself drew on the hell imagery of medieval art. 'He said that there were pale figures like the ghosts in that film, many, many of them crawling on the ground. Some of them were stuck in the water, covered in mud, and swallowing the dirty water in terrible suffering. Some of them were trapped, and trying to get out. But he couldn't tell which of them were the spirits of people who had already been found, and which of them were those like my daughter, who were still missing.'

Naomi began to seek out other means of reaching the dead. The introductions were easily made – many of the Okawa mothers were consulting one psychic or another. Having started out a sceptic, she found herself holding conversations with Koharu herself.

The medium, whose name was Sumi, ran a small coffee shop in the city. Sometimes, Naomi and Shinichiro went to see her in person; sometimes Koharu's utterances were conveyed over the telephone, and even by email and text message. But Naomi was quickly persuaded of their authenticity. Sumi conveyed so perfectly the tone and character of the Koharu that her family remembered –

the chattiness, bossiness and sweetness of a girl about to become a teenager. Through Sumi, Koharu dictated a detailed list of presents that were to be given in her name to members of the family – a particular kind of drawing pad and pencils for her brother, a pink bag for her little sister. She instructed Naomi to serve the family with powdered green-tea sweets, which she had always loved. But apart from the convincing childishness, there was an unexpected maturity in much of what she said, which might have been that of the medium, but which seemed at times to be the authority acquired by those, even in their young years, who have passed through death.

Koharu asked in detail about the well-being of her family, especially her siblings, and showed great concern about her mother's career. 'She seemed to think that Sae, the baby, would be OK,' Naomi said. 'But she wanted me to give a lot more attention to Toma, who was older. And she told me to finish my maternity leave and go back to work. All of this helped, it helped us so much to carry on with an ordinary life, even after death. It was so welcome.'

What neither the medium nor the spirit ever seemed able to say was the thing Naomi most wanted to know: the resting place of Koharu, or her bodily remnant. 'Sumi told us that finding the remains is not everything. She said, "You might think that the kids want their parents to find them, that they are desperate to go back home. But they are already home. They are already in a very good place. And the more you bury yourselves in the search, the more desperate you will become."'

Naomi's friend Miho visited another medium, and drew the deepest consolation from her conversations with her missing daughter, Hana. 'It was just like talking to her,' Miho said. 'It was just as if Hana was standing there, at my side. She said that she was in heaven, and that she was very happy. The woman knew all about our daily life, how Hana talked, the kinds of expressions she used. If she said that she was suffering, if she'd been crying for help, and saying, "Mum, get me out of here!", I wouldn't have been able to bear it. But the words I heard always made me feel calmer.'

Sometimes the messages from the dead contradicted one another. One of the first things Hana told her mother, Miho, was that she should not harbour any blame or resentment towards the teachers at the school. 'The teachers are crying in heaven, and that is hard for us,' she said through the medium. 'They are suffering, and watching them makes us children feel sad.' But another psychic, at another time, told Miho the opposite: that the children were bitter and angry towards the teachers for letting them die so needlessly, for failing to lead them to the obvious places of safety and survival.

What It's All About

The young man who had given her the crystal, the psychic who described cinematic spectres writhing in the mud, said to Naomi Hiratsuka, 'Your child will come to you in a dream. She will show you images of the place where she will be found. They will be like slides in your mind.' But when she found what she was looking for, it didn't happen like that at all.

Naomi's thinking about the search for the children changed over time. Her faith in the supernatural began to flag; instead, she invested it in her digger and its muddy yellow arm. The conversations with her daughter were consoling, but Sumi, who could relay eerily specific messages from Koharu, became evasive when asked about the location of her body. 'So many of us were consulting psychics, and people with those powers,' Naomi said. 'And we were all hearing different stories. When you think about it, someone must have been making a lot of money.'

Naomi took to visiting Koharu's old classroom. In the weeks that they had spent there, the men of the Self-Defence Forces had restored to the school an extraordinary, and even disturbing, degree of order. The windows and doors were broken, but the rooms had been swept, almost scoured, and the sediment of sludge deposited by the wave had dwindled to a smear of muddy dust. Warped textbooks had been carefully stacked and shelved; sodden dressing up-clothes had been restored to their box – a red wig, a fairy's wings. On Koharu's locker, the four characters of her name were still visible; Naomi left sweets and soft drinks there, to lure her daughter back. And the cleaner the classroom got, the sadder she became.

A many-fingered peninsula groped out into the sea between Ogatsu and Oppa Bay, a territory of rocks, pines and seagulls. The village of Naburi was at the end of the road, fifty houses in a tight triangle of land hard up against the hills. A concrete pier sheltered a little harbour; rocky, unpeopled islands were visible in the bay. A hundred and eighty people lived there, most of them over seventy years old. Japan had countless isolated, ancient populations such as this, places of sharp, harsh beauty and little else, which offered nothing at all for the young, and little reason for anyone else to stay, except habit, or resignation, or an overpowering love of fishing and the sea.

The water had reached a height of thirty-five metres here: 115 feet, as high as an eleven-storey building, almost four times as high as the tsunami predicted on the radio. But as soon as he had felt the earthquake, an old fisherman named Yuichiro Kamiyama had moored his boat and gone about the houses, chivvying the villagers up the steep hill. From there, they watched the water withdrawing from the harbour, and returning unstoppably to overwhelm first the sea wall, then the road and then the alleys dividing the wooden houses, until it lifted them up and spun them around on its frothing surface. The water rose and rose through the pines on the hillside towards the spot where the dumbfounded villagers were watching. A few feet below where they crouched, it slowed and withdrew.

The sight reminded Kamiyama of the summer Festival of the Dead, when illuminated paper lanterns are set adrift on the tide to guide the spirits back across to the far world. 'The houses receded all together, along with the sea,' he said. 'They were all in a row, like the festival lanterns, floating out over the sea wall. And the electricity poles too, with the wires between them. Those wires are strong – they didn't break. They were all taken back intact into the sea. Perhaps I shouldn't say so, but it was beautiful.'

There was nothing left of Naburi. 'It looked as if time had gone backwards,' said Kamiyama. 'It looked like a place in an ancient era, before humans came.' But in the whole village only two people had died, both of them after returning down the hill to retrieve precious items forgotten in the evacuation. 'With something like a tsunami, a decision has to be made very quickly,' Kamiyama said. 'What's needed is immediate action by someone with initiative. You don't have time to hold a meeting. So long as someone says, "Go to the mountain!", without any doubt or hesitation, then people will go.'

By August, five months later, the fishermen were buying new nets and boats and beginning to go out to sea again. Early one morning, they noticed a commotion among the gulls, thirty feet out in the harbour. The birds were crying and circling something, with dives and pecks. One of the boats went out to have a look, and then the police were called, and three officers arrived in a patrol car and went out with the fishermen to retrieve the object in the water. 'It was the calmest day of the season,' Kamiyama remembered. 'The water was so still and clear. They brought her onto the quay here, with all the gulls overhead. We shouldn't think ill of the birds. We shouldn't imagine them pecking her flesh. We should thank the seagulls, who showed us where she was, so she could see her mother and father again. Though she died, she was protected by the sea.'

Naomi was in Sendai at her mother's house; later, she felt a sense of failure that she not been at the school when the news came, on duty in the cabin of her digger. It arrived in the form of a text message from the police: another set of remains had been found in Naburi. They had been provisionally identified as those of a woman aged twenty to forty years old. But the body was described as being incomplete. Naomi telephoned the head of the local police, a man she had come to know well, and asked for more information. He told her that, although most of the clothes were absent, the unidentified woman had been wearing an outer set of thick thermal underpants. They were pink, with the motif of a white heart. With this, Naomi knew in an instant that Koharu had been found. The forecast for 11 March had been for cold weather, and possibly snow. And so Naomi had put this warm undergarment out for her daughter, a few hours before the tsunami.

She went to the police station with her husband, and examined the garment with her own eyes. 'I knew immediately that it was hers,' she said. 'And it was reasonable that they thought it was an adult, because Koharu was tall for her age. But then they were asking me, over and over, "Are you sure? Are you sure this is hers? Is there no chance that someone else could have been wearing similar clothes?" And I lost my confidence.'

Naomi asked to see the remains with her own eyes. The policemen looked uncertainly at one another. During the months she had spent in the mud, Naomi had beheld numerous dead bodies, in various states. The last one, in April, had been the twelve-year-old daughter of a friend. 'She was wearing jeans, with a belt,' Naomi remembered. 'Of course, she was not in a normal condition. Some of her hair had come away. But she was recognisable. So I knew the kind of thing to expect. I had a sense of how human bodies change in time, and how it becomes difficult to identify them. But I asked to see Koharu in the hope of some kind of . . . spiritual understanding, some kind of recognition that in seeing part of her body, I was looking at my daughter.

'The police kept asking me, "Are you sure? Will you be OK?" I said that I would.' They led Naomi in, and removed the sheet from the object on the table. She looked at what lay beneath it, and held it in her gaze. 'But it was just a lump of something,' she said. 'Without arms. Without legs. Without a head. And this was my daughter, my little girl. I don't regret seeing her. But the hope that I had, the hope that I would recognise her, was not fulfilled.'

This was the moment Naomi had been praying for through all these months, the moment of certainty and reunion, when death was supposed to settle for a few moments on her palm, like a squawking, flapping bird suddenly made still. But it was not to be. There was no real doubt, to the Hiratsukas or to the policemen, that this was Koharu. But without a positive identification, they would have to wait for the results of a DNA test, which would take months.

Naomi and Shinichiro walked out to their car, dazed. As she was climbing in, Naomi experienced a sudden pain in her back. Her legs locked. She found herself unable to move. 'This had never happened to me before,' she said. 'So I thought it had to be Koharu trying to hold me there.'

She said to her husband, 'I want to call Sumi.' The medium picked up the phone immediately. As soon as she had heard what had happened, she said, 'It is Koharu.' Naomi's paralysis in the car park, the words of the medium – these were enough for the police, who released the body the next day.

The Hiratsukas cremated Koharu on 11 August 2011. It was 153 days since the tsunami. A week later, Naomi was back at the school at the wheel of her digger, searching for Koto Naganuma, Hana Suzuki, Yuto Suzuki and Yui Takeyama, the four schoolmates of Koharu whose bodies had still not been found.

'We used to think that we were bringing up our children,' said Sayomi Shito. 'But then we discovered that it was we, the parents, who were being brought up by them. We thought that the children were the weakest among us, and that we protected them. But they were the keystone. All the other pieces depended on them. When they were taken away, we realised this for the first time. We thought that we were looking after them. But it was the children who supported us.'

I pictured the image that Sayomi had called to mind: an arched stone bridge collapsing; masonry crashing into a river. She went on: 'Nothing is capable of changing the situation. It's not about the passing of time. It's not about kind words. It's not about psychological support. It's not about money. None of that can change anything. There's a space which is empty and which will never be filled.'

For survivors of the disaster, various kinds of assistance – practical and financial – were made available by the government, but there was little in the way of formal counselling or mental-health care. Many of the institutions to which people would instinctively have turned – village, family, workplace – were themselves broken by the wave. But out of the pieces, in the fragmented towns and temporary houses, new forms of community emerged, cemented by loneliness, grief and practical necessity. In Fukuji, a particularly strong and well-organised group of friends formed around Sayomi and Takahiro Shito.

One evening, at Sayomi's invitation, I went to meet them. All were parents of children who had died at Okawa Primary School. These were the hecklers and barrackers of the headmaster and his colleagues, the violators of protocol and convention – but in person they were warm, courteous and patient people, unmarked by visible scars of ego or aggression. At their core were the Shitos and their neighbours, the Satos – Katsura and Toshiro, whose daughter Mizuho had been Chisato's playmate. Hitomi Konno and Kazutaka Sato, whose sons, Daisuke and Yuki, had been best friends in the fifth year, were also members of the group. Then there was a third Sato family: Tomoko and Mitsuhiro, who had lost their only child, a ten-year-old boy named Kenta. The friends met once a week or more; they communicated every day by telephone, email and text. It was through grief that they had found one another, but grief in itself was not what united them. The power of their grief, which gave it form, channelling it like the banks of a river, was rage.

I spent many days with the bereaved of the tsunami, notebook in hand, digital recorder on the table. My questions, or the answers to them, often made them cry. I used to ask myself: What am I doing here? Why should these people talk to me? Sayomi and her friends cried too. But their rage justified it. The conversation propelled itself forward and back, round and round, and on and on. I scarcely had to ask questions at all.

Hitomi Konno said, 'Every day, I think about my children and how each of them would be, if they were here. Today would be a birthday, for example. Or this month one of them would have been taking an entrance examination. In my heart, the children are still growing up. But I can't see them growing up.'

Mitsuhiro Sato said, 'When I think, "If he was alive, he'd be doing this and that", it makes me despair even more. Our child was our dream, and now that dream will never come true.'

His wife, Tomoko, said: 'The feeling of desperately wanting to see him, but never being able to see him, is getting stronger and stronger. If we knew that they were somewhere, if we could only see them for a time, a little time, that would be enough. This need to see him, to hold him and touch him, is getting bigger and bigger.'

There was a silence, marked by sighs. Then Kazutaka Sato spoke. He was a pale man in his mid-forties, with short, tufty hair and weary features. He had been sitting at the table, nodding from time to time, silently listening. Then he said, 'It's the matter of how they died.'

He spoke calmly, almost matter-of-factly, without obvious anger or distress. 'The more we look into it,' Sato said, 'the more we learn. And the better we understand that these were lives which could have been saved. The tsunami was a huge disaster. But there was only one school – just one school in the country – where the children lost their lives like this: Okawa Primary School. That is a fact, and that fact can only be explained by a failure, the failure of the school to save the children's lives. They failed. And they have made no apology, and given no proper explanation. The tsunami – the damage has been huge, and we are all suffering from that. But on top of that, we have to go through the torment of losing our children in this way. That is what it's about, that's what all this is about. It's about how they died.'

The truth about what happened in the tsunami was itself the opposite of a tsunami. There was no grand climax, no crashing wave or rumbling of the earth. The facts came out in trickles and drips, some falling naturally, some squeezed out by wringing hands. The stray words of a surviving child, revealing an unrecognised failure. A document exposing contradictions in the official account. The official account itself, wobbling and bending. Every few months there was a new 'explanatory meeting', at which the bureaucrats of the Ishinomaki Education Board submitted themselves to the anger of the parents. Reluctantly and with trepidation, people came forward to tell their stories. A freelance journalist, Masaki Ikegami, did dogged work submitting freedom-of-information requests for city documents and scrutinising them for inconsistencies.

The account furnished by the surviving teacher, Mr Endo, had seemed at first clear and credible enough. The pupils had evacuated their classrooms, and been lined up and counted off in the playground. A few parents had arrived to pick up their children. An orderly evacuation had begun. As it was under way, the wave had come in. Endo gave an impression of teachers acting with urgency and dispatch, professional men and women conscientiously following procedure, who were helplessly – and blamelessly – overwhelmed by an unimaginable disaster. And this might have made sense within a timespan of fifteen or twenty, or even thirty, minutes. But the earthquake had struck at 2.46 p.m. The hands of the school clock were frozen at 3.37 p.m., when the building's electricity was quenched by the rising water. This was the central question of the Okawa tragedy: what exactly happened between the first event and the second? What was going on at Okawa school for the last fifty-one minutes of its existence?

PART 3

WHAT HAPPENED AT OKAWA

The Last Hour of the Old World

Tetsuya Tadano was a stocky boy of eleven, with close-cropped hair and an air of mild, amused mischief. His family's house was across the rice fields in one of the hamlets at the back of the larger village of Kamaya; every morning, he made the twenty-minute walk to school with his nine-year-old sister, Mina, along the embankment of the river. The eleventh of March was the fortieth birthday of their mother, Shiroe; a small celebration was planned at home that evening. But otherwise it was an unremarkable Friday afternoon.

At lunchtime on that day, the children rode on unicycles in the courtyard and foraged in its margins for four-leafed clovers. It was cold, and a piercing wind came off the river; Tetsuya and his friends stood in a row with their hands in their pockets, and turned their backs on it to keep the chill off their faces. Across the road, the families from the middle school were holding their graduation party. Sayomi Shito emerged from it and experienced that eerie moment of stillness and unease. At 2.45 p.m., the Okawa school bus was waiting in the car park, with its engine running; a few of the smaller pupils had already climbed in. But most of the children were still in their classrooms, finishing up the last school business of the week.

A minute later, the sixth-year class were singing 'Happy Birthday' to one of their number, a girl named Manno. It was in the middle of this song that the earthquake struck. 'It was shaking very slowly from side to side,' said Soma Sato, one of the sixth-year boys. 'They weren't small, fast shakes – it felt gigantic. The teachers were running up and down, saying, "Hold on to your desks."'

In the library, a man named Shinichi Suzuki was waiting for his son, who was in the sick room, having being taken ill earlier in the day. He watched as the water in the school fish tank slopped over its sides in waves. In Tetsuya's class, the fifth year were getting ready to go home for the day. 'When the earthquake first hit, we all took cover under our desks,' he said. 'As the shaking got stronger, everyone was saying things like, "Whoa! This is big. You OK?" When it stopped, the teacher said right away, "Follow me outside." So we all put on our helmets and went out.'

The school building was evacuated with exemplary speed. Scarcely five minutes after they had been crouching under their desks, the children were in the playground, lined up in their classes, in the hard plastic helmets that were stored in each child's locker. Two days earlier they had gone through the same drill. Compared to Wednesday's earthquake, though, this one was several times more frightening. Much later, the city authorities would compile a minute-by-minute log of the events of that afternoon, based on interviews with surviving witnesses. It conveys something of the atmosphere after a big earthquake, of excitement and resignation, light-heartedness and dread:

Child: Everyone sat down and the register was taken. The lower-grade girls were crying, and Miss Shirota and Miss Konno were stroking their heads and saying, 'It's fine.' One of the sixth-grade boys was saying, 'I wonder if my game console at home is OK.'

Child: The lower grades were messing around. There were kids running about.

Child: It must have been a kind of 'earthquake sickness', because there were little kids throwing up.

Child: My friend said, 'I wonder if there'll be a tsunami.'

The alarm of the younger children was renewed by repeated, jolting aftershocks. There were secondary earthquakes at 2.51 p.m., 2.54 p.m., 2.55 p.m. and 2.58 p.m. As early as 2.49 p.m., while the vibrations of the mother quake were still jangling outwards across northern and eastern Japan, the Meteorological Agency issued a warning: a twenty-foot-high tsunami was expected; everyone on the coast of north-east Japan should evacuate to higher ground.

Eleven adults were present in the playground, among them the six class teachers; the special-needs teacher, Ms Suzuki; the school nurse, Ms Konno; Ms Kawabata, the school secretary; and Junji Endo, the head of teaching. In the absence of the headmaster, Teruyuki Kashiba, the senior teacher was Toshiya Ishizaka, his fifty-four-year-old deputy. It was Ishizaka who was listening to the battery-powered radio on which the tsunami warning was being broadcast, again and again. It was on him that the fate of those waiting in the playground depended.

Many people found it impossible to forgive Ishizaka, even in death. But those who knew him well remembered him with love. He grew up inland; the Chile tsunami, which struck when he was three, would have been just a story to him. He was a soft, sensitive man, who formed deep friendships with his young pupils, which continued long after they had grown up. 'He certainly wasn't a handsome kind of guy,' I heard from one woman who had been taught by Ishizaka twenty-five years earlier in another, inland school. 'A bit short, not fat, but certainly chubby. He was always smiling. His smile was what struck me. He didn't drink or smoke, which was unusual for a man back then.'

She described the summer night when Ishizaka took his pupils out to look up at the sky and learn the names of the constellations; and the weekend when he had invited the entire class of thirty children to his mother's home. 'He put us on the train, and then drove in his car alongside the track,' she said. 'He was keeping parallel with the train, and waving to us. We were so excited! He attached great importance to solidarity within the class, to getting everyone to work and act together. In all my days of school life, the two years with him were the most memorable and important.'

Some of the Okawa parents conveyed a different impression. They agreed about his gentleness, his warmth and affability. All remarked on the depth and frequency of his bows, and the politeness of his language. But there seemed in this to be an unvoiced suggestion that, even in a society that esteems formal courtesy, the deputy head's behaviour went beyond the demands of good manners, and crossed the line between respect and obsequiousness.

There were more aftershocks at 3.03 p.m., at 3.06 p.m. and at 3.12 p.m. At 3.14 p.m., the Meteorological Agency updated its warning: the tsunami was expected to come in at a height of ten metres, or thirty-three feet.

The teachers in the playground formed a huddle beneath the cherry trees and engaged in a discussion in low voices.

Like many Japanese institutions, the operations of Okawa Primary School were governed by a manual: among the documents that Ms Kawabata, the school secretary, brought out from her office into the playground, there would certainly have been a copy of this. The Education Plan, as it was called, was reviewed annually and covered everything from moral and ethical principles to the protocol for sports days, parents' meetings and graduation ceremonies. One section was devoted to emergencies, including fire, flood and epidemic. It included a form that was to be filled out and returned by each family, listing the names, telephone numbers and addresses of parents, guardians and anyone authorised to pick up a child from the school. This information was supposed to be updated every year. Kashiba, the headmaster, had not done this, which suggests, at the least, mild laxity in disaster preparedness.

The Education Plan was based on a template which was adjusted according to the circumstances of each school. Even in Japan, none but a handful of schools needed to make provision for volcanic eruptions, for example; those located inland could confidently strike out the section on tsunamis. Ishizaka, who had revised the manual under Kashiba's supervision, had chosen to retain it, but he had left unchanged the generic wording of the template:

Primary evacuation place: school grounds.
Secondary evacuation place, in case of tsunami: vacant land near school, or park, etc.

The vagueness of this language was unhelpful. The reference to 'park, etc.' made little sense out here in the countryside, where there were fields and hills, but no parks as such. As for 'vacant land', there was an abundance of that – the question was: where?

The school bus was waiting in the car park. It had a capacity of forty-five; at a squeeze, the whole school and its staff could have relocated to the heights of the Ogatsu Pass in two journeys. On the eastern edge of the village were two more roads that led up into the hills, one of them to a hilltop Shinto shrine in a forest clearing. But there was a still closer and more obvious place of safety.

Three features bounded the village of Kamaya in a rough triangle: the river to the north-west, the paddy fields to the east and, to the south, an unnamed, forested hill, 725 feet at its highest point. In places, the slope presented a strenuous, even perilous climb up steep and thicketed sides. But at one point there was a gentle and accessible path, familiar to all at the school. Until a few years ago, the children had gone up there as part of their science lessons, to cultivate a patch of *shiitake* mushrooms. This was a climb that the smallest among the children could have easily managed. Within five minutes – the time it had taken them to evacuate their classrooms – the entire school could have ascended hundreds of feet above sea level, beyond the reach of any conceivable tsunami.

But the Education Plan, so minutely prescriptive about other elements in the life of the school, made no clear adjudication about a place of evacuation. In the villages by the sea, including Aizawa, where Junji Endo used to teach, teachers and children were ascending without hesitation up steep paths and cliff steps. In Okawa, deputy headmaster Ishizaka stood in the playground and found only these words to puzzle over: *vacant land near school, or park, etc.*

The school appeared to have suffered no important damage, but while the aftershocks continued, it was judged to be imprudent to go back inside. It was Junji Endo, as the second-ranking teacher present, who darted in and out of the school buildings on this or that errand, while the class teachers kept an eye on their pupils and discussed what they might do. The roll call revealed that a third-year girl was missing; Endo went back in, and found her cowering in the toilet stalls. Many of the children were cold; it was Endo who retrieved their coats and gloves, and who took them to a discreet corner of the playground when they needed to relieve themselves. Occupied thus, he spent little time in active conversation with the other teachers. But it was clear what course of action Endo favoured, and what would have happened if he had been in charge.

'The deputy head took the helm, and the class teachers were attached to their classes,' he wrote later. 'I was running round, and I had no idea what they were discussing.' He recalled one brief conversation with Ishizaka, after checking for stragglers inside the

school. 'I asked, "What should we do? Should we run to the hill?"
I was told that it was impossible with the shaking.'

But Amane Ukitsu, one of the survivors from the sixth year,
recalled a much more dramatic intervention. Endo, she said, had
re-emerged from the school, calling out loudly, 'To the hill! The
hill! Run to the hill!'

His alarm was picked up by Hitomi's son, Daisuke, and his
friend, Yuki Sato, who made their own appeals to their sixth-year
teacher, Takashi Sasaki.

We should climb the hill, sir.

If we stay here, the ground might split open and swallow us up.

We'll die if we stay here!

The boys began to run in the direction of the *shiitake*-mushroom
patch, Amane remembered. But Endo was overruled, the boys were
ordered to come back and shut up, and they returned obediently
to their class.

Two distinct groups of people were beginning to gather at the
school. The first were parents and grandparents, arriving by
car and on foot to pick up children. The second were local
people from the village – to complicate matters further, Okawa
Primary was itself designated an official place of evacuation for
Kamaya. And a drastic difference of opinion, verging at times
on open conflict, was manifesting itself in the attitudes of the
two groups.

The parents, by and large, wanted to get their children out
and away as soon as possible. 'I kept looking at the cars arriving
and wondering, "Is Mum going to come?"' said Fuka, the twin
sister of Soma Sato. 'I was so worried. When she appeared I
burst into tears. Mum couldn't stop crying, either.' At least
one teacher, Takashi Sasaki, actively discouraged families from
leaving the school. 'Teacher said, "You'll be safe here," Soma

remembered. 'Mum said, "Our house is higher up. We'll be safer there."'

From the education board's log:

Child: My mum came to pick me up, and we told Mr Takashi that I was going home. We were told, 'It's dangerous to go home now, so better stay in the school.'

Parent: I told Mr Takashi, 'The radio says that there's a ten-metre tsunami coming.' I said, 'Run up the hill!' and pointed to the hill. I was told, 'Calm down, ma'am.'

The local people also pooh-poohed the danger. The village head of Kamaya, Toshio Takahashi, appears to have been particularly outspoken on the subject. Everyone central to the discussion is dead – but from the fragmentary glimpses provided by the survivors, it is clear that there was an active effort to lobby the deputy headmaster to keep the children in the school playground:

Child: There were teachers who said, 'Let's escape to the mountain', but then there were teachers and local people who said, 'It's safer at the school.'

Parent: The deputy head was consulting with local people, four or five of them, in their seventies or older. 'Will the mountain at the back collapse? I want the children to climb it. Is it impossible?'

Child: The deputy head said it was better to run to the mountain, but someone from Kamaya said, 'We're fine just here.' They seemed to be arguing.

Child: The deputy head and the headman of Kamaya were quarrelling. [The deputy head said] 'Let them climb the mountain.' The headman said, 'It won't come this far, so let's go to the traffic island.'

'The teachers were panicking,' said one parent. Another described how the hair and clothes of Ishizaka were plastered to his head and body by sweat, despite the coldness of the day. But a third said that although the teachers 'were not calm, they weren't panicking, I think'. This atmosphere of strain and irresolution confused people who stepped into it. Tetsuya Tadano and his sister Mina were relieved to see their mother, Shiroe. 'It seemed that she actually wanted to escape with us to higher ground,' said Tetsuya. 'But all the parents and guardians were just standing around. She said, "Wait a minute, I need to pick something up from home." So I just gave her my bags and stayed where I was.'

It was a weekday afternoon, and the working people of Kamaya were away at their shops, factories and offices. Most of the parents who came to the school were full-time mothers and housewives; most of the villagers offering their opinions were retired, elderly and male. It was another enactment of the ancient dialogue, its lines written centuries ago, between the entreating voices of women, and the oblivious, overbearing dismissiveness of old men.

Toshinobu Oikawa was a white-shirted, grey-suited man in his late fifties who worked in the local branch of the Ishinomaki town government. He was in his office, across the bridge from the school on the north bank of the river, when the earthquake struck. Within five minutes the first warning, of a twenty-foot tsunami, was received from the Meteorological Agency. The town office had a back-up generator, but the failure of electricity in the rest of the district had disabled many of the loudspeakers through which the municipality broadcast important announcements. Within fifteen minutes, Oikawa and five of his colleagues were climbing into three cars mounted with rooftop speakers of their own, and setting out to deliver the warning in person.

The roads they drove along were fissured by cracks. In places, earth and stones had slid onto them from the hillsides above. They crossed the Kitakami Great Bridge and drove through Kamaya towards the communities most at risk from a tsunami, the villages closest to the sea around the Nagatsura lagoon. They were driving through the outer margins of Kamaya when Oikawa became aware of something extraordinary taking place two miles ahead of them, at the point where the sea met the land.

The place was Matsubara, the spit of fields and sand where a ribbon of pine forest grew alongside the beach. There were 20,000 of the trees. They were a century old. Many of them were more than sixty feet high. And now, as Oikawa watched, the sea was overwhelming them, swallowing up their pointed green peaks and tearing up the forest in a frothing surge. 'I could see the white of the wave, foaming over the top of the trees,' he said. 'It was coming down over them like a waterfall. I could see it with my own eyes. And there were cars coming in the other direction, and the drivers were shouting at us, "The tsunami is coming. Get out! Get out!" So immediately we made a U-turn and went back the way we'd come.'

Within seconds they were driving through Kamaya again. More aftershocks were taking place. But it was as if the entire village had fallen under a spell.

Oikawa's colleague, Sato, was shouting through the car's loud-speaker, 'A super-tsunami has reached Matsubara. Evacuate! Evacuate to higher ground!' Municipal announcements in Japan are typically delivered in tones of glazed calm; those who survived remembered the pleading, almost crazed quality of this one. 'There were seven or eight people standing around the street, chatting,' Oikawa remembered. 'They paid us no attention. I saw the patrol car parked in front of the village police box. But the policeman wasn't passing on the warning, and he wasn't trying to escape, either. We passed the school. We were driving fast, we didn't stop, and we couldn't clearly see the playground. But they must have heard our message too. The school bus was just standing there.'

* * *

The old men of Kamaya didn't think of themselves as living by the sea.

A tsunami was a coastal hazard, an affliction of beaches, harbours and fishing communities, places hard up against the waves. But Kamaya was a farming village, a category apart. Between Okawa Primary School and the beach at Matsubara was a distance in a straight line of two and a quarter miles. Screened by the houses and shops of Kamaya, the sea was inaudible and invisible. One local woman described to me the surprise, among many other shocks, of looking out from what had formerly been Kamaya after its human structures had been wiped away. 'It was only after the houses had gone that I noticed it,' she said. 'I had always thought of us as living inland, alongside a river. But now, with the houses gone, all of a sudden there was the ocean.'

The Kitakami was the gate through which the tsunami gained admittance to the land. And the river channelled and concentrated it, binding it tighter and stronger, and loosed it over the fragile embankment.

In Kamaya, people were doing what they always did after an earthquake: tidying up. Among them was a farmer in his sixties named Waichi Nagano, who lived in a big house out in the fields. 'I heard all the warnings,' he said. 'There was the loudspeaker car from the town hall going up and down, saying, "Super-tsunami imminent: evacuate, evacuate!" There were a lot of sirens too. Everyone in the village must have heard them. But we didn't take it seriously.'

Nagano was the fifth generation to have inhabited and farmed this land. Families such as his possessed an ancestral consciousness, composed of personal memory, historical anecdote and local lore: nowhere in that storehouse of hereditary experience was there any recollection of tsunamis. 'Until then, no tsunami had ever damaged Kamaya,' Nagano said. 'We knew people in Ogatsu once had a tsunami, and we knew about the Chile earthquake. But they didn't have the slightest effect on this village. So people thought it could never reach here. People felt safe.'

The experience of the generations, the reassurance of the ancestors – these beat louder in the blood than the voices from the loudspeaker cars, screeching, 'Evacuate! Evacuate!'

Nagano was in his shed, gathering up his scattered farming tools, when his wife called to him from the front of the house. There he saw the tsunami coming over the embankment 600 yards away and smashing into the buildings in front of it. He bolted inside and shouted to his daughter and granddaughter. The four of them jumped into two cars and began to manoeuvre onto the road. Nagano's wife suddenly opened the door, saying, 'My bag – I forgot my handbag.' 'No! No!' Nagano shouted. 'Please get back in the car.' It was 200 yards to the point where the road began to rise in its ascent up the hill. Seconds after they reached it, the waters rushed in behind them.

Nagano looked back from the hill to see his home in the rice fields, and Kamaya behind it, being overwhelmed by the sea. Within a few seconds the house had broken up and disappeared. Little more than a minute had passed between the moment when he first glimpsed the tsunami and now, as he stared down, panting, over the destruction of his home, his fields, his village, the inheritance of five generations. 'It was a scene of hell,' Nagano said. 'It was just hell. It was as if we were in a dream. We could not believe what was happening.'

In the playground, the children were becoming restless. A mood of bored resignation had established itself. The tidy lines in which each class had been standing dissolved into seated circles on the ground. Local people from the village sat on mats and cushions, which they had brought from their homes. It was cold. People shared blankets and hand-warmers, and the teachers extracted from a storeroom two open-topped metal drums in which fires could be lit. There was no sense of anything much happening, or that anything was likely to happen very soon.

Children continued to leave with their parents, and said their goodbyes to friends and teachers. After-school activities were cancelled; plans by her friends in the sixth year to continue celebrations of Manno's birthday were deferred. 'Manno was right next to me,' said one girl. 'I had promised her a birthday present after basketball practice. I said, "I won't be able to give it to you after all. I'm sorry." She said, "That's OK."'

Not everyone in Kamaya was indifferent to the warnings. The chronological log produced by the education board refers to several local people who repeatedly urged an evacuation. In the official account, they are identified only by capital letters. It is not clear what became of them:

Parent: F (local person) ran over yelling, 'Run! There's a tsunami coming.' Someone, I don't know who, said, 'What? That's a bit scary, isn't it?'

Parent: I was told by D, 'The tsunami will come at 3.30', and he showed me his mobile phone and said, 'We only have twenty minutes left.'

Parent: A man next to the bicycle shed pointed to the mountain and said loudly, 'There's a tsunami coming, so climb to high ground!' I don't know if the school staff heard him.

At 3.25 p.m. Oikawa and the three loudspeaker vans drove past, blaring their desperate warning. In the school playground, the teachers were preparing to burn wood in the oil drums to keep the children warm.

At 3.30 p.m., an elderly man named Kazuo Takahashi fled his home next to the river. He too had ignored the warnings, until he became abruptly aware of the sea streaming over the embankment beside his house. It seemed to be coming from below the earth, as well as across it: metal manhole covers in the road were being lifted upwards by rising water; mud was oozing up between the cracks that the earthquake had opened in the road. Takahashi directed his car towards the closest place of evacuation, the hill behind the school. On the main street of Kamaya he saw friends and acquaintances standing and chatting. He rolled down his window and called to them, 'There's a tsunami coming. Get out!' He passed his cousin and his wife and delivered the same warning. They waved, smiled and ignored him.

Takahashi parked his car next to the village community centre, adjacent to the school. The other Mr Takahashi, the village head who was so vigorously opposed to evacuation, was helpfully directing the cars. As he climbed out and made for the hill, Kazuo Takahashi became aware of a large number of children issuing forth from the school in a hurry.

Among them was Tetsuya Tadano. He had remained in the playground with his class; after disappearing on her vague errand, his mother, Shiroe, had not returned. Mr Ishizaka, the deputy head, had been absent from the playground. He reappeared suddenly, with an unexpected instruction. 'A tsunami seems to be coming,' he called. 'Quickly. We're going to the traffic island. Get into line, and don't run.' Obediently, the children stood up and filed out of the playground. They left in their classes, the oldest children first. But as some walked, some trotted and others ran, the classes quickly began to merge and overlap.

Tetsuya and his friend Daisuke Konno were at the front of the group. The traffic island was less than 400 yards away, just outside the village at the point where the road met the Kitakami Great Bridge. But instead of leaving through the front entrance of the school, the children were led out of the side, along the foot of the hill and then down a narrow alley that connected with the village street. It was as he approached this junction that Tetsuya saw a black mass of water rushing along the main road ahead of him.

Barely a minute had passed since he had left the playground. He was conscious of a roaring sound, and a sheet of white spray above the black. It was not emerging from straight ahead, from the direction of sea. It was streaming in from the left, from the river, the direction in which the children had been ordered to run.

Some of those at the front of the line froze in the face of the wave. Others, including Tetsuya and Daisuke, turned at once and ran back the way they had come. The rest of the children were continuing to hurry towards the main road; the little ones towards the back were visibly puzzled by the sight of the older children pelting hectically in the opposite direction.

At the top of the alley, the two boys found themselves at the foot of the hill. This was the steepest and most thickly forested section of the slope, difficult to climb at the best of times. At some point Tetsuya became aware that Daisuke had fallen, and he tried, and failed, to pull his friend up. Then Tetsuya was scrambling up the hill. As he did so, he looked back over his shoulder and saw the darkness of the tsunami rising behind him. Soon it was at his feet, his calves, his buttocks, his back. 'It felt like the huge force of gravity when it hit me,' he said. 'It was as if someone with great strength was pushing. I couldn't breathe, I was struggling for breath.' He became aware of a rock and a tree, and found himself trapped between them, with the water rising about him. Then darkness overcame him.

Inside the Tsunami

Everyone who experienced the tsunami saw, heard and smelt something subtly different. Much depended upon where you were, and the obstacles that the water had to overcome to reach you. Some described a waterfall, cascading over sea wall and embankment. For others, it was a fast-rising flood between houses, deceptively slight at first, tugging trippingly at the feet and ankles, but quickly sucking and battering at legs and chests and shoulders. In colour, it was described as brown, grey, black, white. The one thing it did not resemble in the least was a conventional ocean wave, the wave from the famous woodblock print by Hokusai: blue-green and cresting elegantly in tentacles of foam. The tsunami was a thing of a different order, darker, stranger, massively more powerful and violent, without kindness or cruelty, beauty or ugliness, wholly alien. It was the sea coming onto land, the ocean itself picking up its feet and charging at you with a roar in its throat.

It stank of brine, mud and seaweed. Most disturbing of all were the sounds it generated as it collided with, and digested, the stuff of the human world: the crunch and squeal of wood and concrete, metal and tile. In places, a mysterious dust billowed above it, like the cloud of pulverised matter that floats above a demolished building. It was as if neighbourhoods, villages, whole towns were being placed inside the jaws of a giant compressor and crushed.

From the hillside where they had narrowly escaped to safety, Waichi Nagano and his wife, Hideko, could see the whole scene spread out below them, as the water swept in pulsing surges over the embankment and across the village and the fields. 'It was a huge black mountain of water which came on all at once and destroyed the houses,' he said. 'It was like a solid thing. And there was this strange sound, difficult to describe. It wasn't like the sound of the sea. It was more like the roaring of the earth, mixed with a kind of crumpling, groaning noise, which was the houses breaking up.'

There was another fainter noise. 'It was the voices of children,' said Hideko. 'They were crying out – "Help! Help!"' On the hill above, where he had half climbed, half floated to safety, Kazuo Takahashi heard them too. 'I heard children,' he said. 'But the water was swirling round, there was the crunching sound of the wave and the rubble, and their voices became weaker and weaker.'

How does it feel to die in a tsunami? What are the thoughts and sensations of someone in those final moments? Everyone who contemplated the disaster asked themselves these questions; the mind fluttered about them like an insect around a flame. One day, I mentioned it, hesitatingly, to a local man. 'Do you really want to know the answer to that question?' he asked. 'Because I have a friend who can tell you.'

He arranged the meeting for the following evening. His friend's name was Teruo Konno and, like Toshinobu Oikawa, he worked in the branch office of the Ishinomaki town hall. Oikawa was the model of the local bureaucrat: quiet, patient, dogged. But Konno was an imaginative and restless character. As a boy, he had dreamed of leaving Tohoku and travelling the world. His parents, seeking to quell this impulse, had discouraged him from going to university, and Konno had spent his life in the place where he grew up, and his career in local government. In March 2011, he had been deputy-head of the local development section, responsible, among other things, for 'disaster counter-measures'.

Few people were more knowledgeable about the menace of earthquakes and their particular threat to the Kitakami area. 'Our assumption was that there would be another big quake,' Konno said.

'There hadn't been a tsunami since the 1896 and 1933 quakes, so we expected that too.' There was no doubt that the small village where the town office was located, situated at the mouth of the river, two and a half miles downstream of Kamaya, would be in its path. Konno and his colleagues bent their efforts to ensuring that they would ride it out.

The two-storey branch office had been built on a rise fifteen feet above sea level, and its ground floor had been elevated a further ten feet above that. Essential utilities, such as electricity and communications, had been installed on the uppermost floor. On the wall was a digital read-out that recorded the intensity of tremors as they occurred.[*] As recently as the previous August, the city government had conducted a drill in which police, fire brigade and local officials acted out their roles in case of an earthquake and tsunami.

When the moment finally arrived, Konno experienced it with the calm detachment of a disaster professional.

'It came in three stages,' he told me. 'When the shaking first began it was strong, but slow. I looked at the monitor. It showed an intensity of upper five, and I knew that this was it.' Even as the rocking continued, he was calling to his staff to make a public announcement: a tsunami warning, he knew, would soon be issued. 'But the shaking went on,' Konno said. 'It got stronger and stronger. The PC screens and piles of documents were all falling off the desks. And then in the third stage, it became worse still.'

Konno gripped his desk in a tumult of competing sounds. Pieces of office furniture were rattling and colliding as they shunted

---

[*] 'Intensity' refers to the effect an earthquake has on the ground, and varies from place to place, depending on their distance from the epicentre (by contrast with magnitude, which is a single number, measuring the energy released by a tremor). The Japan Meteorological Agency measures intensity on a scale of one to seven. Intensity 1 describes hardly noticeable shaking. At intensity 7, people and objects are hurled around, landslides occur and many buildings are damaged and destroyed.

across the room. Filing cabinets were disgorging their files. Now he looked up again at the wall-mounted read-out of seismic intensity: it displayed only an error message. Then, gradually, like the slowing of a beating heart, the shaking and the panic eased, and the employees of the Ishinomaki Kitakami General Branch Office sprang to their appointed tasks.

The emergency generator rumbled into life, the toppled television was lifted off the floor and reconnected, and the tsunami warning was relayed through the municipal loudspeakers. Oikawa and his men were dispatched to those communities where the loudspeakers had failed. Just as had been planned, representatives of the police and the fire brigade relocated to the town branch office. 'Everything functioned very well,' Konno said. 'No one was hurt, everyone was calm, and there was only slight damage to the building. We had drilled for this. Everyone knew who should do what, and what to do next.'

Soon there were fifty-seven people in the branch office. Thirty-one of them were locals who had evacuated from more vulnerable premises to the safety of the strong, modern building. They included six children from a nearby school, the counterpart of Okawa Primary School on the north side of the river, as well as eight old people from the local day-care centre. Three of them were in wheelchairs; four more had to be physically carried upstairs. Volunteers sprang forward to help them safely and comfortably up to the sanctuary of the second floor.

At 3.14 p.m., the Japan Meteorological Agency revised the estimated height of the imminent tsunami from twenty feet to thirty-three feet. But at some point the back-up electricity generator had failed, and Konno and his colleagues never received this information. It would have made no difference anyway.

The building, mounted on its elevation, faced inland, with its back to the river and its front entrance facing the hills over the small village below. From his window, the only water Konno could see was a sluggish brown stream, little more than a drain, which trickled into the Kitakami. 'That was the first thing I noticed,' he said. 'The water in the creek had become white. It was churning and frothing, and it was flowing the wrong way. Then it was overflowing, and there was more water coming in from the river behind, and it was surrounding the houses. I saw the post-office building, lifting up and turning over in the water. Some of the houses were being crushed, but some of them were lifting up and floating.' The destruction was accompanied by that mysterious noise. 'I never heard anything like it,' Konno said. 'It was partly the rushing of the water, but also the sound of timber, twisting and tearing.' In the space of five minutes, the entire community of eighty houses had been physically uprooted and thrust, bobbing, against the barrier of the hills.

Nothing in Konno's simulations and hazard maps had prepared him for this. 'People in the office were looking down on it, amazed,' he said. 'It was unbelievable. It was as if it was happening somewhere else. But at the time I was thinking, "Well, this is it – a twenty-foot tsunami." And I assumed that would be the end of it.'

Through the window, he observed that the car park below was being washed over by black water. At the same moment, a profound shudder went through the whole building. Even without being able to see it, Konno understood what had happened: the large plate-glass windows on the ground floor had broken under the pressure of the wave, which was washing through the lower part of the building.

'It was like the bursting of a dam,' he said. 'Desks, chairs, documents were washing out of the other side. It felt like another earthquake. It was shaking the whole building again. The lights and the panels in the ceiling were falling down.'

The town officials, the police, the firemen, the schoolchildren, the old people and their carers looked on helplessly as the water surged. Konno, remembering the disaster drills, gave the order that everyone should move into a corner room, structurally the strongest part of the building. As he closed the door on them, there was another mighty impact. One of his subordinates ran to report to Konno what happened: the roof of the large public hall next door had lifted off and collided with the branch office.

Konno returned to his desk. The speed of events was difficult to grasp. Until moments ago, he had been leading a trained team in the execution of a well-rehearsed and rational plan. Now he, and all those around him, were facing death. The forces acting on the building were pushing it to the extremes of its resistance. The ground floor was completely underwater; now the wave was rising through the upper floor. Konno climbed onto his desk, as black water sucked and slapped around it with violent force. Then there was another, immense percussion, and suddenly he was tumbling through open air.

The outside world was cold; Konno had the sensation of falling through it very slowly. He was able to take in the sight of the building from which he had just been propelled, with water surging out of all its windows. He was aware of another colleague, a man named Abe, falling through space alongside him: the image of Abe's surprised, bespectacled face lodged in his mind. Then he was in the water.

It was churning and raging with violent internal motion. Konno described it as 'like being in a washing machine'; he was paralysed by the water's grip. He was aware of having being forced down, and of touching asphalt – the surface of the car park, which was now the bottom of the sea. And he understood that his life was coming to its end. 'It's true what people say. You see the faces of your family, of your friends. It's true – I remember it. All those faces. The last words in my mind were, "I'm done for – I'm sorry." It's a feeling different from fear. Just a frank feeling of sorrow, and regret.'

As he was viewing the gallery of his past, Konno found himself able to move his neck, and then his arms and legs and, kicking and thrashing, he propelled himself upwards and broke the surface.

He cast around for something to hold on to. A tree branch came into his grip, but it was too small. He exchanged it for a thicker spar of timber. On the surface, he could make out Abe, minus his glasses, gripping onto a sturdy log and being carried north, away from the river and towards the hills. But Konno was spinning in the opposite direction, towards what had been the river and was now the sea.

Having faced death without fear, now he became afraid. 'It was like being sucked into a whirlpool,' he said. 'I went under again, and again I thought this must be the end. And then, somehow, I was released from it, and I was in the middle of the river in a slow and quiet stream.'

He caught hold of a wide wooden panel, the section of a house's outer wall, a stable support compared to the rotating tree branches. Gripping this, he drifted steadily towards the bank again and the hills that rose out of the flood. He could tell, more or less, where the submerged embankment and road must be; he imagined lowering his feet in the shallower reaches and wading to safety. But just as hope was returning, the tsunami began to withdraw, and the stampeding waters reversed direction.

Konno found himself being carried back out into the stream and towards the river's mouth. Familiar landmarks passed at racing speed. He saw the outline of his office building – it had not collapsed after all. Clinging to his raft, Konno was rushed downstream by the withdrawing tide, through the river's gaping mouth and out towards the horizon of the Pacific Ocean.

He lost all sense of time passing. He could see, or hear, no other living creature. It was as if the whole world had succumbed to the flood and he was its only survivor. His Ark was that section of wooden wall, six feet by three, which he half gripped, half sprawled over. It saved his life – a smaller, less stable support would quickly have exhausted his energy and cast him off. Although he had crossed the threshold from river to sea, he remained within the broad sweep of Oppa Bay, and he never lost sight of the land. After the first great pulse of the tsunami had pulled him back, the next one surged in and bore him back up the river again.

He was swept beyond the starting point of his journey towards the spot where a small park had formerly been, below a high section of embankment. The water was pouring over it in a black waterfall; Konno floated at the top, teetering on its brink. He was afraid that in the churn of the waterfall he would lose consciousness, and momentarily he did. When he came to, he was suspended on a crust of jammed and overlapping rubble. Among it was the red-tiled roof of a house, sturdy and intact around its wooden frame. He pulled himself up onto it, and for the first time since falling from his office he was out of the water.

Then began what he described as the most frightening part of his ordeal, as he suddenly became aware of the profound cold.

'A wind began to blow,' he said. 'A violent snowy wind. It was so cold. I had only a wet shirt, no jacket, no shoes. I started shivering. I could see the hills. They were close, and I am a good swimmer. But I was so cold and I knew that I would not make it. My senses were failing me again. I started counting. I wanted to know how long it would take before the tsunami reversed and took me out to sea again. I got to one hundred and sixty – I remember that number. And then the roof I was lying on began to move.'

As his raft spun on the water, Konno began to lose himself again. Then into his failing vision came a place that he knew well. It was the home of an elderly lady named Mitsuko Suzuki, an old friend and formerly a teacher at the local nursery school. Her house was built a little way up the slope in a protective fold of the hill. Its ground floor was flooded, but the upper storey was clear of the water. From it, he heard a voice call out, 'Hang on there!'

It was Mrs Suzuki. She had seen the roof, and the prone figure clinging to it, without recognising who it was. And now, as if guided by her voice, the floating roof was edging towards her house. It came to a stop, wedged up tight against her front door.

The face of the old lady looked down on him. 'Young Teruo!' she said. 'What are you doing here? Climb up. Climb up!'

'I can't, Mrs Suzuki,' Konno answered. 'I have no strength.'

'What are you talking about? No strength? Just come up.'

Now the wave was renewing itself and pulling the roof away from the house again. It was Konno's last chance. He forced himself up and found himself in a spaghetti of fallen electrical cables. 'I was tangled up in them,' he said. 'I held onto them. And then I was swimming into her house through the front door. It was dark. Mrs Suzuki was upstairs. She was calling my name and shining a torch. I don't know how I managed. I lost my memory of all that. But I got upstairs.'

It was after five o'clock. Konno had spent more than two and a half hours in the water. He had saved himself from drowning, but now he was dying of hypothermia. He began to display the mania associated with the condition. Mrs Suzuki described to him later how, even at the extremity of exhaustion, he had acted like a madman, pulling open her drawers and cupboards, throwing their contents on the floor and scrabbling to find dry clothes. The old teacher soothed him, undressed him, laid him in her own bed and rubbed warmth back into him. Konno remembered nothing of this. He was conscious only of something he called 'the golden hand'. 'It was Mrs Suzuki's hand,' he said. 'But it was also the hand of a Buddha. It was curved, soft, warm. I don't think I ever saw her

physically, during that time. I couldn't open my eyes. But I saw
the soft, round Buddha with golden hands.'

He woke abruptly the next morning, electrified by anxiety. From
Mrs Suzuki's window, he could see that the water had retreated;
ignoring her anxious pleas, he made his way towards the town
office. He wanted to find the others who had been sheltering there,
the people whom he had herded into the secure room. It was no
more than a few hundred yards from the old lady's house. Picking
through snow and rubble in a pair of slippers, it took him an hour.
He scaled a rise from which the office was visible, and immediately
understood that the worst had happened.

The building itself was a gaping shell. The area all around it was
littered with bodies, half submerged in muddy pools, draped over
railings. Most terrifying of all was the complete silence. 'It was a
world without sound, without any sound at all,' said Konno. 'I
was trembling with terror.'

A single other survivor from the town office had washed up to
the hill and been helped to safety. Everyone else had died – the
policemen, the firemen, the children and the old people on walking
sticks and in wheelchairs. Abe, whom Konno had seen bobbing
towards the hills, had reached them, alive. But there he had lost
his strength and died of exposure during the night.

What was it that spared Konno when so many others died?
Was it physical strength or mental determination – or just the
lucky timing of a last deep breath of air before he plunged into
the water? His body was black with bruises where objects in the
water had collided with him, but his face was unmarked, and his
worst injuries were three broken fingers. He returned immediately
to work, organising refugees, identifying bodies, consoling the
families of the bereaved.

They were dreadful, crushing tasks, even for one who had not
gone through such an experience. But Konno found that it had
left him with an indifference to mental hardship, and an absence

of trepidation of any kind. He had no fear, of life or of death. He was like a man who had suffered a dangerous disease, to survive with complete immunity to future infection. The prospect of his own extinction – now, soon or far in the future – was a matter to him of no concern at all.

The River of Three Crossings

Tetsuya Tadano came to on the hill, blinded by mud and with the roar of the tsunami in his ears. His limbs were immobilised by spars of debris and by something else, something wriggling and alive, which was shifting its weight on top of him. It was Kohei Takahashi, Tetsuya's friend and fifth-year classmate. Kohei's life had been saved by a household refrigerator. It had floated past with its door open as he thrashed in the water, and he had squirmed into it, ridden it like a boat and been dumped by it on his schoolmate's back. 'Help! I'm underneath you,' Tetsuya cried. Kohei tugged him free. Standing on the steep slope, the two boys beheld the scene below.

Tetsuya's first thought was that he and his friend were already dead. He took the raging water to be the River of Three Crossings, the Japanese equivalent of the River Styx. Those who have led good lives cross the river safely by bridge; evil-doers must take their chances in the dragon-ridden waters. Innocent children, being neither sinful nor virtuous, rely on a kindly Buddha to make their passage, and to protect them from the depredations of hags and demons.

'I thought I'd died,' Tetsuya said. 'Dead . . . the River of Three Crossings. But then there was the New Kitakami Great Bridge, and the traffic island. And so I thought this might be Kamaya after all.'

The water, which had receded, began to surge up the hill again. The two boys tottered up the slope. Tetsuya's face was black and bruised. In the churn of the tsunami, the ill-fitting plastic helmet that he wore had twisted on its strap and dug brutally against his eyes. His vision was affected for weeks; he could make out only dimly what was going on in the water below.

Kohei's left wrist was broken and his skin was punctured by thorns, but his vision was unaffected. Whatever was visible of the fate of his school and his schoolmates, he saw it. He would never talk publicly about it.

Tetsuya became aware that an expression of glazed sleepiness was passing over Kohei's face. 'Hang on, I thought – that's dangerous,' Tetsuya said. 'I can't have him saving me, then dying on me.' But his friend was becoming more and more detached from the here and now. Tetsuya's mind, too, began to drift and wander. He struggled even to remember what day it was. His little sister had been in the schoolyard too; his mother, who had disappeared on her vague errand, must be out there somewhere. He thought of the soldiers of the Japan Self-Defence Forces: surely by now they must be on their way. He called out to the soldiers: *Help! Help!* 'But they didn't come,' Tetsuya remembered. 'And while I was thinking about all these things, Kohei had fallen asleep.'

With their loudspeakers blaring evacuation warnings, Toshinobu Oikawa and his colleagues from the town office had raced out of Kamaya and up to the traffic island opposite the Great Bridge. To his dismay, cars were still coming into the village from the opposite direction, towards the oncoming tsunami. They pulled in, with the aim of setting up a checkpoint to force drivers to turn back. Hardly had they parked when the water began to pour over the embankment.

'It came down over us like a waterfall,' Oikawa said. 'We ran. There was no time to think.' The only place of safety was a steep slope on the other side of the same hill that backed onto the school. Four of them reached it and scrambled clear, by a matter of seconds. One man, Sato, was caught by the water, but was dragged and yanked out by his colleagues. The sixth man, Hideyuki Sugawara, was trapped in his car and tumbled away by the waters, never to be seen alive again.

From the hillside they watched the tsunami swallow up the road and the traffic island. That was the place of evacuation chosen by the deputy headmaster, Ishizaka – if any of the teachers or children had ever reached it, they would have perished there under thirty feet of water. By reckoning the distance the tsunami had travelled since it broke over the pine forest, and the time that had passed, Oikawa calculated its speed – more than forty miles an hour. The pines, carried by the water, added greatly to its destructive power – sixty-foot-long battering rams, which clubbed and crushed whatever they encountered. Where they met the bridge, the trunks became entangled in its arches, turning it into a kind of dam and diverting the tsunami's flow over the downstream embankment – in other words, over Kamaya. 'It made it much worse,' said Oikawa. 'There was still water going under the bridge, of course. But the barrier of trees was pushing some of it back, over the village and the school.'

The construction of the embankment was of uneven quality: in places, the water washed it away like a child's sandcastle, leaving the houses behind it completely exposed. The hamlet of Magaki suffered this fate. 'Mr Sato, who was with us, lived in Magaki,' Oikawa remembered. 'He watched his own house being washed away. His parents, his daughter, his grandchild were in the house. He lost all of them. He was shouting, screaming, "My house, my house!"'

One of the men had with him a video camera, and at one point he turned it on. The 118-second film is the only recording of the tsunami in full spate in the Okawa area. In the hands of the stricken cameraman, the image veers wildly back and forth between the black river, the green girders of the bridge and Magaki, already reduced to a single house. Suddenly, the camera is pointing up at trees and the sky; then it is lying on the ground amid stalks of dry grass. The voice of the man holding the camera can be heard calling out, 'Is the school OK? What about the school?'

Shivering in his sodden clothes, Sato made his way down the far side of the hill with one of his colleagues. The remaining three, led by Oikawa, climbed up it, in search of survivors. Rubbing their gloveless hands, they called aloud as they peeped between trees. Eventually their cries were answered by a strong voice, that of old Kazuo Takahashi, who had run up the hill past the fleeing schoolchildren.

Takahashi was a fierce and irascible old man. Reporters who called on him to ask about his experiences were sent packing. He had no interest in hearing it, but he was one of the heroes of that day. Half a dozen lives were saved by him at the meeting point of the land and the wave.

The tsunami had caught up with him as he climbed the hill, but he found his feet and outran it. He was aware of cries all around, and one voice close at hand. He ran to it and found a woman trying to save a young girl, who was trapped between floating rubble. Takahashi, risking his own secure footing, reached down into the water and dragged her out. This was Nana Suzuki, from the first year of Okawa Primary, the youngest of the children to survive the tsunami. Striding along the margins of the hill, Takahashi pulled to safety five more people, most of them elderly.

He led the survivors to a clearing on the hill, where they settled, shivering, on the ground. A cigarette lighter was produced, and a fire kindled with twigs and fragments of bamboo. From time to time, human calls could be heard through the trees, and Takahashi marched off in pursuit of them. After uniting with Oikawa's team, they found Tetsuya and Kohei and seated them around the sputtering fire.

Fourteen people were gathered there, all told. It was by now completely dark, snowing and profoundly cold. Most of the survivors were in wet clothes, and one old man was barefoot. No one spoke much. They fed the fire with twigs on which frost was forming. They propped up a branch close to the flames, draped with wet garments. There were no tears or hysteria; but no attempts at mutual encouragement, no songs to keep up the spirits. The minds of all those on the hill were turned to those who were not present – parents and grandparents, children and grandchildren, siblings and spouses, who must still be down there, somewhere.

Among the survivors was a married couple in their sixties, who had been thoroughly drenched by the tsunami. The woman clutched to her what Oikawa took to be a glossy black doll. Then he saw the doll moving feebly. It was a tiny dog, which had entered the water white and had come out dyed by evil-smelling mud. 'It was the same with the shirts we wore,' Oikawa said. 'In the tsunami, everything which was white became black.'

The woman's husband had no visible wounds, but it was obvious that he had suffered dreadful internal injury. He could not speak at all. From the beginning, his breathing was shallow and laboured. No one present on the hill had any medical expertise, and he needed help urgently. The main road was a few hundred yards away; to the village of Irikamaya it was less than a mile. But it was pitch black, in a forest littered with obstacles and slippery with ice. Each man and woman on the hill was completely absorbed by the personal struggle against the cold. The idea of abandoning the fire, even in pursuit of help for a gravely injured man, was insupportable. They laid him alongside the fire and tried to keep him warm. Abruptly, at around 3 a.m., his gasping stopped.

'No one got upset by it,' Oikawa said. 'Even his wife didn't display much grief. In those circumstances, after what they had all managed to survive, that thing – I mean, death – was not frightening there.' It was snowing, steadily and heavily, and the earth was freezing. Tetsuya and the other two children were falling asleep on the cold ground. 'Usually, you would stop that,' Oikawa said.

'You would stop a child from falling asleep in that kind of cold. But we let them sleep.'

Around six, the sun rose. The three children, the dog and the ten surviving men and women stirred and picked themselves up from the ground. At the high-water mark of the wave, someone found a mandarin orange and a packet of custard creams, which the children shared. None had the strength to carry the corpse, which remained behind them on the hillside. They picked their way down to the road and along it to Irikamaya, where refugees were gathering from all over the district. There they encountered another survivor – Junji Endo, the single teacher left alive, who must surely know what had happened at the school.

PART 4

THE INVISIBLE MONSTER

In the Web

The first place I ever lived in Tokyo was a harbour island reclaimed from the edges of the Pacific Ocean. I had been there less than two weeks when my first earthquake struck. The tremor passed while I was still asleep, leaving the faintest smudge on my conscious mind: a sudden wakefulness, fugitive unease, evasive as an exhalation of smoke. I woke up, without understanding why. I felt a tugging need to switch on the light and sit up. I felt very much like a solitary foreigner in a strange city.

Over breakfast, the Japanese family with whom I was staying told me about earthquakes. Last night's tremor had been small, but unusual in that it had come and gone with a single jolt: usually they rumbled on, and the abruptness of the event suggested that the stirring of the crust was incomplete and that there was more movement to come. There were earthquakes all the time, they said, every few weeks at least – some unmistakable, some difficult to distinguish from the routine rumbling of the city: construction work, passing trucks, the vibration of underground trains. The last one to cause any alarm had been six months ago: all the joints of the apartment block creaking, the ceiling lights swinging crazily, neighbours crying out in alarm. And one day, of course, there would be a truly huge tremor, a repeat of the Great Kanto earthquake, which shook Tokyo and Yokohama before the war and started fires that killed a multitude. The Tokyo earthquakes came round on a regular cycle, and the next one was already overdue.

I knew this. Everyone who comes to Japan acquires this information within a few days of arriving. The first thing you learn about Tokyo is that it won't be there for much longer.

My friends talked with gossipy animation – there was evidently a mischievous pleasure in imparting this frightening information to a new arrival. They spoke with a kind of scandalised amusement, and with no visible alarm or trepidation. Earthquakes, the mass destruction of human life, the obliteration of the city were matters of lively breakfast conversation, of no more concern than a violent rain shower or an unseasonable fall of snow.

Sometime in the next few years, it is generally assumed, Tokyo will be shaken by an earthquake powerful enough to destroy large areas of the city and set off fires and tsunamis that will kill many tens of thousands of people. The reasoning is straightforward. Every six or seven decades, for several centuries, the Kanto plain, on which Tokyo, Yokohama and Kawasaki have merged into a single megalopolis, has been devastated by a vast tremor. The last one, which killed 140,000 people, took place in 1923. Seismologists point out that it is not, in fact, as simple as this – that past Tokyo earthquakes have originated in different faults, on separate and overlapping cycles, and that a sampling of a few hundred years is, in any case, too small to infer a pattern. But, for more nuanced reasons of their own, they agree with the conclusion: that widespread destruction is inevitable and, in geological terms, imminent.

In speaking of natural disasters, large casualty figures quickly acquire an air of unreality. To put them into perspective, consider the victims of the two atomic bombs. In Hiroshima in August 1945, 70,000 people were killed at once, and by the end of the year 60,000 more had died of injuries and radiation sickness. The Nagasaki bomb was less destructive, with a total of about 74,000 deaths. In 2004, the Japanese government predicted that an earthquake under Tokyo could kill as many as 13,000 people – one-tenth of a Hiroshima. Six years later, it considered a scenario in which a tremor originating in one fault sets off earthquakes in two more, and concluded that across the country 24,700 people could die – one-third of a Nagasaki. Projections made after the Tohoku disaster became gloomier, or more realistic. In 2012, a new study concluded that an earthquake and tsunami originating in the Nankai Trough could take 323,000 lives along the south-central Pacific Coast and cause 623,000 injuries.

This was not the speculation of cranks or activists, but the carefully researched finding of Japan's Cabinet Office, a deeply cautious organisation instinctively averse to alarmism. It took into account the many precautions and protective measures that Japan has developed – the sturdy construction, and sea walls, and regular evacuation drills. Despite all of these, its conclusion was blankly horrifying: the Nankai earthquake, which might strike at any time, could kill more people than four atomic bombs.

What is it like to live with knowledge such as this in daily life? What goes on inside the heads of those living under sentence of earthquake?

Recurring questions come to mind every few days, sometimes every few hours, especially in a new or unfamiliar quarter of the city. Sitting in a car on an elevated expressway, or walking through an underground shopping centre, you ask yourself, more in curiosity than in alarm: what if the Big One struck now? Are the pillars beneath that flyover strong enough? Would that plate-glass window hold? What would become of the large and rusty water tank on top of that old building? Finding a place to live crystallises the situation with particular clarity. Question one: is this apartment conveniently located, well appointed and reasonably priced? Question two: will it crush me to death when the ground starts to shake?

The answer, in the case of almost all modern buildings, is no. One of the unexpected consequences of the March 2011 disaster was to diminish anxiety about earthquakes. Even in Sendai, the big city closest to the epicentre, the damage caused by the tremors alone was impressively slight. There were cracks and broken windows; the ceiling of the main hall of the station partially fell in; and on the edges of the city, older houses – especially those built on hill-sides – slumped and slid on their foundations. But there were no big fires; no large modern buildings came close to collapse, and most of them suffered no significant damage at all.

In a disaster caused by an earthquake, in other words, only a tiny proportion of the victims was killed by the earthquake itself. More than 99 per cent – all but a hundred people or so – died in the water. And to survive a tsunami, it was not enough to be in a strong building; it also had to be tall. During an earthquake, open ground – an uncluttered beach, for example – is the safest place to find yourself. In a tsunami, such exposure is deadly. Mentally, a rebalancing took place as one menace receded and another loomed. There was no improvement in the overall sense of security; those who lived through March 2011 simply exchanged one set of imaginings – of fire and blunt impact – for new mental images of death by drowning.

I live and work in strong buildings, and on elevated ground. My home, my office and my children's schools may be badly shaken and structurally damaged, may even be rendered uninhabitable, but it is unlikely they will collapse or be inundated. Japan's wealth and advanced technology protect it from disaster better than anywhere else in the world. But the safety of any one individual depends entirely on where he or she is when the moment comes.

Over dinner one evening in Tokyo I found myself among a group of friends discussing the very worst place to be in a big earthquake. One of us suggested the Tokyo monorail, a slender ribbon of steel and concrete on which trains from the airport glide high over the chemical and petroleum tanks in the south of the city. Someone else imagined being trapped in the subway, amid fracturing tunnels and blackness. My own phobia was the flimsy pedestrian bridges that extend across big roads, often sandwiched between a six-lane highway below and an expressway above. But as we talked, I became aware of the restaurant in which we were sitting. It was a dark, narrow snuggery on the eighth floor of a cramped and decrepit old building. Behind the counter, the chef was cheerfully pouring oil onto a pan that flared with a foot-tall plume of flame. The partitions, doors and the mats on which we were sitting were made of wood, paper and rushes.

'Why does it not upset people more,' the journalist Peter Popham asked, 'the fact that they might any day be roasted alive, gassed to death, buried in a landslide or in the wreckage of their own homes?' People in Tokyo abandon the city from time to time, or lose their minds, or take their own lives, for the same reasons that they do such things anywhere in the world. But no one goes mad over earthquakes. Why not? What does it do to the unconscious, even to the soul, to exist with such precariousness?

The first time I lived in Japan I was eighteen years old. I had come to Japan in search of strangeness and adventure – I had come precisely to seek out excitements such as earthquakes. But they also seemed to explain something about the city I was experiencing with such intensity. I spoke no Japanese, and knew almost no one in Japan. Tokyo, with its vastness and impenetrability, answered to something in my loneliness. I left the Japanese family with whom I had been staying on the edge of the bay, and found a room in the suburbs and a job at an English conversation school. On the morning train, I stared at the ideograms in a Japanese textbook. I spent my evenings in bars with red lanterns at their doors, with new friends, most of them foreigners as transient and untethered as me. On the last train home, I exchanged smiles with Japanese girls. It was close to the height of Japan's 'Bubble' economy, the moment when Tokyo was briefly the richest city in history. The force of money was tearing down the old neighbourhoods and throwing them up again in steel and glass. The city, as I inhabited it, was as dazzling as a filament and as thin as tissue paper. It felt, in my excitement, like a place that was physically trembling, and that could at any moment come crashing down. It seemed entirely appropriate to learn that this was literally true.

'Far from being dull to the dangers, acute awareness of them gives Tokyo people's lives tone and brio,' wrote Popham, during this same period. 'The satisfaction of being a cog in the most elaborate and well-oiled machine in the history of the world is given an almost erotic twist by the knowledge that the machine is poised over an abyss.' Tokyo, he concluded, is 'a city helpless to save itself, and reconciled at some quite deep level to destruction and loss of life beyond all but the nuclear nightmares of other cities.'

'Now I will tell how Octavia, the spider-web city, is made,' says Kublai Khan, in Italo Calvino's *Invisible Cities*:

> There is a precipice between two steep mountains: the city is over the void, bound to the two crests with ropes and chains and catwalks. You walk on the little wooden ties, careful not to set your foot in the open spaces, or you cling to the hempen strands. Below there is nothing for hundreds and hundreds of feet: a few clouds glide past; farther down you can glimpse the chasm's bed.
>
> This is the foundation of the city: a net which serves as passage and as support. All the rest, instead of rising up, is hung below: rope ladders, hammocks, houses made like sacks, clothes hangers, terraces like gondolas, skins of water, gas jets, spits, baskets on strings, dumb-waiters, showers, trapezes and rings for children's games, cable cars, chandeliers, pots with trailing plants.

Suspended over the abyss, the life of Octavia's inhabitants is less uncertain than in other cities. They know the net will last only so long.

Earthquakes get into your dreams. But their meaning changes as you grow older. When I was young, I was excited by the idea that Tokyo's atmosphere of impermanence was a result of its inevitable doom. But that sense of things falling apart, the conviction that the centre cannot hold, is an adolescent notion: in reality, of course, the tension and insecurity came, not from the city, but from within me.

The earthquake is the thing that all humans face: the banal inevitability of death. We don't know when it will come, but we know that it will. We take refuge in elaborate and ingenious precautions, but in the end they are all in vain. We think about it even when we are not thinking about it; after a while, it seems to define what we are. It comes most often for the old, but we feel it most cruelly when it also takes away the young.

'Some people can't find the words,' said Naomi Hiratsuka. 'They just mutter, "Must have been terrible . . . " and that's it. It's not that they don't feel sympathy. They just don't have a way to express it. But I get sick of hearing the same phrases over and over again. And then I meet people who pretend not to know anything about it, because that's easier for them, just to ignore it and hope it'll go away. Not that I particularly want to talk to people like that.'

She paused and then smiled, as if at a private joke. 'The thing is that if someone doesn't mention it all, I think, "Why?" But if they're full of pity, I don't like that, either. I live my life day by day. I'm not always crying and feeling sorry for myself. Sometimes, even when we're out at the site, digging, we have a chat and a laugh about something. And then we feel self-conscious about people seeing us smiling. I shouldn't have to worry things like that, should I? It's very difficult.'

It is easy to imagine grief as an ennobling, purifying emotion – uncluttering the mind of what is petty and transient, and illuminating the essential. In reality, of course, grief doesn't resolve anything, any more than a blow to the head or a devastating illness. It compounds stress and complication. It multiplies anxiety and tension. It opens fissures into cracks, and cracks into gaping chasms.

From the survivors of the tsunami, I learned that everyone's grief is different, and that it differs in small and subtle ways according to the circumstances of loss. 'The first thing was this,' said Naomi. 'Did you lose your children, or did your children survive? That divided people immediately: the children who lived and those who died.' Thirty-four of the 108 pupils at the school survived the wave – because they had been picked up in time by their parents, or crawled miraculously out of the water. The horror of survival – the destruction of their community, the deaths of so many of their friends – was not to be underestimated. But in the eyes of those whose children had perished, they were the beneficiaries of almost unbearably good luck.

'Some of those who lost their children find it impossible to talk to those whose children survived,' Naomi said. 'In some ways, it's worse for people who were close.' Naomi knew one mother who had collected her children from the school and taken them to safety. Her neighbour had not done so, and her children had died. 'So the neighbour says to her, "Why? Why didn't you take my kids too?" Of course, it doesn't work like that. The school has rules – it wouldn't have been allowed. But once something like that is put into words, that friendship is over.'

Even among the bereaved there were gradations of grief, a spectrum of blackness indiscernible to those on the outside. It came down to a cold-hearted question: once the water had retreated, how much did you have left? Sayomi Shito had lost her beloved daughter Chisato; it would have been unthinkably callous to point out that her two older children, her husband, her extended family and her home were unharmed and intact. But others were acutely aware of Sayomi's circumstances, and the precise degree to which they differed from their own. Naomi, for example, had also lost one child out of three, while her home, husband and the rest of her family had survived. But Sayomi had been able to find and bury Chisato quickly, while Naomi had gone through the prolonged anguish of hunting for Koharu's remains.

Then there were those worse off, who had lost some, though not all, of their children, and the entirety of their homes; and those even more wretched, who had lost their homes and their entire families. And even within this group, the most miserable division of the stricken, there were terrible distinctions. Hitomi Konno, for example, had lost her son and both her daughters, but soon recovered and cremated their bodies. In this, she was better off than Miho Suzuki, who had found her son, but five years later was still looking for her daughter, Hana.

It is true that people can be 'brought together' by catastrophe, and it is human to look to this as a consolation. But the balance of disaster is never positive. New human bonds were made after the tsunami, old ones became stronger; there were countless, and remarkable, displays of selflessness and self-sacrifice. These we remember, and celebrate. We turn away from what is also common-place: the destruction of friendship and trust; neighbours at odds; the enmity of friends and relatives. A tsunami does to human connectedness the same thing that it does to roads, bridges and homes. And in Okawa, and everywhere in the tsunami zone, people fell to quarrelling and reproaches, and felt the bitterness of injustice and envy, and fell out of love.

Naomi Hiratsuka and Sayomi Shito were scarcely more than nodding acquaintances before the disaster. After it, they grew to hate one another. Of all the Okawa mothers, they were the ones whom I came to know best, and their mutual resentment was almost palpable. Sometimes I would visit Sayomi's house after a meeting with Naomi, or vice versa. In exaggeratedly casual tones and with a thin smile, the second woman would ask after the first, and the air in the room became colder.

Their antipathy was a function of the distinct tasks which each had set about with such energy. As Naomi sat in her digger, turning over the earth, Sayomi, her husband and the friends whom I had met that evening were pursuing a systematic investigation into the truth about what had happened at the school. Searching letters were sent to Ishinomaki city hall. Witnesses were sought out, and their accounts compiled. The group held a press conference at which they demanded that Junji Endo come before them again, to account for the anomalies in his story; and there were consultations with lawyers.

To Sayomi, these two tasks – dredging the physical, and bureaucratic, mud – were complementary; Naomi's contempt was baffling to her. 'By pursuing the question of what happened, by forcing the authorities to take responsibility, that will also force them to carry out the search,' she said. 'We talk to the media to keep up the pressure, and so that public concern won't fade away. I never interfered with her taking her digger licence. I've never criticised her. So I wonder why people such as Mrs Hiratsuka try to get us to do things their way.'

But to Naomi, the campaigning of what she called the 'Fukuji group' was a practical hindrance, as well as a social embarrassment. Because they were so outspoken, Sayomi and her friends were assumed by many outsiders to be leaders among the Okawa parents, representative of the whole. But their unashamed directness, amounting, by Japanese standards, to plain aggression, irritated and mortified many. The barracking of the town officials in the public meeting was regarded as unforgivably bad manners. Their denunciations of the education board threatened the delicate architecture of relationships built up by Naomi, who depended upon the goodwill of the city government for diggers, for fuel and for the permissions necessary to continue her search. 'I'm not in the least satisfied with the education board,' Naomi told me. 'But we need them, we need their cooperation, just to do what we have to do.'

Something else distinguished Sayomi and the campaigning Fukuji parents, as Naomi pointed out: all had recovered the bodies of their children quickly – within a couple of weeks, at most. 'From the beginning, it depended on whether you found your child or not,' Naomi said. 'When your child came home, when you had held a funeral, then you naturally moved onto the next question: why did this happen? And then anger could begin. But if your child was still out there, all you could think about was her face, the only thing in your mind was the idea of finding her, finding her.'

Naomi said: 'The question is: what's the purpose of pursuing the truth? What do you expect to come of it? Those people' – and she meant Sayomi – 'say, "Why did it happen? Why did it happen only at Okawa, but not at other schools?" But if you knew all that, then what? They say, "It's for the future, it's for the sake of other children. We want to draw lessons, so that our children didn't die in vain." But is that really all it is? Or are they simply laying blame? When you know exactly what happened, are you any better off? When you've got the truth in your hand, what are you going to do with it?'

What Use Is the Truth?

In all their dealings with the families of the dead children, the bureaucrats of the Ishinomaki Education Board maintained an exterior of calm and fussy courtesy. In the 'explanatory meetings', held several times a year, they sat in a dark-suited line, attending patiently to the distraught mothers and fathers with tilted heads. Their bows were slow and deep. In the most formal registers of language, they expressed their profound and sincere condolences. But about the city's handling of the tragedy of Okawa Primary School there lingered an air of disreputable shabbiness, an odour of suppressed panic and cack-handed cover-up. It seemed, at times, to be as much a matter of incompetence as deliberate conspiracy. But every few weeks emerged some new example of fishiness and ineptitude.

Early on, the education board had conducted an interview with the headmaster, Teruyuki Kashiba. The written record of this conversation contained obvious and inexplicable impossibilities. Kashiba claimed that immediately after the disaster, for example, he had travelled from his inland home to a spot on the Kitakami River in two hours, an impossibly fast journey. He described meetings with people who had no memory of seeing him on that day, and of a visit to a place which, at the time, was under five feet of water.

There were interviews, too, with the surviving children. They had lived through appalling trauma; their psychological state can only be imagined. But, in some cases, there was no parent present for these interviews, or any advance warning that they were to be conducted. When young Tetsuya Tadano was questioned, his interrogators simply turned up at his new school, with no attempt to seek the permission of his father.

Parents who had been present noticed later that certain details were inexplicably omitted from the written summaries of these interviews. The most important of these were the words of Yuki Sato and Daisuke Konno, the two sixth-year boys who had pleaded with their teacher to be allowed to escape up the hill, who had been refused and who had both perished in the wave. A number of the surviving children had recounted this exchange. One of the officials, Shigemi Kato, had referred to it in an early meeting with the parents. This, it became clear, had been a bad and unintentional lapse on his part – ever after, when questioned about it, the members of the education board denied that any of the surviving children had ever told them such a thing. 'I heard my child say during the interview that her friends were saying, "Let's escape to the hill,"' one mother told the meeting. 'But that wasn't written down at all.'

The memos summarising parts of the interviews were identically worded, as if they had been cut and pasted one into the other. No audio recordings had been made; even the name of the person conducting the interview was not indicated. When parents asked to see the written notes taken at the time, they were told that Shigemi Kato had disposed of them.

At a later meeting, Kato was pressed about the boys who had tried to run up the hill. During this exchange, his boss, Moto Yamada, was seen looking at Kato and raising his fingers to his lips as if to silence him. The gesture could be seen on the video recording of the meeting; Yamada repeated the hushing motion three times.

And then there was the matter of the surviving teacher, Junji Endo.

*   *   *

Of the various untruths in Endo's testimony, the most baffling were his claims about the trees. Consistently, in recounting the events after the earthquake, he described the spectacle of pines on the hillside behind the school being toppled by the earthquake and its aftershocks. He recalled being pinioned by two cedars, and how the rising tsunami had lifted them off and miraculously freed him. His account conveyed a vivid impression of panicked survivors, having narrowly escaped death by water, cowering as the hillside shook with the collapse of deadly tree trunks.

There were no fallen trees. Many people tramped up and down the hill in the weeks after the disaster, and not a single one was found. Trees, with flexible trunks and branches, efficiently dissipate the energy of earthquakes: they may shake and bend, but they rarely topple over. The landscape following the disaster was littered with pines, but these had been carried in from the beachside forest, and ripped from their roots not by the earthquake but by the tsunami.

'If it was such a big a quake that so many trees fell down, all the houses would have collapsed too,' said Kazutaka Sato. 'Mr Endo was a nature lover. He must have known that.'

The details of Endo's testimony filtered outwards from the circle of the bereaved and into the community at large. The first person to denounce it was a car mechanic named Masahiko Chiba, whose house had been protected by its elevated position on the far side of the hill from the school. No other house so close to the river had survived the tsunami, and soon survivors – many of them wet, some of them injured – were converging on it. Among them were Junji Endo and Seina Yamamoto, the little boy who had escaped with him.

The two arrived late that afternoon. Chiba's wife was the first to see them – a man in a suit, and a young boy still wearing his white plastic helmet, stepping uncertainly down the hill. 'The man in the suit said, "I could only rescue one,"' Mrs Chiba recalled. 'Those were his first words. I think he said something about

Okawa school, but I had so much to think about that I didn't listen carefully.'

She remembered that the boy's shoes and socks were wet, but that Endo's clothes were dry. He still had his shoes, which he removed before stepping inside. 'He wore a check suit, an indistinct brown-grey colour, and a bit shabby, typical for a teacher,' she said. 'But it was clean and it wasn't wet. I remember this quite clearly.'

One of the refugees staying in the house was an old man who could hardly walk. The following morning, Endo carried him on his back from the house to a waiting vehicle. Only a fit adult could have managed this; there was no sign at all that Endo was injured.

Later, the Chibas read about the teacher's own account of that afternoon: how he had been caught up in the tsunami and almost drowned; how he had lost his shoes and staggered down from the hillside in darkness; and how he had dislocated his shoulder. They were baffled and appalled. 'The account of Endo, the teacher, is lies,' Masahiko Chiba said. 'Ninety per cent of it is lies. But why he lied, I do not know.'

In June, three months after the tsunami, Endo wrote two letters, one to Kashiba, the headmaster, and another addressed to the bereaved parents collectively. They were sent by fax, the day before a meeting between the families and the education board. In one more of those suspicious and inexplicable decisions taken by the board of education, it was six months before these documents were released. In them, Endo added little to the account he had given in person, but described in some detail his own agonised state of mind. 'It's terrible to remember what happened then,' he wrote. 'I go completely pale when I think about it. My hands are trembling as I write . . . There's something wrong with my body and with my mind. I'm being selfish, I know, I'm sorry, but for the time being could you leave me alone? I'm frightened when the phone rings.'

Every request from the families to meet Endo received the same response – a letter from his doctor, explaining that he was recovering from Post-Traumatic Stress Disorder and was too distressed to talk about what had happened. It was impossible to challenge such a diagnosis. But the months passed into years, and the response remained the same. 'I think it's an excuse,' said Kazuhiro Yoshioka, a lawyer who advised the families. 'Every note from the doctor reads like a carbon copy of the last one. He always says that just three more months are needed. And the drugs he's on are no more than you'd be prescribed for insomnia.

'It may be that Mr Endo doesn't want to appear. But the board of education twists facts to avoid responsibility. Perhaps they have gone to him and said, "You stay in the background. Don't say anything. We'll look after this problem."'

The men of the Ishinomaki city government were not villains. In plenty of ways they had behaved heroically. They were local bureaucrats in a small regional city. They were familiar, in theory, with the threat of natural disaster, but nothing in their personal or professional experience could have prepared them for an event of such magnitude and horror. They were themselves victims: many had seen their homes flooded or washed away; some had lost friends and relatives. They were reeling and in confusion, but they never abandoned their sense of public duty, and they kept the motor of administration turning over, despite crushing practical obstacles.

There were no telephones, no mains electricity and no fuel. The city hall itself was flooded by five feet of water; its vehicles were immobilised in the car park. The staff abandoned the mud-slimed ground floor and worked by torchlight in the upper offices. It was not a question of merely cancelling leave – city employees were required to remain on duty around the clock. Step by step, they extended themselves across the stricken municipality, first in the ruined city centre, then into the outer villages, across fields and hills and forests, by bicycle, by foot and in rubber boats. Fifteen of the city's schools, nurseries and kindergartens were flooded, burned or otherwise affected by the disaster; others were serving as evacuation centres for tens of thousands of displaced families. Day by day, the board of education gathered information about the state of schools, the welfare of their children and teachers and arranged supplies of food for the refugees.

As individuals, they were tireless and self-sacrificing; without them, a desperate situation would have been many times worse. But when confronted by their own failure, as they were at Okawa Primary School, personal warmth and empathy were stifled by the instinct of the collective – the instinct to protect the institution against outside attack. Faced with unanswerable reproach, it shrank back into itself, behind scales of formality and claws of bureaucratese. The faces of the kindly, hard-working local men and women who made up the education board dropped from view. Their loyalty was to a higher cause, beyond that of public duty or personal decency – that of protecting the organisation from further damage to its reputation, and above all from legal attack in the courts.

The imperviousness of the city officials, their refusal to muster a human response to the grief of the families, seemed at the beginning to be a collective failure of character, and of leadership. But as time passed, Sayomi and Takahiro Shito, and the other parents of the 'Fukuji group', began to suspect another motivation – an obsession with avoiding anything that could be taken as an admission of liability. The metallic tang of lawyerly advice lingered around many of the bureaucrats' utterances. They were happy to express grief and condolence, and willing to abase themselves in general terms for their unworthiness. But to acknowledge specific negligence on the part of individuals, or systematic, institutional failure – that was a step which no one would take.

Then, the winter after the tsunami, they offered up a sacrifice, of sorts. Teruyuki Kashiba, the headmaster of Okawa Primary School, presented a signed statement of apology addressed to the parents. This 'irremediable situation', he said, resulted 'from my carelessness as headmaster'. 'However much I apologise,' he went on, 'things such as the lack of a proper emergency manual and the failure to promote crisis awareness among the staff cannot be forgiven.' Two months later, he took early retirement.

It looked, on the face of it, like an important concession. But to the Fukuji parents, finely attuned to the nuances of apology, there was something about it – something in the word 'carelessness' – that smacked of evasion. They put it to the test at a meeting a few months later at which Kashiba was present.

Sayomi's husband, Takahiro Shito, addressed the now-retired headmaster, as he sat before the assembled parents. He pressed him on the question of the school's emergency manual, which Kashiba, in his statement of apology, had acknowledged to have been inadequate. 'Reflecting on it now,' Shito said, 'I'd like to hear from you again what you mean by that that word "carelessness".'

'In short,' said Kashiba, 'not to have checked it thoroughly was careless.'

The word for carelessness in Japanese is *taiman*. Shito was fishing for another, and more potent, word: *kashitsu* – negligence.

'Do you not think,' he asked, 'that this carelessness amounts to negligence?'

Sitting on Kashiba's immediate left was a man named Kenetsu Shishido, deputy councillor of the board of education. Perhaps it was the temperature in the overheated room; perhaps it was the effects of a medical condition. Whatever the cause, Mr Shishido displayed signs of intense physical discomfort during Kashiba's exchange with Takahiro Shito. He fidgeted in his chair. He wiped his face and hands repeatedly with a hand towel. At the mention of *kashitsu*, he leaned forward and back, and placed his hand on a document on the desk on which he appeared to be pointing to something. Almost imperceptibly, he muttered to Kashiba out of the corner of his mouth. Then he rubbed the towel over his hands and face again, wiped the back of his neck and attended to an itch in his right ear.

'Headmaster?' said Shito, after moments of unfilled silence.

Kashiba shot a sideways glance at Deputy Councillor Shishido. 'As far as that goes,' he said, looking down now at the papers on the desk in front of him, 'personally, I don't think so.'

'You don't think so?'

'Although I might have overlooked some things, I did what I had to do, so I don't think it's negligence. I wouldn't say that myself.'

Shishido was wiping his face again. This, it had become clear, was not done to quell perspiration, but to mask more muttered remarks to Kashiba.

'We can't hear what Mr Shishido is saying to you,' said Shito. At the mention of his name, Shishido looked up abruptly, with an expression of quizzical innocence.

'Move away from him,' someone else called out. Sulkily, Shishido shifted his chair a few inches to the left.

Then Shito's neighbour, Katsura Sato, stood up to speak. Katsura taught art in a high school in the city of Ishinomaki; she knew from personal experience about the preparations that teachers make in anticipation of disaster. 'None of them was done,' she told Kashiba. 'But still, as headmaster, you told the education board you'd done them. If we'd known, then everyone would have gone to the school to pick up their children. If everyone had gone, many more children would have been saved. Because of your "carelessness" all those children died. It's negligence. Negligence! How long do you intend to put off admitting responsibility? Seventy-four children died, and you still don't get it.'

Shishido was muttering again to Kashiba out of the corner of his mouth. 'Truly,' Kashiba said, after a pause, 'for not being able to protect the lives of the seventy-four children and ten teachers, I feel truly sorry.'

'You *feel* that,' said Katsura. 'But you haven't *done* anything about it. Have you? It's negligence, it's negligence!'

Shishido continued to towel his face and to mouth inaudible words.

'For the fact that I couldn't save seventy-four children and ten teachers,' Kashiba said, 'I apologise.'

'Will you admit professional negligence?'

Shishido wiped his mouth and continued his sidelong muttering.

'I feel sorry,' said Kashiba, 'but . . . '

Katsura Sato almost screamed, '*Will you admit negligence?*'

'I can't make that judgement.'

'Who *will* make that judgement? *Answer!*'

Kashiba was looking at Shishido. Shishido was telling him something.

'I feel very sorry,' Kashiba said, 'but I can only say that I am truly sorry, and I apologise.'

Twenty-three months after the tsunami, the Ishinomaki city government announced the establishment of something called the Okawa Primary School Incident Verification Committee. It consisted of a panel of ten eminences, including lawyers and university professors of sociology, psychology and behavioural science. The committee would spend a year reviewing documents and conducting interviews. Its findings were published in a 200-page report in February 2014.

The committee was funded by the city at a cost of ¥57 million (£390,000). Its mission – 'verification' – turned out to have specific and limited scope: to establish the facts and causes of what happened, but by no means to assign personal responsibility. It concluded that the deaths arose because the evacuation of the playground was delayed, and because the children and teachers eventually fled, not away from the tsunami, but towards it.

The school, the board of education and the city government, the report said, were inadequately prepared for such a natural disaster. The municipal 'hazard map', which indicated areas of coast vulnerable to tsunami, did not include Kamaya. The possibility of a tsunami was not considered in compiling the school's disaster manual, and there were no tsunami evacuation drills. No one in the municipal government had checked on the preparations taken by the school. Teachers at the school, the report concluded, were psychologically unable to accept that they were facing imminent danger.

If any one of these failures had not occurred, the committee concluded, the tragedy could have been avoided. 'These circumstances were not unique to Okawa Primary,' said the report. 'Such an accident could occur at any school.' This seemed at first to be a powerful, and disturbing, conclusion: a warning to the country at large. But its effect was to disperse to the wind any individual blame or responsibility. A terrible thing had happened, the committee was agreeing – but it could have happened anywhere, and to anyone.

The most controversial aspects of the case – such as the silencing of the boys who wanted to run to the hill – were ignored or skated over. To the Fukuji parents, the committee's conclusions were no more than an expensive restatement of what had been obvious for more than two years. The true purpose of the exercise, they concluded, was to shut down disagreement about the tragedy by commissioning 'independent' experts to produce a tepid report, which articulated mild criticisms, while sparing the careers and reputations of the guilty.

No employee of the city of Ishinomaki or its board of education was ever sacked, disciplined or formally reproached over the deaths at Okawa Primary School. Shigemi Kato, who destroyed the notes from the interviews with the surviving children, was promoted the following year to the headmastership of a city primary school.

The committee's report came out in the last week of February 2014, almost three years after the tsunami. The day before the anniversary, on 10 March, came a startling piece of news. The families of twenty-three children who had died at Okawa were suing the city of Ishinomaki and Miyagi Prefecture in the Sendai District Court. They were accusing them of negligence, and demanding compensation of ¥100 million – about £600,000 – for each of the lives lost. It was two years and 364 days since the disaster, the very last moment that it was legally possible to file a case. It was the move they had secretly been planning all along.

The Tsunami Is Not Water

The tsunami had the power of many atomic bombs, but the most impressive thing about it – more astonishing, in its way, than the spectacle of destruction – was the behaviour of those who survived it. Within a matter of hours, hundreds of thousands of people were converging on schools, community halls, temples and shrines, huddling in classrooms, gymnasia, hallways and corridors, anywhere that had space enough to unroll a quilt. They were panicked, grieving and in shock; they included centenarians, newborn babies and everyone in between. For the first few days, there was scant official help. Those left alive had to help themselves, which they did with unsurpassable discipline and efficiency.

Naturally, invisibly, without fuss or drama, order crystallised in the chaos of the evacuation centres. Space was allocated, bedding was improvised and food was pooled, prepared and distributed. Rotas, for fetching, fixing, cleaning and cooking, were quickly established and filled. Everything was eased by the instinctive Japanese aversion to anything that could be judged messy, selfish or otherwise antisocial. And all of it was achieved in an atmosphere of good humour and generosity, which sometimes bordered on the ridiculous.

Among the burdens of working as a foreign journalist in Tohoku was the constant struggle to fend off gifts of food – sweets, rice balls, chocolate biscuits, fish sausage – from homeless refugees who had only enough to feed themselves for the next few days or even hours. People who had recently lost their homes apologised, with pained sincerity, for the inadequacy of their hospitality. There was no significant looting; despite the chronic shortages of everything from petrol to toilet paper, no one took the opportunity of scarcity to raise their prices. I never once saw fighting or squabbling or disagreement; and, most remarkable of all, there was a complete absence of self-pity.

It was impossible not to make mental comparisons. I pictured a school gymnasium in north-east England, rather than north-east Japan, in which hundreds of people were living and sleeping literally head to toe. By this stage, they would have been murdering one another.

Every foreigner who visited the disaster zone in the early weeks was struck by it; it transformed what should have been a harrowing experience into an inspiring one. There were many terrible and fearful scenes, and bottomless pain, but the horror was offset, and almost eclipsed, by the resilience and decency of the victims. It seemed to me at the time that this was the best of Japan, the best of humanity, one of the things I loved and admired most about this country: the practical, unselfconscious, irrepressible strength of communities. And I found myself thinking about history, and those moments when a national shock of one kind or another had galvanised Japan and marked the beginning a new and dynamic era.

There had been the forcible opening of the feudal country in the mid-nineteenth century by American gunships. There was the catastrophic defeat of 1945. Both events had seemed at the time moments of irredeemable humiliation. Both had been followed by decades of resurgence and prosperity. By 2011, that atmosphere of expansive and ambitious optimism was twenty years in the past. Since the collapse of the economic bubble in the early 1990s, Japan had been adrift, becalmed between a lost prosperity and a future that was too dim and uncertain to grasp. The economy was shrinking or stagnant. Companies no longer promised the security of employment for life. The old ruling party, which had led Japan for half a century, was bankrupt of ideas and personalities; but the opposition politicians elected in its place were diffident and inept. So I was not alone in wondering whether this new disaster might turn out to be the force that jolted Japan out of the political and economic funk into which it had slithered.

A multitude of people had died at a stroke. Nuclear furnaces were venting poison into the air. In any country, surely, events such as these would be the catalyst of protest, and action, and indignant movements for change. 'The Japanese people rose from the ashes of the Second World War using our fundamental strength to secure a remarkable recovery and the country's present prosperity,' said Naoto Kan, the prime minister at the time. 'I have not a single doubt that Japan will overcome this crisis, recover from the aftermath of the disaster, emerge stronger than ever, and establish a more vibrant and better Japan for future generations.'

Nothing of the kind was to happen; the promise of rebirth glimpsed in the evacuation centres would go completely unfulfilled.

Japan changed in various ways in the years after the tsunami, but it shed energy and confidence rather than gaining them. Partly, this had to do with a gathering sense of insecurity in East Asia – the crackling belligerence of North Korea, the domineering assertiveness of China. At the core of it, though, was an ever greater disconnection between Japan's leaders and the citizenry they were supposed to represent.

Naoto Kan and the centrist politicians who were in power at the time crumpled before the tsunami. They were the first Japanese opposition party to have won an outright majority; their inexperience and poor judgement had been obvious from the day they took power. In 2009, they had won the country's biggest-ever election victory; three years later, they suffered its fourth-worst defeat. Rejuvenated by its period of opposition, the old Liberal Democratic Party was back in power, as it had been for fifty-three of the past fifty-seven years. Its victorious leader, Shinzo Abe, was the most nationalistic prime minister since the war.

He supported revision of Japan's pacifist constitution, and assumed new powers to deploy its armed forces. He pooh-poohed historical accounts of atrocities committed by the Imperial Army; he was a worshipper at Yasukuni Shrine, where hanged Class-A war criminals were revered as Shinto deities. Despite the nation-wide anxiety about Fukushima, he was unswervingly committed to maintaining Japan's nuclear reactors. Opinion polls showed that his plans for Japan's economy were widely supported. But his views about nuclear power, about wartime history, and the anger they excited among Japan's Asian neighbours, were the cause of deep unease.

At a moment when it most needed unifying leadership, Japan faced a democratic crisis. One party stood convicted of gross incompetence. The other was led by a man whose ideology was drastically at odds with most of the population. Many of those who voted for Shinzo Abe did not like or approve of him. But he was decisive, consistent and he had a plan, more persuasive than any other, for restoring to Japan its economic well-being. The weakness of the opposition was so extreme that many Japanese felt they had no choice.

In government, Abe faced protests of his own – against the restart of the reactors, against his plans to allow Japanese soldiers to deploy overseas and against a sinister new state secrecy law. I followed these demonstrations and talked to the marchers; and I was always struck by the peculiar intensity of the opposition to Abe. It was not only about his nationalist enthusiasms; something in his personality excited in the demonstrators a deep, personal loathing. He was a lackey of big business and the powerful nuclear industry, they agreed; and a militarist who could end up leading Japan back into war. Japanese do not easily reach for invective, even towards their politicians. But many of the slogans denounced him as a fascist; some of the posters depicted Abe with the moustache of Adolf Hitler.

One old marcher told me that he had lived through the war, and the devastation it had brought. He remembered the incendiary bombing of Tokyo; his cousin, a young conscript soldier, had died in the atomic bombing of Hiroshima. And now he found himself in a country in which radioactive fallout once again drifted across the land, with a prime minister who was slowly leading his people back towards militarism. 'It feels to me as if history is going into reverse,' he said. 'Who could stand by and watch such things happen?'

A huddle had formed about us as we talked on the margins of the demonstration. People, young and old, were nodding in agreement. Behind us, slogans were being shouted through a powerful amplifier: 'Against the Abe government! Against war!'

If he was against Abe, I asked the old man, then who did he prefer? Where were the wise and responsible leaders? Who should be leading Japan?

His face displayed puzzlement, then surprise and finally embarrassment. The protesters standing around us glanced silently at one another; a few smiled sheepishly. I suggested the name of Naoto Kan's successor, the feebly uncharismatic leader of the disgraced centrist party, now in opposition; and people shook their heads in disgust. There must be someone, I said. But no one had any ideas. I was standing among some of the most politically motivated people in Japan. Shinzo Abe was a hate figure to them, almost a bogeyman. But they could propose not a single person to take his place.

What accounts for this democratic deficit, this failure of the political system to generate a dynamic politics? It is one of the mysteries of modern Japan.

Technically, nothing is missing; all the moving parts are there. Japan has an unambiguous written constitution, an independent judiciary and a free press. There are multiple political parties; elections are uncontaminated by coercion or corruption. And yet there is a stagnancy and lack of conviction to Japan's political life. In North America and Europe, there is no lack of odious and incompetent leaders; but there is a sense of creative friction and of evolution, of a political marketplace, in which ideas and individuals less popular and effective yield, over time, to those that prove themselves fitter for purpose, and where politics – even if it has its wrong turns and dead ends – is at least in constant motion. In Japan, this is not the case; even seventy years after the war, a genuinely competitive multi-party system has still not established itself.

After the tsunami had destroyed their homes, the survivors of the wave mobilised and organised, and took control of their fate. They did this instinctively, because it appeared to them the natural and moral thing to do. They also did so because they didn't expect official help. In any comparable disaster in the West, its victims would quickly and shrilly have been demanding to know: where is the government? In Japan in 2011, that was a question that was rarely heard.

At the time, such low expectations were an asset, a spur to resilience and self-reliance. But low expectations are corrosive to a democratic system. It is not universally true – there are in Japan many people who are deeply and conscientiously engaged. But it is common in discussing parliamentary politics to encounter indifference, disgust and, above all, a paralysing resignation. Our leaders are terrible, people seem to be saying – but what can *we* do about it? It is as if politics itself is a natural disaster of which the Japanese are the helpless victims, an impersonal misfortune beyond the influence of common men, and which can only be helplessly accepted, and endured.

One-tenth of the world's active volcanoes are in Japan – the entire archipelago, in fact, consists of an immense range of volcanoes jutting out of the sea. Late every summer, typhoons churn into motion in the north-west Pacific and spend themselves on its long coast. The rain they deposit loosens the soil, which slides down the steep mountainsides in rivers of mud. In geological terms, Japan is in an appalling situation, on top of not one, but two so-called 'triple junctions' – points at which three of the Earth's tectonic plates collide and grate against one another. Fire, wind, flood, landslide, earthquake and tsunami: it is a country of intense, elemental violence. Harsh natural environments often breed qualities that take on the status of national characteristics – the dark fatalism of Russians, the pioneer toughness of frontier Americans. Japanese identify in themselves the virtue of *nintai* or *gaman*, variously rendered as endurance, patience or perseverance. Foreign journalists covering the disaster liked to refer to the 'Stoicism' of the survivors, but Japanese *gaman* is not a philosophical concept. The conventional translations failed to convey the passivity and abnegation which the idea contains, the extent to which *gaman* often seems indistinguishable from a collective lack of self-esteem. *Gaman* was the force that united the reeling refugees in the early days after the disaster; but it was also what neutered politics, and permitted Japanese to feel that they had no individual power over, and no responsibility for, their national plight.

I happened to visit Okawa during the election campaign that brought Shinzo Abe to power. Nobody I met displayed any curiosity about the election, or even an awareness that it was taking place; it was as though it was occurring in a separate dimension, parallel with, but invisible to, the one through which ordinary human beings moved.

Posters along the road bore the slogans of the competing parties and photographs of their candidates. Vans mounted with loudspeakers drove through the villages, blaring out their names. It was impossible not to think of Mr Oikawa and the men from the town office, driving along these same roads with similar equipment, broadcasting their message about the coming of the tsunami, which was similarly ignored.

'I'm not saying that they should have been rioting, and *gaman* or *nintai* – these qualities clearly had a positive role on the immediate aftermath,' said Norio Akasaka, an academic specialist in the culture of Tohoku. 'But people had all kinds of demands and complaints and dissatisfaction. They should have spoken out – against the national government, against the nuclear-plant operator. Their complaints were not made. They kept those things within themselves, through endurance, through patience. And that was a bad thing.'

Sometimes in Japan I wondered if it didn't come down to a simple proposition: would you tolerate a certain amount of whingeing and squabbling and disorder, even a bit of looting and profiteering, if such selfishness was accompanied by a willingness on the part of ordinary people to fight a bit, to shout down authority and to take responsibility for the people they elected?

There was another set of slogans that were ubiquitous at that time, employing a different Japanese word. *Ganbarō* is an exhortation to overcome challenges and hardships: the simplest English translations would be 'persevere', 'stick at it' or 'do your best'. *Ganbarō* is what you say to a child studying for exams, or to an athlete competing in a tournament. Banners reading *Ganbarō Tohoku!* were often to be seen in stations and public buildings. They were intended as declarations of solidarity by those – the great majority in Japan – who were personally unaffected by the disaster. But as an expression of sympathy, let alone condolence, it was a curious expression.

Was it really a source of consolation to people newly homeless and bereaved to be told, in effect, to tough it out, like a marathon runner? *Ganbarō* always seemed to me a word in which empathy with those suffering was compromised by the implication that what they were going through would be good for them in the long run.

*   *   *

Tohoku people were famous for their *gaman*. It was what had forti-
fied them over the centuries against cold, poverty and unreliable
harvests. It was also, I suspected, what had made them susceptible
to their historical role as Japan's exploited – inured to selling off
their daughters, and sending off their sons as cannon fodder in the
empire's wars. People spoke nostalgically of Tohoku as a repository
of 'the old Japan', by which they meant a slower, gentler, rural
way of life, a 'village society' unsullied by urban ugliness and the
viruses of greed and commercialism. But this outward simplicity
masked a deep conservatism, a repression so deeply internalised
that it was experienced by its victims as common sense. The people
of the old Japan shut up and got on with it – and shutting up was
the crucial element. They worried deeply about what other people
would think if they stood up and argued. They rejected change,
and efforts at change – the idealised village was a world in which
conflict, and even disharmony, were immoral, a kind of violence.

It was a hidden world, of which I only ever caught glimpses.
By definition, those whose mouths have been stopped by social
convention do not talk about it to an outsider. I encountered it
through the stories of those who did speak out, such as Naomi
Hiratsuka, whose father-in-law regarded grief as an expression of
weakness; and in the accounts of the old men of Kamaya who
refused to believe in the possibility of a tsunami. Most eloquent
of all was Masahiko Chiba, the car mechanic into whose house
Junji Endo, and dozens of other refugees, had staggered on the
afternoon of the disaster.

Over the next three days, more than a hundred strangers fetched
up at the Chibas' two-storey house, to be fed, clothed and sheltered. They included local people, passing motorists, local government officials and young Tetsuya Tadano and the handful of other
surviving children from Okawa Primary School. The Chibas used up
their stores of food, and gave away all their own clothes and those
of their children and grandchildren. Afterwards, many of those

whom they had helped, including the Okawa children, returned to express their gratitude to Chiba and his wife. Junji Endo was not one of them; nor were any of the local bureaucrats. And after he spoke publicly about the discrepancies in Endo's story, Chiba told me, he began to become aware of an invisible force of disapproval and reproach.

It came as no surprise. 'In the village society, if you speak out, you will be ostracised,' he said. 'There's a common assumption that if you talk too much, or do anything controversial, the authorities won't help you. They won't repair the road by your house. They won't give the benefit of official services. That's what people assume. We were lucky – our home and our business survived, and we didn't need their help. But plenty of people round here lost their families, their homes, their possessions. People like that are not going to speak out, or criticise the local government.'

It was vanishingly subtle. No one said anything explicitly angry or reproachful – it was the Chibas' friends who cautioned them, for their own good, to remain silent. But the fact was that out of eleven car-repair businesses operating in the local area, only two, including theirs, survived the tsunami. And as the months wore on, Chiba saw official business from the local government offices and their employees consistently going to his rival.

'The children were murdered by an invisible monster,' Sayomi Shito said once. 'We vent our anger on it, but it doesn't react. It's like a black shadow. It has no human warmth.' She went on, 'The tsunami was a visible monster. But the invisible monster will last for ever.'

I asked, 'What is the invisible monster?'

'I wonder myself what it is,' said Sayomi. 'Something peculiar in the Japanese, who only attach importance to the surface of things. And in the pride of people who cannot ever say sorry.'

I was sitting with Sayomi and Takahiro in the Shito family's big wooden house. It was late at night; we had been there since dusk.

I had asked all the questions in my notebook. Now the conversation had taken on a different quality – meandering, flickering between the particular and the general, between anger and sadness; marked by shifts, jumps, silences.

Sayomi's family had lived in this village, Fukuji, for 500 years. One of her ancestors had been a samurai who had travelled to the far north-east from distant Kyoto, Japan's most magnificent and snobbish city. As a teenager, Sayomi had come to loathe the pressure of being a member of a grand old family and to long for escape and independence. But her two older sisters quickly found husbands and left home, and there were no brothers. So when Sayomi married Takahiro, he was legally adopted by her parents as their son, a common practice among families without a male child. Thus Sayomi was pulled back to the centre of the family against which she had rebelled, and became the inheritor and custodian of the line of descent.

The banks of the Kitakami were remote from the sophistication of the city, but Sayomi's forebears took a rich harvest from the sea, the river, the lagoon, the fields and the forests. The hills cut the villages off from one another, but the water connected them. There was a sense even now of the water being older than the land, and of having a claim on it which had been only reluctantly surrendered. It was hinted at in the names of places miles inland, with no obvious connection to the sea. The land on which Okawa Primary School had been constructed was called Nirajima – 'Chive Island'; close to Fukuji was Shioden: 'Salt Field'. As a child, Sayomi had dug up ancient shells from paddies that had once been under the ocean. The only sites of antiquity were stone monuments and Shinto shrines; and these, almost always, were positioned upon high ground.

'Those rice fields were the sea once,' Sayomi said. 'Now they are the sea again. That's the thing about water – water always tells the truth. There's no argument to be had. Water goes freely where it must.'

Takahiro said, 'Everything made by men will be destroyed by nature in the end. Mountains and river, the creations of nature – they will remain. Everything human, that will go. We need to reconsider the respect we give to nature.'

In the months and years afterwards, Takahiro received invitations to give talks around the country to groups interested in the tragedy of Okawa. He accepted out of a sense of duty; he assumed that he would encounter people alert to the human component of disaster, anxious to learn how they themselves could reduce the chances of falling victim to similar catastrophe. 'But I was shocked,' he said, 'by how low their level of awareness was.' Takahiro's audiences expressed sympathy, and polite horror at what had happened, but it was as if they viewed it through the wrong end of a telescope, as something small, curious and remote from their own lives. 'For them, it was someone else's problem,' he said. 'They didn't recognise it as the kind of thing that could happen again in the future, even happen to them. Perhaps it's the same with nuclear power. Everyone played down the dangers for all those years, and the result was this sudden, terrible situation. In Okawa School too, the teachers played everything down, took nothing seriously.'

Takahiro was a strong, healthy man in his forties. He spoke calmly; nothing in his tone suggested that he was in the grip of powerful emotions. But, as he continued, I could see that his hand was trembling.

He said, 'If they don't take this opportunity, even now when so many people have died, you can't ever expect them to change the way they think or act. That's why we are pursuing the real cause of the tragedy. If they consider this disaster, but refuse to look into its core, the same tragedy could be repeated. But that's how Japan functions, which the national government can do nothing to change.'

In this, and in many of the conversations I had in Okawa, it wasn't completely clear to me who 'they' were. I was about to ask, when Takahiro said: 'As a citizen of this country, I'm ashamed of that. I think it's embarrassing. But it's something that I have to say. By telling this story, even though I am ashamed of it, perhaps we can change the situation.'

The Shitos were victims; but the shame was theirs too. 'They' meant 'us', meant everyone. The tsunami was not the problem. Japan was the problem.

'I tell them that the tsunami is not just water,' Takahiro said, in a rush. 'The tsunami is a lethal weapon that can kill you in an instant. Don't think of it as water. The first thing the tsunami hit was the forest that blocked the wind from the sea. The trees are swept away, and it is those trees which break the houses, and then the rubble of the houses which hits the people. And then everything is gone. Trees, houses, rubble, people – everything. That's how the tsunami attacks. It's not water.'

Predestination

Secretly, Naomi Hiratsuka sometimes used to wonder how long she could continue searching for the lost children. But she never asked herself why she did so.

After the remains of her daughter, Koharu, were recovered in August 2011, there were four who still remained missing. Yui Takeyama, who was seven years old, had died at the school alongside his sister and his mother. His surviving father, overwhelmed by grief and tied down by a full-time job, took no part in the extended search. Yuto Suzuki, a twelve-year-boy, had been off sick and was at home in the care of his family when the wave struck – so it was arguable whether he counted as one of the victims of the tragedy at the school. Masaru Naganuma, the father of seven-year-old Koto, was the most indefatigable of all the searchers, going out alone every hour he could, in digger and boat, looking for his son in ocean, lagoon and in the earth. But the parent to whom Naomi became the closest was Miho, the mother of the only girl still missing, nine-year-old Hana Suzuki.

Miho had lived with her son and daughter by the Nagatsura lagoon, one of the communities to have been completely swept away by the tsunami. She and her husband, Yoshiaki, had both been at work inland on that afternoon. Miho's elderly parents-in-law had died in the home they all shared. Both her children died at the school; the body of her son, the older of the two, had been found after eight days. Miho and Naomi spent months together looking for Hana and Koharu; they acquired, after a time, something of the intimate ease of sisters. Naomi, the younger, was focused and determined, the well-organised teacher adept at dealing with paperwork and officialdom, who got her heavy-vehicle licence and trundled her own digger out in the mud. Miho, gentler and less assertive, was the one who waited supportively on the margin with towels and refreshments, ready, whenever needed, to wade out in long boots and pick through the objects turned up by the digger's claw. In 2012, police searching the lagoon had lifted out the body of an elderly couple in a submerged car; later that year, the head of a missing young woman had been recovered nearby. But, since the discovery of Koharu, no more children from Okawa school had been found. When Miho, with shaking hands, pulled bones out from the mud, they always turned out to be those of chickens from an obliterated poultry farm.

Miho loved to draw. It was an enthusiasm that she had shared with Hana, who had spent hours creating cartoon faces in the distinctive style of Japanese *manga*, with big eyes and mouths, spangled with stars and teardrops and rainbows. One of the mediums whom Miho consulted had reported to her the consoling news that, even in the afterlife, Hana was still busily making pictures.

The shrine in front of the school was decorated with three letters, written and coloured in felt-tip pen and illustrated with *manga* faces. They had been drawn and written by Miho and were addressed to her daughter. The first was faded by sun, and spattered by rain and mud. 'Dear Hana,' it began:

Mum and Dad moved to Grandpa's place. There are so many things there that your big brother and you used to play with, so remembering the two of you, I cry all the time. I always used to say, 'Don't cry!' to your big brother and you, but now your mum cries so easily at anything at all. I'm sorry . . .

Today, Grandma and I came here again wanting to see you, just to breathe the same air with you. Even that helps. But, always I want to hear your voice, see your smile. I want to be with you.

The second was less weathered and was written on a piece of paper cut into the shape of a heart:

Dear Hana,

I'm sorry that I can't find you. I come every day, wanting to see you. You must be around here. I'm so sorry that I can't find you, Hana. You don't appear in our dreams and Dad, Mum, Grandpa and Grandma are sad. I'm sorry I can't do anything for you. I'm so sorry. If I could see you in my dreams, I would hug you tight.

The third letter, on the day I first saw it, was so crisp that it might have been left that morning:

Dearest, dearest Hana,

Did you like your funeral?* We made a display of ♪ and ◠ in flowers. I hope that you and your big brother were glad to see them. That was the only thing that Dad and Mum could do for you.

I wanted to prepare many dresses for you on your wedding day, even a traditional long-sleeved kimono in black like a bride in the old days . . . But Mum and Dad's dream will just be a dream now.

If you can read this letter, do come back to Mum and Dad, Hana.

* * *

After losing her home and village, her children and her parents-in-law, Miho spent four years living in a metal 'temporary residence' on the outskirts of Ishinomaki. No one in the community knew her or her husband, Yoshiaki; no one asked about their circumstances; and this was how they wanted it to be.

For one in Miho's situation, even the company of other bereaved mothers was difficult to bear. The only people from whom she did

---

* Like other families who failed to recover the remains of their loved ones, the Suzukis nonetheless conducted a funeral ceremony for their daughter at a Buddhist temple.

not feel isolated were Naomi and their common friend Akemi, both of whom had spent long weeks searching for their own daughters. 'They were the only people I could talk to,' she said. 'Akemi's girl was found on the forty-ninth day, and Koharu was found long after that. So they understood how I felt. And they talked to me normally – they treated me like an ordinary person. With the other families, I was always aware of the way they were looking at me and thinking about me – that they saw me as the most tragic one of them all. And that just made me feel worse.'

Miho was forty-three at the time of the tsunami; Yoshiaki was six years older. Neither had brothers or sisters; each was the sole inheritor of the family line. The prospect of having another child now seemed remote, and they were stricken by the sense, peculiar to the religion of the ancestors, of having been orphaned by their own children. There was the practical fear of growing old and sick with no one to care for them; and then there was spiritual anxiety about ongoing care and reverence after death, in the absence of descendants to pray not only for them, but for their own parents, grandparents and generations past. 'When one of us dies, who will look after the other?' Miho asked. 'Who will bury us? Our closest relatives are cousins, or even more distant than that. We feel such anxiety about the future. When I think about it, it suffocates me.'

Miho gave up her job as a doctor's receptionist; the search for Hana became the centre of her life. She was at the school every day, to help Naomi and Masaru in their diggers. She resolved that she would look for Hana for at least two years. In the foremost part of her mind, she harboured no illusions; as the months passed, she gave up hope of finding a body, even an incomplete one – bones, a single bone, even a fragment of flesh or a strand of hair would have been enough. But in her car, Miho always kept a full set of Hana's clothes in case – just in case – they should happen upon her miraculously biding in some overlooked spot, hidden and alive.

Towards the end of 2012, though, she stopped going to the school. After careful thought about the emotional, as well as the financial, costs, she and Yoshiaki made the decision to undergo fertility treatment at the big hospital in Ishinomaki. The doctor was the same man who had delivered Hana eleven years earlier and he was optimistic: Miho, he told her, was in good health, and although she was in her mid-forties, there was no physical reason why she could not conceive again. But she would no longer be able to stand in the mud every day; the task of making a new child made it harder to look for the lost one. And at about the same time came another piece of news: Naomi Hiratsuka, who had always promised that she would continue the search for the missing children, was giving up.

The practical difficulties of searching the mud were increasing every month. The chances of finding even fragmentary remains were dwindling. For all this, though, Naomi insisted that if it had been up to her, she would have gone on looking. The decision had not been made by her, and it had not been made by her husband or father-in-law. It was her dead daughter, Koharu, who decided.

Naomi had once again become close to Sumi, the medium who had proved so adept at relaying Koharu's voice from the other world. The two women met every few weeks, spoke often by phone and exchanged text messages and emails. Through Sumi, Koharu would make requests for sweets and snacks placed as offerings on the *butsudan*, and urge her mother to pay greater attention to one or other of her surviving siblings. Naomi was still on maternity leave from her job as a high-school teacher; the moment came when she had to choose whether to return to her job or abandon it. At the time that she was contemplating this important decision, Koharu made her feelings strongly felt.

'The medium told me that Koharu wanted me to go back to work,' Naomi said. 'She said that she had always wanted to be a teacher when she grew up. And so she wanted me to do what she could not. The medium told me, "The way to use your talent is not just to stay in the house and search for the missing children, but to do something active outside the home."'

And so, in April 2013, Naomi found herself back in the classroom, at a junior high school in Ishinomaki. It was two years since the disaster, and three years since she had last worked. And yet the jolt she experienced came not from the strain of teaching, but from the children she taught. 'My class were fourteen year olds,' she said. 'In other words, they were Koharu's class.' Every time she looked up from her desk, Naomi faced children exactly the same age that her daughter would have been, if she had survived beyond the age of twelve.

She confronted a question: how to address, within the world of the school, the fact of Koharu's death? Many people knew what had happened, of course, and those who didn't only had to search for Naomi's name on the Internet to bring up the interviews she had given over the years. She did not want to be defined by her loss, but she did not want to be evasive about it, either. Sometimes the subject came up indirectly – like the occasion when one of the girls asked Naomi how many children she had. Was the answer two, or three? Naomi wondered. Neither felt correct. 'They were good children, and they trusted me,' she said. 'I didn't want them to pity me, but I didn't want them to think that I didn't trust them, either. I sensed that they wanted me to talk about it, but I couldn't. For one thing, I couldn't be sure that I wouldn't cry.'

She left it until the very last week of the school year. She brought thirty-six copies of a book about Okawa Primary School, published by a group of the bereaved mothers, and gave one to each of her students. And she told them the story of Koharu and what had happened to her. At the end, she invited questions. The class of fifteen-year-olds sat in stupefied silence. 'But I wanted them to know,' Naomi said. 'I don't believe that stuff, which you sometimes hear, that the children who survived must "live their lives for those who died". There are a lot of people around here who have feelings of guilt for surviving. We don't want children growing up that way. I told them that you have to make a life for yourself. No one should ever need to feel that they are living their life for someone else.'

Work, and the care of two younger children, left Naomi with little energy for anything else. It was the very best thing for her peace of mind. 'Teaching was a kind of therapy for me,' she said. 'Very honestly, the more I work, the less I think about Koharu. I persuade myself that is a good thing.'

Koharu herself confirmed that it was – or this was the message relayed by Sumi. The more time she spent with the medium, the more Naomi appreciated, and depended upon, her soothing words, and her account of the existence into which her daughter had entered in the other world. Once, Naomi made plans for a winter holiday in Okinawa, the warm southern island where she had gone to university. She was going to catch up with old college friends – and Sumi said that she would come along too. 'She said that she'd always wanted to go to Okinawa,' Naomi told me. 'And she said that Koharu wanted her to go, to console the spirits of those who died in the war.'* It might have seemed a surprising suggestion from a twelve-year-old girl, but this, the medium explained, was part of the progression of a human spirit on the other side. Immediately after the end of her human life, Koharu had retained much of her individual character – her lovable girlishness and sense of humour. But now she was evolving into what Japanese call *hotoke-sama* – an enlightened soul, purged of the dross of human personality, the terminal stage of the soul's pilgrimage into death. 'The kind of

---

* A quarter of a million people died in the battle of Okinawa, the bloodiest of all the battles of the Pacific War.

things she tells me these days, through the medium, aren't always what you'd expect from a sixth-year,' Naomi told me. 'They're not just personal matters, but more general. She's becoming more . . . authentic, somehow. She's coming closer to god, or to Buddha. She's not a little child any more.'

Sumi's explanation went even further than this. Far from being a tragedy, she told Naomi, Koharu's death, and all the events that had followed on from it, had been predestined. 'It is difficult to convey, and it was difficult to understand,' she said. 'But my husband and I both came to think that things are decided in advance.'

Death, the woman explained to Naomi, is preordained at birth. More than that, the individual soul selects the time and manner of its own death. In other words, Koharu – and, by implication, the legion of others who perished in the wave – had chosen to die that day. 'According to the medium, it's destiny,' Naomi told me. 'She says that those who die as children are elevated to a higher stage than those who die in old age. And knowing that is a comfort to me.'

Naomi, who survived the disaster with two living children and an intact family home, found her daughter, buried her, returned to her career and made an accommodation with death. Miho, childless, middle-aged, isolated in her metal hut, was unable to do so. And at some point, difficult to define, the close friendship between the two women turned to sourness and mistrust.

Both were shy of talking about it, but it seemed to have been Miho who turned away. Every spring, as the March anniversary drew near, she became intensely depressed and withdrawn. At these times Naomi kept a respectful distance. 'After I started my job again, I was busy,' Naomi said. 'But we would speak from time to time – for a year, it all seemed normal. Then it started to become difficult to reach her. One day, I went round to where she was living. I didn't call in advance, just turned up. I got the impression she didn't want me there at all.'

Naomi puzzled over the reason for Miho's coldness. She did not believe that it was about the search for the missing children, from which Miho was also withdrawing. It was about the hunt for something more elusive, divisive and dangerous – the truth of what had happened at the school.

In the beginning, Naomi and Miho's solidarity had been cemented by a common isolation, a shared sense of standing alone against the world. They despised the arrogant bureaucrats of the board of education; but they also had a shared contempt for the 'Fukuji group', and what they saw as the aggressive self-righteousness of people such as Sayomi Shito. The search for the children had consumed all their reserves of emotional, as well as physical, energy. But when Miho stopped going to the school, in the tense hiatus of her fertility treatment, she found herself with leisure to think through matters that she had never closely considered before: the way, as she came to think of it, that teachers had permitted the deaths of her children.

'We couldn't find Hana,' she said. 'So we had to find the truth. We couldn't just leave this as one more of those things that no one is to be blamed for. I can't accept that. The more time passes, the more strongly I feel this.'

Naomi was torn by the contradictions of her own situation. 'Seventy-four of them perished,' she said, 'and no one was taking responsibility. And that feeling, that outrage – of course, we have that feeling too. Someone has to take responsibility for what happened.' But the only people capable of doing so were the teachers at the school and members of the education board – the colleagues and direct superiors of Naomi and her husband.

Naomi's husband, Shinichiro, was a promising and ambitious teacher who had no intention of sacrificing his career by taking on his bosses in a campaign to heap condemnation on his own dead colleagues. 'For a while, I felt that I wanted to take legal action,' Naomi said. 'But my husband never agreed.'

A lawyer from Sendai held an open meeting for bereaved parents who wanted to learn more about the possibilities for legal action. Miho attended, and was surprised to encounter Naomi there. The atmosphere between the two women was chilly. To Miho, her former friend's presence was 'insincere'. It was obvious that the Hiratsukas would never join in legal action against other teachers. She half suspected them of having come to spy on the proceedings, and to report back, although to whom it was not clear.

Later that year, Shinichiro Hiratsuka was promoted to deputy headmaster of a big school in Ishinomaki. Miho's fertility treatment failed; mental stress and anguish, her doctor speculated, were interfering with the production of the hormones necessary for the creation of a new life.

The Rough, Steep Path

Miho and Yoshiaki Suzuki became leading figures in the legal action against the Ishinomaki city government, which had been launched so unexpectedly and at the last possible moment. It was striking, to anyone familiar with Western modes of litigation, that it had taken so long to get under way. If a comparable tragedy had happened in Europe or the United States – scores of children dead, piercing questions about the competence of the authorities – there would have been lawyers swarming over it from the beginning. But in Japan there was an instinctive aversion to taking legal action, and a sense that those who did so were themselves breaking some profound unwritten law.

It was seen, or felt to be seen, as a failure of *gaman*, a violation of the unwritten codes of the village society. There was an assumption that unpleasant consequences – social disapproval and exclusion, even victimisation – were in store for those who sued, particularly those who took on the government. People became vague and tongue-tied when pressed over this; they struggled to come up with particular examples. It was about the nagging sense of being talked about behind your back; an obscure guilt in the hearts of people who knew they had done nothing wrong. And the discomfort of stepping outside the snug, warm, paralysing web of compliance that Japan weaves around its people, a fuzzy, enveloping tangle in which constraint is inseparable from the sense of being protected, and where the machinery of coercion rarely has to be applied from outside, because it is internalised so efficiently within the mind.

It takes an unusual kind of personality to be deaf to those snickering interior voices. By comparison with the West, the damages awarded by Japanese courts were low – even if they won their case, the Okawa parents would be lucky to receive half of the ¥100 million they were demanding for the life of each child. Kazuhiro Yoshioka was the lawyer who represented them, and even he sympathised with the reluctance of ordinary people to resort to the courts.

'It's not the kind of abuse that is obvious or explicit,' he said. 'But people feel themselves, in quite an insidious way, to be reproached. If a relative works at the local authority, that relative may be ill spoken of. At school, sons and daughters might be referred to as the children of someone who went to court. Cutting remarks online. It's often hard to see it clearly or to pin it down, but such people end up feeling rejected by society. Often people prefer to stay under the warm futon and endure their anger and sorrow, rather than go to court.'

Japan's civil-justice system, like its democracy, appeared on the face of it to be beyond reproach. Judges were independent; bribery and intimidation were almost unknown. But at its core the system expressed a bias in favour of the status quo and the private and public institutions that upheld it. Judges, Yoshioka told me, were derisively referred to as 'flounders' – flatfish who dwelt on the ocean floor, with their eyes positioned on the top of their bodies, always anxiously looking upwards. There was no explicit conspiracy to deliver verdicts one way or another, no direct orders from on high, just an understanding, as natural as the instinct of an animal, about how the world worked and where self-interest lay. 'If someone brings a lawsuit against an institution, against a big company or a bank, or a local government,' said Yoshioka, 'in Japan the institution will almost always win.'

It was eight months after the disaster when the first of the Okawa parents, Sayomi and Takahiro Shito, came to talk to him. He gave them two pieces of advice. The first was to muster as large a group of complainants as possible, to attract the attention of the media and establish an institutional presence of their own. The second was to bide their time, and to make use of the legal resource that their opponents in the city government were unwittingly providing for them – the infuriating 'explanatory meetings'. 'Once you've filed a case,' Yoshioka said, 'no one connected with it will talk any more – they'll just say that the matter is in the courts, and use that as an excuse to say nothing. Even if you summon them to court, you get each witness in the stand for no more than an hour or two. But those explanatory meetings went on for three or four hours each. And there were ten of them.' Rather than rushing to sue, it was better to draw out the city officials while their guard was down, encourage the media to report it all, and quietly accumulate as much ammunition as possible.

The families who took up the case were housewives, joiners, builders, factory workers; none had expertise in forensic inquiry. 'A lot of people would assume that these ordinary blokes out in the countryside wouldn't be capable of making a cross-examination, for example, and putting sharp questions,' Yoshioka said. 'Well, they'd be surprised. These are pretty smart people, quite capable of following a line of inquiry and pinning down the other side.'

Yoshioka made no attempt to rehearse the families for the meetings. 'I intervened as little as possible,' he said, 'and sometimes it got quite rough. People lost their tempers – they shouted, "Idiot!" and "Return my child!" Those kinds of words serve no purpose in the legal sense. But the people facing them, hearing those words of grief, seeing the parents of dead children exposing their hearts – I was glad for them to talk like that, because it forced those officials to respond.

'I also tried to think about what this case was really about. Usually, it's simple – if the lawyer wins, he's done his job. But these families were fighting for their beloved children, the children they had lost. Even if they did win, it wouldn't end their suffering. It's not about a victory. It's about finding out what happened to their children in the last moment of their lives, and why.'

In Japanese justice, nothing happens quickly; it was not until April 2016 that witnesses appeared to give evidence in the case against Ishinomaki City and Miyagi Prefecture, co-defendants in the case. In the two intervening years, there had been half a dozen hearings at which lawyers for both sides debated matters of law and narrowed down points of contention. The plaintiffs' claim was that the city, in the person of the teachers at Okawa Primary School, had been guilty of negligence – *kashitsu*, the word that Kashiba, the headmaster, had resisted so tenaciously – in failing to protect the children in its care. The case centred on two questions. Could the teachers have foreseen the coming of the tsunami? And, if so, could they have saved the children from it?

The city insisted that the answer to both these questions was no. The school was two and half miles from the coast; even the mightiest tsunami in living memory – the one released by the Chile earthquake in 1960 – had done no harm this far inland. The school building, and the village around it, obscured the teachers' view of the ocean; the spectacle of the wave overwhelming the forest of pines at the sea's edge had been invisible to them. As soon as Deputy Headmaster Ishizaka had become aware of the water coming over the river bank, he ordered the children to flee – but by then, tragically, but unavoidably, it was too late.

Yoshioka countered these arguments. The school may have been a good distance from the ocean, but the tsunami had come over the river bank, and that was only a hundred yards away. The village of Kamaya was scarcely above sea level at all, and had experienced conventional flooding from the Kitakami River in the past. Ishizaka had had the choice of several paths of evacuation – at least three different routes up the hill behind the school, or via the waiting school bus – all of them to places higher and safer than the spot he chose, the traffic island on the river's edge. And there were multiple reasons for believing that not only should the teachers have anticipated a tsunami, but that they did in fact do so. 'If we prove that they could have foreseen the tsunami,' Yoshioka told me, 'then we can win this case.'

The public gallery at the Sendai District Court was full on 8 April 2016 when the former headmaster, Teruyuki Kashiba, gave his evidence; so many members of the public queued to get in that the available seats had to be allocated by lottery. All the familiar faces were there. Takahiro Shito, the Konnos, the Suzukis and Hideaki Tadano, the father of the young survivor, Tetsuya, sat behind their lawyers. There were bureaucrats from the board of education, and local journalists who had been covering the story from the beginning. But the courtroom possessed a quality of tension and formality that the explanatory meetings never had. It was imparted by the presence of the three dark-robed judges who swept in, as everyone in the room rose to their feet; and by the oath that Kashiba read aloud at the witness stand.

'I swear to tell the truth, according to the dictates of my conscience,' said the headmaster, small and plump in his charcoal-grey suit, 'without omission or addition.'

Kashiba was first questioned by one of the city's lawyers, who walked him through the basics of the defence case. He talked about the school's emergency manual, which set out clearly the actions to be taken in case of fire or earthquake. The school had carried out regular drills to prepare for such eventualities, and their effectiveness had been demonstrated when the strong, but lesser, earthquake had shaken the area on 9 March 2011, two days before the catastrophe. Kashiba had been at school that day; the children had evacuated calmly and quickly; the teachers had confidently discharged their designated duties. Okawa Primary School did not bother to hold tsunami drills, for a simple reason: no one had any reason to anticipate such an event. And, whatever the plaintiffs asserted, the paths up the hill were completely unrealistic as a route of evacuation. Kashiba had climbed them himself and found them steep, treacherous and overgrown with brush or bamboo.

But here lay the flaw in the defence case. If the tsunami had truly been unimaginable, something that had not even crossed the minds of the teachers at the school, then why give any thought at all to the need to escape from one, any more than from an asteroid impact or zombie apocalypse?

Yoshioka's cross-examination of Kashiba lingered on this contradiction. He pressed the headmaster for details about the precursor earthquake on 9 March. A tsunami warning had been issued that day too, but for a wave of no more than twenty inches – scarcely noticeable to a casual observer, and incapable of causing damage. Nonetheless, as the children waited in the playground, Junji Endo, third in the school hierarchy, had conscientiously gone down to the river to scan its waters and confirm that nothing was amiss.

Kashiba was asked about an exchange which he had that day with Endo and Ishizaka, his deputy. Details of this conversation had been let slip by the headmaster himself; it was one of the choicest of the revelations that came out of the 'explanatory meetings'. After the children had returned safely to their classrooms, the three men had talked in the staffroom for several minutes about the evacuation, and the lessons to be learned from it. 'We discussed what we should do if a tsunami reached Okawa Primary School,' Kashiba told the court. 'In such circumstances, could we escape by climbing up behind the bamboo grove? As it's rough and steep, perhaps we couldn't. We didn't reach a conclusion.'

He was shown a set of photographs that he had taken himself from the hill behind the school. It had been a blazing day of summer at the beginning of the long holiday. The photographs showed the red-roofed school set among the colourful jumbled roofs of the village, with the shining river and rice fields beyond. They had clearly been taken from a good way up the slope – a slope that, Kashiba insisted, was too dangerous for children to climb, even to save their lives.

'Take a look at these pictures,' Yoshioka told the witness. 'Photographs one and two were taken by you on the twenty-first of July 2009.'

'I remember it,' said Kashiba.

'How did you get up there?' Yoshioka asked him.

'I think that I climbed up behind the back of the little hut and through the bamboo grove.'

'The route you walked – children could climb up there too, couldn't they?'

'I think that would be very dangerous.'

'What was your physical condition when you took those pictures?'

The headmaster paused for a moment. 'I weigh eleven stone,' he said. 'With a height of five foot one.'

A moment passed in which this information registered with the court, along with the visual image of the short, podgy man standing at the witness stand.

'At such a height and weight,' asked the lawyer, 'wouldn't it be easier for a child to climb than for you?'

The starkest evidence of all that the school had, in fact, anticipated the disaster was in the emergency manual itself.

Earlier versions of the document had adapted the basic template to strike out all references to tsunamis, on the basis that they were irrelevant to Okawa school. But beginning in 2007, these had been restored. The teacher who carried out the task was the deputy headmaster, Toshiya Ishizaka.

The section labelled 'On the occurrence of an earthquake' was renamed 'On the occurrence of an earthquake (tsunami)'. In a list of actions to be taken, the instruction 'collect information' became 'collect information (also tsunami-related)'. And Ishizaka had added a new directive among the list of tasks to be ticked off by teachers during an earthquake evacuation: 'confirm the occurrence of a tsunami, and lead the school to the place of secondary evacuation'. The place of secondary evacuation was added, but with wording unchanged from the template: 'in case of tsunami: vacant land near school, or park, etc.'

Kashiba's obvious discomfort in the witness stand reached its peak in discussion of the emergency manual. At first, he found himself unable to recall why the revisions had been undertaken at all. Yoshioka reminded him: the education board had summoned a meeting of headmasters at which they had been instructed to review their procedures. The logic of the changes seemed inescapable. The manual had formerly made no mention of tsunamis. It had been changed to make provision for a tsunami. Why? Because there was a danger of a tsunami. With every question, Yoshioka seemed to tighten his grip on Kashiba; with every answer, he wriggled in the lawyer's grasp. At one moment, Yoshioka furiously reminded him of the risk of perjury.

'What prompted these revisions?' the lawyer asked.

'Deputy Headmaster Ishizaka added them,' Kashiba said, 'so I don't know.'

'During the time you were in charge at the school, three additions to the manual were made.'

'Perhaps, I think, awareness about tsunamis was gradually increasing.'

'So you came back from the headmasters' meeting and told Mr Ishizaka what to do.'

'I just never expected a tsunami to reach the school at all,' said Kashiba. 'So I thought it would be fine if we just put the word in.'

'But if you thought a tsunami would never come, why did you bother to put any word in at all?'

'We were told to put in the word "tsunami", so we did.'

'But why did you support putting it in?'

'I thought . . . it would be fine.'

The atmosphere in the courtroom was strained and grave. At various points there was stifled weeping from the seats where the families sat. But on hearing from the headmaster that their children had been protected from a tsunami by nothing stronger than words, the parents broke into bitter and incredulous laughter.

There May Be Gaps in Memory

Sometimes Tetsuya Tadano wanted to be a policeman when he grew up, and sometimes he wanted to be a firefighter. He loved judo and swimming, but his mum often had to nag him to do his homework. In other words, he was a conventional, playful eleven-year-old boy. But of all the people I met, it was Tetsuya who had the greatest love and fascination for Okawa Primary School, an enthusiasm close to passion.

Everyone else emphasised the school's ordinariness and normality, as if this absence of qualities enlarged the grossness of the tragedy. But in Tetsuya's eyes, it was a wondrous place, not so much for its pupils and teachers, whom he loved and respected, as for its physical eccentricities. Most Japanese schools are flat-roofed cubes, which vary only in their size. Okawa Primary School was the work of an architect of ambition and imagination. The main building was constructed not as an angular block, but on a curving perpendicular; from it projected a secondary wing, which spread into a twelve-sided pavilion. Tetsuya talked about the inner courtyard where the children rode their unicycles,* and the pond where they threw insects for the bloated ornamental carp. Planted along the front of the school were cherry trees, which every April put out a foam of pink blossoms. On one outer wall, the pupils had painted pictures of the children of the world in the national dress of their respective countries. Tetsuya described the view from the upper

---

* Unicycles, along with wooden stilts, are a feature of Japanese primary schools: the idea is to promote good balance.

classrooms of the paddy fields and the river, and the play of the elements on the building's materials. 'When the weather was fine,' he said, 'the roof was red. But when it rained, the colour changed into this blend of purple and blue, a dark blue. And the whole building looked fantastic.'

Before 11 March 2011, Tetsuya lived with his family in Yachi-naka, the hamlet immediately behind Kamaya. His father, Hideaki, worked at the paper mill in Ishinomaki. He had fled from the tsunami to a hill in the centre of the city. When the waters receded, he borrowed a bike and pedalled to the big inland sports centre where the refugees from the Okawa area had gathered. There Hideaki learned the fate of the school and his village. But there, almost alone among the desperate parents, he found his own son, Tetsuya, scratched and battered, with a patch over his injured right eye – but alive.

Tadano was head of the local volunteer fire corps, which went into action at times of natural disaster as an auxiliary to the professional fire brigade. Fathers of children from the school were exempted from duty in Kamaya, on compassionate grounds, but he led his men anyway, lifting bodies out of the mud. His wife, Shiroe, was found five days after the disaster, his father after eight days and his nine-year-old daughter, Mina, the day after that.

Father and son moved out of the sports centre to the home of Hideaki's sister. Later they found a house of their own on the outskirts of Ishinomaki. They often went back to the site of where they had lived. All that was left of the family home – all that remained of any of the houses in Kamaya – was the outline of its concrete foundations. Even the doctor's clinic, the husk of which had outlasted the wave, had quickly been bulldozed. Only the school survived to show that there had ever been a village here at all – cracked, windowless, exposed in places to the elements, but still recognisable.

Upon its ruin, a remarkable feat had been performed. Early on, soldiers and recovery workers had removed the rubble of trees, cars and broken houses that enmeshed the building, but the work had not ended there. The school's interior, and its contents, which had been churned and befouled by the inrushing water, had been tenderly sifted and restored, as if awaiting the return of children and teachers. The small desks with their iron legs had been lined up in rows. There were heaps of miscellaneous objects: a sewing machine, abacuses, a recorder and a wall clock, its hands suspended at 3.37. Outside each classroom was a row of hooks still labelled with the names of the children whose coats had once hung there.

Tetsuya took comfort in his visits to the school. So much had changed, so suddenly, that his old life – and the lives of his mother, sister, grandfather, schoolmates – flickered in his mind sometimes, with the insubstantiality of a dream. The presence of the school assured him that he, and they, had lived. Memory lived on in its walls and spaces. During one of his wanderings through the deserted classrooms, Tetsuya uncovered a dictionary bearing the name of his little sister, Mina, written in her own childish handwriting.

Then one day his father told him that the city government would soon reach a decision about the future of the surviving buildings. The consensus was that the remaining structures should be demolished, the site levelled and all traces of Okawa Primary School removed from the earth.

All along the north-east coast, those who had survived the tsunami were considering how to deal with what it left behind. Not the mundane mess of broken houses and commercial buildings, which was steadily being heaped and cleared, but the symbolic ruins: those sites of particularly acute or vivid tragedy, as well as the jarring juxtapositions thrown up by the wave's force. There was the Disaster Prevention Centre in Minami-Sanriku, where a young

woman named Miki Endo famously remained at her post, duti-
fully broadcasting evacuation warnings, even as she, and forty-
two of her colleagues, were swallowed up. There was the *No.18
Kyotoku-maru*, a 200-foot fishing boat, which was deposited in
a residential street in the port of Kesennuma; and the *Hamayuri*,
a 190-ton catamaran that came to rest on the roof of a hotel in
Otsuchi. And then there was the 'miracle pine' of Rikuzen-Takata,
the single lonely survivor of a coastal forest of 70,000 trees, and
the object of intense efforts to keep it alive. There was a precedent
in Japan for preserving ruins associated with death and disaster:
the Atomic Bomb Dome in the city of Hiroshima, a former public
hall whose skeletal shell is a place of international pilgrimage and
a world-famous symbol of the horrors of nuclear war.

Local campaigns were established to preserve these relics, but
they were controversial and divisive. To some people, the tsunami
ruins were emblems of survival and hope, and a necessary warning
to future generations of the power of the sea. To many others,
they were reminders of a horror they were struggling to forget.
Some pointed out the value of such sites as tourist attractions, in
towns that now had less than ever to draw visitors from outside;
for others, that was exactly the reason why the ruins should be
expunged. 'A lot of people want to pray for the souls of the dead
in a calm, peaceful environment,' Naomi Hiratsuka told me. 'They
don't want pitying eyes upon them. The bodies of some of the
children were recovered from inside the school – that's the kind
of place it is. You don't want buses parking there, and sightseers
on package tours.'

The arguments also turned on money, and on the irrationality,
as some people saw it, of devoting resources to maintaining ruins
at a time when many people still lacked permanent homes. But
they also seemed to express opposing convictions about the best
way of dealing with mental trauma: whether to face it, articulate
it and struggle to accept it – or to thrust it out of view.

As time passed, the supporters of preservation lost several of their battles. The hulks of the *Kyotoku-maru* and *Hamayuri* were hoisted away and scrapped. The surviving iron frame of the Minami-Sanriku Disaster Prevention Centre was condemned to demolition. Salt in the soil slowly killed the roots of the miracle pine.* A survey of the families of children who died at Okawa school revealed that 60 per cent of them wanted it to be razed. 'If you remain silent, it will definitely go,' Hideaki Tadano told Tetsuya. 'If you want to speak out, the time to speak out is now.'

Of the seventy-eight children who were caught up in the water, only four had come out alive. Three of them disappeared from view, anxiously protected from scrutiny by their families. Tetsuya's father, Hideaki, used to see one of them from time to time; he was struck by an air of anguished repression about the boy, as if he had been instructed not to speak, or even to think, about the fact of his escape from death. Only Tetsuya chose to talk publicly about his experience. To journalists, he was a gift – a child of the tsunami, both a victim and a survivor, authentically boyish in manner, but lucid, articulate and, on the face of it, remarkably undamaged by what he had seen. Okawa Primary had been re-established in another school and Tetsuya attended it with the other survivors, most of them children who had been picked up by parents or grandparents in the fifty-one minutes between earthquake and wave. He spoke willingly about the experience of being caught in the tsunami and the unanswered questions about what had happened, and why. His father was vigilantly alert to his son's mental state, but he encouraged these engagements. There was no systematic provision of mental-health

---

* After it died, the authorities in Rikuzen-Takata spent ¥150 million (£1.2 million) on cutting the tree up, hollowing it out and reassembling it with fake twigs and needles. The Minami-Sanriku Disaster Prevention Centre was later reprieved.

care for the children of Okawa Primary School: for Hideaki, Tetsuya's conversations with sympathetic reporters amounted to a kind of therapy. 'And it was all easier,' Hideaki told me, 'with other people around. There was a restaurant where we all used to go as a family, and to go there with a TV producer, all talking about what they were going to film, was fun. To go there alone, just Tetsuya and me – that was too sad, because of all that we remembered.'

Hideaki was aware of an atmosphere of unvoiced disapproval from the community of the bereaved, and he understood it well. 'I am the father of a survivor,' he said, 'but I am also the father of a child who died at the school. Plenty of people – the kind of people who have lost two or three children – they don't want to turn on the television and see the faces of the children who survived.' But no one, surely, had a greater right to express his opinion than Tetsuya?

He began talking to journalists about the fate of the school buildings, and his belief that they should be saved. He made a speech on the subject at a public event in Sendai. With his father, he took the bullet train to Tokyo to give talks at two famous universities. A handful of other young people began speaking up in support of Tetsuya, former pupils at the school, whose younger siblings had died there – including the surviving daughters of Katsura Sato and Sayomi Shito, and Amane Ukitsu, the sixth-grade girl whose mother had picked her up just in time. The group of six children began to meet every week to discuss tactics and muster their resolve. 'The Atomic Bomb Dome in Hiroshima was preserved because people took action,' Amane said. 'Nothing changes until somebody stands up.'

Early in 2014, Tetsuya spoke at a symposium at Meiji University in Tokyo. It was a solemn and intimidating occasion, the biggest gathering he had ever addressed. 'I lost my mother and sister in the tsunami,' he told the audience. 'And my grandfather, who used to look after me. The grief did not come immediately, but now, at last, I feel the sadness and the pain.'

He talked about the word *gareki*, meaning 'rubble' or 'debris', and used to refer to the detritus of the tsunami. To most people, it was a neutral, colourless term, unthinkingly employed; but for Tetsuya, it hurt to hear it. 'Our possessions,' he said, 'are now called *gareki*. Until the disaster, they were part of our life. Now, they contain our memories. I don't like to hear all those things referred to as "rubble".' And now the school, where he had been so happy, and where his friends and sister had died, was also to be treated as *gareki*. 'If the school is demolished, people in the future will not know what happened here,' he said. 'I don't want the building to be destroyed.'

It was a matter of concern to his father that even in the early days after the tsunami, Tetsuya rarely showed signs of being overcome by emotion. But after delivering these words to the university audience, he began to slump in his seat. Hideaki had to lead him off the podium to a quiet room. Asked what was wrong, he laid his head on the table. 'I started thinking about how everyone died, and how they must have felt,' he said. 'Thinking about that, I felt very heavy.'

The final decision about the school lay with the mayor of Ishinomaki. In February 2016, he called a public meeting to debate the question of the school's future. This time Tetsuya did not appear in person, but he recorded a video message, pleading for the school to be preserved. Naomi Hiratsuka's husband, Shinichiro, was one of those who argued passionately for it to be demolished. A wrenching and unbridgeable gulf separated the opposing sides; whatever the decision, the result would be pain. To some, the ruin of the school represented the destruction of their beloved children; to others, it was their last surviving trace.

The following month, the mayor made his decision. The school would be preserved, and a memorial park built around it. But a thicket of trees would be planted so that those who chose to could pass by without ever looking the ruin in the face.

Two weeks after the testimony of Kashiba, the former headmaster, a second hearing was held at which further witnesses were sworn in and examined. To spare them the ordeal of a court appearance, Yoshioka, lawyer for the families, decided not to call as witnesses any of the surviving children. But Miwae Ukitsu, the mother of the sixth-year girl, Amane, did give evidence. She had been off work and at home on the day of the earthquake; she recounted how she had immediately driven the two miles to the school after hearing the tsunami warning on the radio. She went straight to her daughter's teacher, Takashi Sasaki, who was standing in the playground with his class. 'I told him, "On the car radio, I heard that the height of the tsunami is getting higher, so please run up the hill quickly,"' she said. 'I took his left arm, and I pointed at the hill and I said, "There's a tsunami coming. Twenty feet high, they said." I was upset, I was shouting loudly. He was completely unconcerned. He patted my shoulder, and said, "Calm down, ma'am."'

Mr Sasaki asked Mrs Ukitsu to take Amane home. The girl was weeping uncontrollably and it was upsetting the other children. Her mother was struck by this, for Amane was not a tearful or touchy child. As Amane explained later, she had heard her two classmates, Yuki Sato and Daisuke Konno, arguing with the teacher.

Sir, let's go up the hill.

We should climb the hill, sir.

If we stay here, the ground might split open and swallow us up. We'll die if we stay here!

And she was thinking of a dream she had had a few days before, of all of her friends caught up in a churning, chaotic swirl. Remembering the nightmare, she became uncontrollably afraid.

*   *   *

The nineteen families who went to court did so for different reasons, and with varying degrees of alacrity and hesitation. For some, the prospect of a financial pay-out, after years of grief and hardship, was like rain after drought. For others, the idea of placing a value on the lives of their dead children was unbearably distasteful. But everyone I met agreed on one thing: the most important thing was not the money, but the prospect of uncovering the truth about what had happened at the school. These declarations began to puzzle me after a while – for the families, after years of investigation, knew a great deal already.

The speedy evacuation from the school buildings, the long sojourn in the playground, Sasaki's offhand confidence, Ishizaka's indecisiveness, and then the panicked flight into the mouth of the tsunami – all of this has been established in documents and eyewitness accounts. The board of education might slither and swerve around the question of responsibility, but it was clear what had taken place, and who had failed. What further 'truth' remained to be uncovered? When I put this question to Sayomi Shito, she answered with a single word: 'Endo'.

After his single appearance at the first of the explanatory meetings, Junji Endo had gone to ground. With him, in the eyes of many of the parents, the truth had also vanished from view. This was the point of going to court – to force Endo out of hiding and compel him to come to the witness stand, where he would finally give voice to the evasive truth. 'It's very simple,' said Yoshioka. 'There is one living adult witness who was present at the school. The families want to know in his own words exactly what happened to their children in those last moments, how they were washed away by the tsunami, how they died.'

Endo continued to insist that he was psychologically unfit to appear in court. The judges, if they chose, had the power to order his appearance, and Yoshioka requested them to do so. In the meantime, he attempted to manage the expectations of his clients.

To win their case, he pointed out, they had to show that the teachers could have foreseen a tsunami – Endo might be useful in achieving this, but there were other routes to proving the same thing. Even if he did appear as a witness, it was likely that, having been coached by the city's lawyers, his evidence would be vague and misleading. The parents nodded their understanding, but the lawyer knew how much was invested in the hope of seeing and hearing this one man.

What exactly was it, I asked Sayomi Shito, that she expected to learn from Endo that she didn't already know, or couldn't guess?

'Everything that happened then.'

'Such as what?'

'What kind of sky it was,' she said. 'How the wind was blowing. What kind of atmosphere there was. What the mood was among the children. Did the teachers seriously try to save their lives? Did the children feel cold? Did they want to go home? How was my child? Who was the last person to talk to her? Who was beside her when she ran away? Was she holding hands with anyone? Even knowing all of this, none of it will bring Chisato back. But everything that happened then – that is what I want to know.'

The last hearing of the Sendai District Court was on 21 April 2016. Afterwards, the lawyers made their final written submissions. The document prepared by the city of Ishinomaki was twenty-three pages long; lawyers for the second defendant, the government of Miyagi Prefecture, presented just nine pages. Yoshioka submitted a 400-page book, dense with diagrams, graphs, statistics and legal argument. He was a calm, poised man, but afterwards he seemed as close as such a personality could ever get to jubilation. 'I was talking about it with my colleague, and we can't think of a single reason why we might lose,' he told me. 'Not one – and that's a rare thing.' From first filing to last submission, the case had taken two years and three months. By the standards of Japanese justice, Yoshioka said, that was 'extremely quick'.

But the chief judge ruled against calling Junji Endo as a witness. He was not obliged to set out his reasons, but Yoshioka took it to be a good sign. The plaintiffs, it implied, had successfully argued their case by other means. The judges did not need another witness to persuade them; and they would, in any case, have been reluctant to impose upon a man diagnosed with mental illness.

'As long as he's alive, I believe that he will cross our lives again at some point,' said Sayomi. 'It may not be in court. But we will have a chance to meet him, and listen to what he has to say. It's not just Endo whose life has gone to pieces. He's not the only one suffering mentally. I don't just mean that our lives have changed. I mean inside our heads. Since that day, everyone has something wrong with them.'

PART 5

GONE ALTOGETHER BEYOND

Consolation for the Spirits

Reverend Taio Kaneta, priest and exorcist, described to me the night after the tsunami, a moment remembered with intense clarity by people all over northern Japan. His inland temple had been untouched by the water, but the earthquake had knocked out power and light across Tohoku. For the first time in a century of human development, the land was in a state of historic, virgin darkness. No illuminated windows blazed upwards to obscure the patterning of the night sky; without traffic lights, drivers stayed off the unlit streets. The stars in their constellations and the blue river of the Milky Way were vivid in a way that few inhabitants of the developed world ever see. 'Before nightfall, snow fell,' Kaneta said. 'All the dust of modern life was washed by it to the ground. It was sheer darkness. And it was intensely silent, because there were no cars. It was the true night sky that we hardly ever see, the sky filled with stars. Everyone who saw it talks about that sky.'

Kaneta was personally safe, and isolated by the power failure from a full understanding of what had happened. But he recognised that the world had changed. He had learned enough about the unprecedented magnitude and submarine epicentre of the earthquake to know that a tsunami must have followed. The closest stretch of coast to his temple was Shizugawa Bay, thirty miles away. His mind was filled with an image of the waters of the bay, awash with bodies. 'A magnitude 9.2 earthquake,' he said. 'When something that powerful occurs, the Earth moves on its axis. So many people, all over Tohoku, were looking up at the sky on that night, filled with intense feelings. And looking at the stars, I became aware of the universe, the infinite space all around and above us. I felt as if I was looking into the universe, and I was conscious of the earthquake as something which had taken place within that vast expanse of empty space. And I began to understand that this was all part of a whole. Something enormous had happened. But whatever it was, it was entirely natural; it had happened as one of the mechanisms of the universe.

'It's engraved in my mind: the pitiless snow, and the beautiful shining, starry sky, and all those countless dead bodies drifting onto the beach. Perhaps this sounds pretentious, but I realised that when I began my work, giving support to people whose lives had been destroyed, I had to attend to the hearts of human beings and their suffering and anguish. But I also had to understand those sorrows from the cosmic perspective.'

He experienced at that time a sensation of dissolution, of boundaries disappearing. It was the enactment of a Buddhist concept: *jita funi*, literally 'self and other: undivided' – the unity of being apprehended in different times and places by mystics of all religions. 'The universe wraps everything up inside it, in the end,' Kaneta said. 'Life, death, grief, anger, sorrow, joy. There was no boundary, then, between the living and the dead. There was no boundary between the selves of the living. The thoughts and feelings of everyone melted into one. That was the understanding I achieved at that time, and it was what made compassion possible, and love, in something like the Christian sense.'

It was a singular, unrecoverable moment. A catastrophe had occurred. But because it was so new, was still unfolding in fact, no one could reckon its breadth and its height. In the Kitakami River, Teruo Konno was clinging to his raft. The mothers of Okawa Primary School were listening to the reassuring broadcast on the radio, confident that they would see their children the next day. Standing beneath the stars, Kaneta glimpsed the scale and horror of what had happened, but he did so imaginatively, and in his imagination the disaster took on the lineaments of a profound spiritual truth. It would be a long time before he possessed such clarity again.

Of all the people I encountered in Tohoku, none made a stronger impression than Taio Kaneta. It was not his Buddhism that interested me the most – the fact of his being a priest often seemed incidental to who he was, no more than an interesting detail of personality. He was a natural teller of stories, a man of learning and intellectual honesty, and of rich empathy. And he had that gift of imagination which I had been seeking for myself – the paradoxical capacity to feel the tragedy on the surface of the skin, in its all cruelty and dread, but also to understand it, to observe from a position of detachment, with calm and penetration. Kaneta did not jump back from the disaster, as I always did – back on the bullet train, back to Tokyo, back to my desk on the tenth floor. He was immersed in the necessity of dealing with the corpses of the dead, although he had lost none of his own loved ones. He allowed the catastrophe to change his life, but he did not become its victim. He was strong enough to admit doubt, and confusion, and his own physical and mental weakness. It was these qualities that enabled him to console the living, and to communicate with and command the dead. But there was a mental cost for those who straddled the boundary between the two worlds. In Kaneta's case, it would almost break him.

When the funerals were done, and after the possessing spirits had been driven out of Takeshi Ono, Kaneta turned to face what the tsunami had left behind and looked for ways of making himself useful. In Buddhism, the forty-ninth day after death marks the moment when the departed soul enters the afterlife. He gathered a group of fellow priests, Shinto and Buddhist, as well as a Protestant pastor, to perform a ritual march to the town of Shizugawa, a town almost completely obliterated.

They set out in the morning from a temple inland. The Shinto priests wore their extravagant black lacquered hats; the Buddhists were red-robed and shaven-headed; the pastor had his dog-collar and silver cross. The landscape through which they walked was broken, and corrupt with decay. Bulldozers had cleared ways through the rubble, and piled it into looming mounds of concrete, metal, wood and tile. The heaps had been incompletely searched; cadavers were folded inside them, unrecovered and invisible, but obvious to everyone who passed. 'There were strange smells,' said Kaneta, 'of dead bodies, and of mud. There was so much rubble, and mementoes of people's lives still lying around on the ground. We had to take care where we stepped to avoid trampling on photographs.'

The procession of vividly dressed men moved through the ruins, holding aloft a placard bearing characters meaning 'Consolation for the Spirits'. They walked for four hours. Machines were pawing at the rubble as they passed. Workers in hard hats picked at the debris, and waved them gruffly away from the caterpillar tracks. The men of religion began to feel self-conscious. They began to suspect that, rather than helping, they were an unwelcome obstruction to the clean-up operation. But there were ordinary people here too, standing about with a dazed air, or picking at the rubble of their former homes. 'They were looking for the bodies of their loved ones,' said Kaneta. 'When they saw us marching past, they turned and bowed their heads. They were praying desperately to find their loved ones. Our hearts were so full when that happened. I have rarely been more conscious of suffering.'

As they marched, Kaneta and his group had intended to chant sutras and sing hymns. But here, among the stench and mess, their voices failed them. 'The Christian pastor was trying to sing hymns,' said Kaneta. 'But none of the hymns in his book seemed right. I couldn't even say the sutra – it came out in screams and shouts.' The priests lurched uselessly through the rubble in their rich robes, croaking the scriptures, getting in the way. 'And when we got to the sea,' said Kaneta, 'when we saw the sea – we couldn't face it. It was as if we couldn't interpret what we were seeing.'

He said, 'We realised that, for all that we had learned about religious ritual and language, none of it was effective in facing what we saw all around us. This destruction that we were living inside – it couldn't be framed by the principles and theories of religion. Even as priests, we were close to the fear that people express when they say, "We see no God, we see no Buddha here." I realised then that religious language was an armour which we wore to protect ourselves, and that the only way forward was to take it off.'

Monku stood for the Japanese word 'complaint' and the English word 'monk', but there was a third allusion in the name of Café de Monku, the mobile event that Kaneta organised for survivors of the wave, to offer refreshment, companionship and counselling by stealth. 'I love jazz,' he said, 'and above all I love Thelonious Monk. Bebop – such brilliant, peculiar music. Loose phrasing, those dissonant sounds. It seemed to me that it reflected what people's minds were like after the disaster – the tempo of people's minds and hearts. It was the perfect music for the occasion.' At Café de Monku, Kaneta took off his priest's robes – in the struggle to help the survivors of the disaster, a jazz fan was as much use as a Buddhist.

The 'temporary residences' were laid out in rows on vacant land on the margins of the inland towns. Kaneta would arrive with a group of priests and helpers and set up in the community meeting room. They would brew tea and coffee, set out cakes and biscuits. The inhabitants of the metal huts would begin to arrive, most of them elderly. Kaneta would stand up and address the room, a tall, smiling, bespectacled figure, dressed in a simple indigo tunic.

He would welcome everyone, introduce his helpers and make teasing jokes. 'Mr Suzuki is here to give you a massage round the shoulders, if you want one,' he said. 'Ah, what a massage! You should try it. His massage is so relaxing that you may actually find yourself slipping into the next world. But you needn't worry, if that happens – we have lots of priests on hand.'

Hot drinks would be poured, and plates of food passed around. Trays were set out with lengths of coloured cord and beads of glass; the old people would sit on the floor at the low tables and string Buddhist rosaries. The priests inscribed and blessed *ihai* memorial tablets, for those who had lost them. There were more jokes and chuckling; but often Kaneta was to be seen sitting apart with one person or another, engaged in a private and visibly tearful conversation. Thelonious Monk would be playing.

Everyone in Japan was looking for consolation. The more time passed, the harder it became to find. After the immediate struggle for survival, and the arduous weeks in the evacuation centres, the homeless were dispersed across the country in the homes of relatives, in rented accommodation and in the grim temporary residences. But the period of acute crisis, in some ways, had been the easy part. When survivors moved out of the cramped, but cheerful, communal shelters to the relative privacy of the metal containers, grief and loss rose up like a second wave.

'Immediately after the tsunami, people were worried about surviving for the next hour,' said Naoya Kawakami, a Protestant pastor whom I met at Café de Monku. 'Then they got to the shelters and worried about getting through the day. Things settled down, they were provided with food and something to sleep on, and they were anxious about the next fortnight. Then they were given temporary homes and their lives were secure, in a sense. They were not going to starve or freeze. But after the practical problems were resolved, the anxiety they felt was as strong as ever. It stretched ahead indefinitely into the future. It could no longer be soothed by just giving them things. The things will never be enough.'

The metal boxes were lonely and sterile after the companionable crowding of the evacuation centres, but as the years passed, they were made cosy. Flowers and ornamental cauliflowers were planted; neighbours became friends. But then permanent homes became available, and the new communities began to shrink and break up. The homes were awarded by lottery – those who won moved to new purpose-built apartments; those who lost were left behind, at least until the next allocation. 'Some people lose, and keep on losing,' one of the priests told me. 'They have an acute sense of abandonment. Sometimes, they wake up and find that their neighbours, the winners, have disappeared without saying a word. They're too embarrassed to say their goodbyes.'

Pastor Kawakami said, 'In the beginning, they could talk about their anxieties, and how they could be resolved. I need a rice ball for my child. I need a cardboard box to put my possessions in. People have those now. But they still have their anxiety, and the anxiety that remains is too big to speak of. It comes out in anger, in the breakdown of relationships, between individuals and between groups. There is resentment, disharmony, a failure of understanding. These are people of goodwill, but they are becoming stubborn. So many people are seeing ghosts these days, and it's because of trauma. People talk of seeing ghosts, but what they're talking about is troubles back home.'

Japanese had been dying in tsunamis as long as the Japanese islands had existed. And every tsunami had brought forth ghosts. One of them was recorded in a famous old book of Tohoku folklore called *The Tales of Tono*. It told the story of a man named Fukuji who survived the Sanriku tsunami of 1896, and who lived with his two surviving children in a shack on the site of the family house. One moonlit summer night, he got up to relieve himself on the beach.

'This night, the fog hovered low,' the book records, 'and he saw two people, a man and a woman, approaching him through the fog.' The woman was his wife. The man was another villager, who had been in love with her, until the woman's family had chosen Fukuji as her husband.

As if in a dream, Fukuji followed the couple and called out his wife's name. She turned to him, smiling, and said, 'I am married to this man now.' Fukuji, half or fully asleep, struggled to understand. 'But don't you love your children?' he said. The woman's pale face became paler, and she began to weep. Fukuji, uncomprehending, looked miserably at his feet. His wife and her lover moved soundlessly out of sight. He started to follow them, and then remembered that both his wife and the man had died in the tsunami. 'He stood on the road thinking until daybreak and went home in the morning,' the story ends. 'It is said that he was sick for a long time after this.'

No one knew the literature and folklore of Tohoku better than Masashi Hijikata and he understood immediately that, after the disaster, hauntings would follow. 'We remembered the story of Fukuji,' he said, 'and we told one another that there would be many new stories like that. Personally, I don't believe in the existence of spirits, but that's not the point. If people say they see ghosts, then that's fine – we can leave it at that.'

Hijikata was born in Hokkaido, Japan's northernmost island, but he had come to Sendai as a university student, and had the passion of the successful immigrant for his adopted home. He ran a small publishing company whose books and journals were exclusively on Tohoku subjects. It was Hijikata who explained to me the politics of ghosts, and the opportunity, as well as the risk, they represented for the people of Tohoku.

'We realised that so many people were having experiences like this,' he said. 'But there were people taking advantage of them. Trying to sell them this and that, telling them, "This will give you relief.'" He met a woman who had lost her son in the disaster, and who was troubled by the sense of being haunted. She went to the hospital: the doctor gave her antidepressants. She went to the temple: the priest sold her an amulet, and told her to read the sutras. 'But all she wanted,' Hijikata said, 'was to see her son again. There are so many like her. They don't care if they are ghosts – they want to encounter ghosts.

'Given all that, we thought we had to do something. Of course, there are some people who are experiencing trauma, and if your mental health is suffering then you need medical treatment. Other people will rely on the power of religion, and that is their choice. What we do is to create a place where people can accept the fact that they are witnessing the supernatural. We provide an alternative for helping people through the power of literature.'

Ghosts were not only inevitable, they were something to celebrate, part of the rich culture of Tohoku. Hijikata revived a literary form that had flourished in the feudal era: the *kaidan*, or 'weird tale'. *Kaidan-kai*, or 'weird-tale parties', had been a popular summer pastime, when the delicious chill imparted by ghost stories served as a form of pre-industrial air conditioning. Hijikata's *kaidan-kai* were held in modern community centres and public halls. They would begin with a reading by one of his authors. Then members of the audience would share experiences of their own – students, housewives, working people, retirees. He organised *kaidan*-writing competitions, and published the best of them in an anthology. Among the winners was Ayane Suto, whom I met one afternoon at Hijikata's office.

She was a calm, neat young woman, with heavy black glasses and a drooping fringe, who worked in Sendai at a care home for the disabled. The fishing port of Kesennuma, where she grew up, had been one of the towns worst hit by the tsunami. Ayane's family home was beyond the reach of the wave, and her mother, sister and grandparents were untouched by it. But her father, a maritime engineer, worked in an office on the town's harbour front, and that evening he didn't come home.

'I thought about him all the time,' Ayane said. 'It was obvious something had happened. But I said to myself that he might just be injured – he might be lying in hospital somewhere. I knew that I should prepare for the worst. But I wasn't prepared at all.'

Ayane passed painful days in Sendai, clearing up the mess caused in her flat by the earthquake, thinking constantly about her father. Two weeks after the disaster, his body was found.

She arrived back at her family home just before his coffin was carried in. Friends and extended family had gathered, most of them casually dressed – everything black, everything formal, had been washed away. 'He hadn't drowned, as most people did,' Ayane said. 'He died of a blow to the chest from some big piece of rubble. In the coffin you could only see his face through a glass window. It had been a fortnight, and I was afraid that his body might have decayed. I looked through the window. I could see that he had a few cuts, and he was pale. But it was still the face of my father.'

She wanted to touch his face for the last time. But the casket and its window had been sealed shut. On it lay a white flower, a single cut stem placed on the coffin's wood by the undertaker. There was nothing unusual about it. But to Ayane it was extraordinary.

Ten days earlier, at the peak of her hope and despair, she had gone to a big public bathhouse to soak in the hot spring water. When she came out, she retrieved her boots from the locker, and felt an obstruction in the toe as she pulled them on. 'It was a cold feeling,' she remembered. 'I could feel how cold it was, even through my socks. And it felt soft, fluffy.' She reached in and removed a white flower, as fresh and flawless as if it had just been cut.

A minor mystery: how could such an object have found its way into a boot inside a locked container? It faded from her mind, until that moment in front of her father's coffin, when the same flower presented itself again. 'The first time I'd had the feeling that this might be a premonition of bad news,' Ayane said. 'Dad might not be alive any more, and this might be a sign of his death. But then I thought about it later, about the coolness of the flower, and the whiteness of the flower, and that feeling of softness against my toe. And I thought of that as the touch of my father, which I couldn't experience when he was in his coffin.'

Ayane knew that the flower was just a flower. She didn't believe in ghosts, or that her dead father had sent it to her as a sign – if such communication was possible, why would a loving parent express it in such obscure terms? 'I think it was a coincidence,' she said, 'and that I made something good of it. When people see ghosts, they are telling a story, a story that had been broken off. They dream of ghosts because then the story carries on, or comes to a conclusion. And if that brings them comfort, that's a good thing.'

Committed to print as a *kaidan*, published in Hijikata's magazine, it took on ever greater significance. 'There were thousands of deaths, each of them different,' Ayane said. 'Most of them have never been told. My father's name was Tsutomu Suto. By writing about him, I share his death with others. Perhaps I save him in some way, and perhaps I save myself.'

Having treated, fed and sheltered the tsunami's victims, the struggle began to prevent an invisible secondary disaster of anxiety, depression and suicide. A survey carried out a year after the disaster revealed that four out of ten survivors complained of sleeplessness, and one in five suffered from depression. There was a surge in alcoholism, and in stress-related conditions such as high blood pressure. It was a struggle to measure the crisis because of the difficulty in compiling accurate data – in the town of Rikuzen-Takata, for example, most of the social workers who would have carried out the surveys had drowned.

Café de Monku, so simple in form, came to seem an essential emergency measure. The good it did to the tsunami refugees was obvious from their faces. Requests were coming in from all over Tohoku; Kaneta and his priests were setting out their tea and biscuits once a week or more. But he also had a busy temple to run, and all the routine obligations of a town priest – funerals, memorial ceremonies, visits to the sick and lonely, mundane tasks of administration. To everyone who knew him, it was obvious that he was taking on too much; hesitantly, and then with greater urgency, friends and family cautioned him to rest. But his presence, as comforter, organiser and leader, had become indispensable to so many people; there seemed to be no way to extricate himself from their need. The physical collapse that came at the end of 2013 was inevitable and overwhelming.

Painful blisters erupted on his skin. He was so exhausted that he could hardly get out of bed. For weeks he did nothing, except sit in front of the television and strum on his guitar. 'I don't remember what I watched,' Kaneta said. 'I watched in a stupor. I didn't even listen to jazz. I was a step away from depression. I had to stop doing everything, or else.'

It was the culmination of three years of physical, psychological and spiritual crisis, but two things served as immediate triggers. One was a series of speeches that Kaneta gave in different parts of the country about the experience of the disaster. Like Sayomi Shito's husband, Takahiro, he travelled outside the zone of disaster in the hope of communicating to the outside world the pain and complexity of the situation there. Like Takahiro, he came away with the crushing sense of having failed to express himself or to have been understood.

The second experience was set in motion by a young woman whom I will call Rumiko Takahashi. She had telephoned Kaneta one evening in a state of incoherent distress. She talked of killing herself; she was shouting about things entering her. She too had become possessed by the spirits of the dead; she begged the priest to help her.

Save Don't Fall to Sea

The Sendai District Court delivered its verdict on 26 October 2016. I took the bullet train up that morning from Tokyo. It was a warm, piercingly bright day of early autumn. Five and a half years had passed since the tsunami, and there was no obvious sign that such an event had ever taken place. The towns and cities of Tohoku were humming with the money that was being injected into the region for its reconstruction. One hundred thousand people still lived in metal houses, but these upsetting places were tucked away out of sight of the casual visitor. None of the towns destroyed by the wave had been rebuilt, but they had been scoured completely of rubble. Coarse, tussocky grass had overgrown the coastal strip, and those ruins that poked through it looked more like neglected archaeological sites than places of continuing pain and despair.

The court building was a short taxi ride from the station. Inside, I joined a queue and drew a lucky ticket for the public seats. An hour remained until the hearing began. I stood outside at the front of the courthouse, where reporters and photographers were milling lazily; a ripple of animation passed through them at the arrival of a procession, slowly making its way through the sunshine. It was the plaintiffs in the case, the mothers and fathers of the Okawa children, walking along the pavement, three abreast. Apart from Naomi Hiratsuka, all the parents I had got to know best were there. They wore black. Several carried framed photographs of their sons and daughters. The three men at the front held a wide banner. Around its margins were the faces of the children, the twenty-three children named in the case, photographed at home, at school or

234

playing outside, laughing, smiling or solemn. In the centre was a sentence of Japanese, the characters carefully hand-painted with an ink brush: *We did what our teachers told us.*

It was a profoundly dignified spectacle. The group entered the courthouse and split into smaller groups, as plaintiffs and defendants, lawyers, journalists and members of the public waited for the proceedings to get under way. There was no obvious anxiety or tension; there was comradely pleasure in the coming together of old allies and acquaintances. But everyone present was conscious of the possibility of defeat. Yoshioka had made his case as well as he could, but certain facts remained unalterable. The plaintiffs were a small group of individuals; the defendants were a city and a prefecture; and Japanese courts were conservative. 'Whatever the verdict today,' said Takahiro Shito, 'it will just add to the sum of all the other experiences we have had up until now. It was our responsibility to do this, as parents. This is part of what it means to bring children into the world. Of course, I'm worried about the verdict going against us. But if it does, it would mean that a school does not have to protect the lives of its pupils. And that should never be the case.' The parents had just come from a meeting with their lawyer, Shito said. The delivery of the verdict would take only a matter of moments, he had told them; it would be obvious in the first few seconds which way it was going to go.

The doors of the courtroom were opened, and everyone took their places. The five defence lawyers sat on the right, and on the left were the black-clad parents. I looked across at them from the public seats. How many hours I had spent talking to them over the years, in conversations filled with intense, and sometimes unbearable, detail. Grief was in their noses like a stench; it was the first thing they thought of when they woke in the morning, and the last thing in their minds as they went to sleep at night. They had spoken about each stage of the lives of their children, in childhood, infancy, even in gestation. They remembered the school, and the community of families of which it was the focus. They described the disaster and its unfolding, the blows of realisation that followed, and the asphyxia of loss and of survival. Like the plot of a fiction, these remembrances culminated in belief in a mystery, in things missing, removed and deliberately hidden – a conspiracy, in other words, which not only worsened the pain of grief, but rendered it incomprehensible. It expressed itself in impotent, inward-turning anger, and in unanswered questions about particular individuals. Why did this one not do his job? Why did this one tell a lie? Why will that one not speak to us?

There had indeed been a cover-up, but of a pitifully unambitious and ill-executed kind: inconsistent, banal and transparent. There was no grand plan, no mastermind – even to call it a conspiracy was to grant it a dignity and cunning that Kashiba and the mediocrities of the Ishinomaki Education Board never possessed. A group of unexceptional men had failed dismally. They didn't even try very hard to deny their failure, just to contain it within manageable bounds. They were stubborn, clumsy and charmless, personally and institutionally. But if Kashiba had fallen to his knees and confessed his negligence, and if Junji Endo had come forward and wept out his story once again – nothing that mattered would be significantly changed.

The true mystery of Okawa school was the one we all face. No mind can encompass it; consciousness recoils in panic. The idea of conspiracy is what we supply to make sense of what will never be sensible – the fiery fact of death.

Extinction of life: extinction of a perfect, a beloved child: for eternity.

Impossible! the soul cries out. *What are they hiding?*

A door opened noiselessly, and all at once the three judges – a young woman and two middle-aged men – were seated in their black gowns. The judge in the centre began speaking, fast, quietly and without inflection. The Japanese he used, formal and legal-istic, was beyond my grasp. So I focused instead on the faces of the listening parents – there, surely, I would immediately be able to read the verdict, in their anger or jubilation. The faces looked intently at the judge. They frowned in concentration; their features were blank and expressionless. And then, as suddenly as it began, it was all over, and the occupants of the court were standing up and filing out.

The dark-clad parents were on their feet too. They exchanged no words or glances; they looked grave and even grim; they looked like people who had received deeply troubling news. And yet, towards the end, I thought I had been able to follow part of the judge's ruling, the part when he seemed to be ordering the defendants to pay what sounded like a very large sum of money.

I stepped out into the corridor where the Japanese reporters were huddled, comparing their notes. I had not misunderstood. The Okawa parents had won their case – they had been awarded more than £11 million. All their children were still dead.

The final judgment ran to 87 pages. It surveyed in detail the actions taken by the teachers, and found no fault in their behav-iour immediately after the 2.46 p.m. earthquake. It was 'not inappropriate', the judges insisted, to keep the children at school. For the first forty minutes that they waited in the playground, even after the first radio warnings, 'it cannot be said that the teachers could foresee the danger of being hit by a tsunami'. But then, at 3.30 p.m., the vans from the city office had careered past, blaring their frantic warning about the sea breaking over the beachside forest of pines. At that point, seven minutes before it eventually arrived, 'the teachers could have foreseen the coming of a huge tsunami to Okawa Primary School'. The place of evacu-ation that was eventually chosen, the traffic island by the bridge, was 'inappropriate'. 'The teachers,' the judgment said, 'should have evacuated the children up the hill at the back, which was unobstructed.'

The damages – ¥1.43 billion* – were less than the ¥2.3 billion that had been demanded, but still at the high end of those habitually awarded by the courts. Once legal costs were accounted for, the plaintiffs would receive some ¥60 million – about £470,000 – for each child lost. Japanese judges were expert at forging compromise and delivering verdicts in which both sides won something of the argument, neither was humiliated, and vindication was impossible to tease out. This was not such a judgment. It was a decisive legal victory, an unambiguous assignment of responsibility, which nonetheless completely failed to concern itself with the things that mattered to the parents the most.

It expressed no opinion about the actions of Kashiba, the headmaster, before or after the tsunami. It absolved the teachers from blame over the chaotic emergency manual. It was silent about the evasions of the board of education, about the disposal of the notes on the interviews with the children, about the untruths of Junji Endo, and about his failure to give an account of himself. A little while after the verdict, three of the fathers came before the cameras with another carefully hand-brushed placard. 'We prevailed,' it read. 'The voices of the children were heard!' But there could hardly have been less sense of triumph; as they talked about it afterwards, the families of the dead children expressed nothing stronger than relief at the absence of defeat.

'As far as the death of my daughter goes, we won, I suppose,' said Hideaki Tadano. 'But my son, Tetsuya, and me – we have been beaten. They've been beating us from the moment it happened, with their lies and their evasions. This verdict lets them get away with it – the falsifications, the hiding of evidence. That kind of thing should never be tolerated. I don't want a world in which that kind of thing is allowed.'

*　　*　　*

---

* At the time this was worth about £11.1 million, or $13.6 million.

'December is the time when the day is the shortest,' said Reverend Kaneta. 'And then midwinter comes, and the light begins to return. That was the moment for me. When the days began to get longer I recovered my energy. For three years, stress had been stored up inside me. It was pent up. Over the winter, I let it go.'

Months of precious inactivity healed Kaneta. With the crisis past, he returned to the life of his temple. The world around him was unchanged, still shadowed by grief and by ghosts. But the priest had been renewed. 'For a long time, I felt that everything I had learned had no reality,' he said. 'But the reality returned. It was a revival of my faith. When I was on the verge of collapse, it came back to me from a deeper level.'

He began to rediscover the clarity that he had glimpsed in the starry sky on the first night of the disaster. The question with which he struggled – the question put most insistently by survivors – was the oldest one of all. 'What does life mean, in the face of death?' Kaneta said. 'That was what people wanted to know. An old woman told me, "My grandchild was washed away before my eyes. I am ninety years old, and I lived. What am I supposed to make of that? Can you answer me, priest?" People who survived wanted to understand their survival. For a long time, I couldn't explain it to them.'

Kaneta said, 'What determined life or death? No Buddhist priest knows, no Christian pastor – not even the Pope in Rome. So I would say, "There's one thing I can tell you, and that is that you *are* alive, and so am I. This is a certainty. And if we are alive, then there must be some meaning to it. So let's think about it, and keep thinking about it. I'll be with you as we think. I'll stay with you, and we will do it together." Perhaps it sounds glib. But that is what I could say.'

I asked Kaneta about Okawa Primary School. He was a specialist in grief and suffering, and an instinctive ally of the small man and the underdog. The death of the children was the single grossest tragedy of the whole immense disaster, a distillation of its arbitrariness and horror. So it was striking, at first, to hear him talk of it in tones of such detachment.

He had often been to the school and prayed there; a nearby community of temporary homes had hosted Café de Monku. But the local priest had discouraged Kaneta and his team from ministering directly to the families of the children; and he knew none of them personally. 'Of course I know that seventy-four children died there,' he said. 'And that it was widely reported, and that the families brought a legal case. But I don't want to set what happened there apart from, or above, anywhere else. There are places all over this land, places little known or forgotten, where many people died, where many are grieving.'

I asked him what kind of consolation a priest could offer to people such as the parents of Okawa school, and he was quiet for a moment. 'You have to be careful,' he said. 'You have to be very careful in asking this of people who have lost their children. It takes long months, long years – it might take a whole lifetime. It might be the very last thing that you say to someone. But perhaps all that we can tell them in the end is to accept. The task of acceptance is very hard. It's up to every single person, individually. People of religion can only play a part in achieving that – they need the support of everyone around them. We watch them, watch over them. We remember our place in the cosmos, as we work. We stay with them, and we walk together. That's all we can do.'

We were sitting in the priest's quarters of Kaneta's temple. His wife was pouring tea. Sunlight broke on the paper screens across the windows; the room smelled of incense and tatami mats. An everyday moment of beauty in a Buddhist temple in the heart of Japan: it was natural, in such a place, to assent to ideas of harmony, to acknowledge the existence of essential principles beyond the weak grasp of human thinking. There were few men whom I respected more than Kaneta. But in my guts, I rejected what he said.

I had had enough of Japanese acceptance; I was sick with a surfeit of *gaman*. Perhaps, at some level of superhuman detachment, the deaths of the Okawa children did make possible insight into the nature of the cosmos. But long before that remote point, in the world of creatures who lived and breathed, they were something else as well – an expression of human and institutional failure, of timidity, complacency and indecision. It was one thing to recognise a truth about the universe, and man's small place within it; the challenge was how to do this without also submitting to the cult of quietism that had choked this country for so long. Japan had enough serenity and self-restraint. What it needed now was people like the Shitos and the Tadanos and the Suzukis: angry, scathing, determined people, unafraid to step out of the ranks and fight, even if all that the contest amounted to was the losing struggle with death.

How to balance affirmation of life with acceptance of its inevitable end? How to keep death in its place, to live under its regime, without submitting to it as tyrant? As if in response to these unvoiced thoughts, Kaneta told a famous story about the Buddha. One day, he was visited by a mother holding in her arms the body of her baby. The woman was grief-stricken and refused to accept the child's death. She had come to beg the famous teacher to perform a miracle, and to bring the infant back to life. 'Go out, and find a house where no son or daughter, no husband or wife, no father, mother or grandparent has ever died,' the Buddha told her. 'Bring from there white mustard seeds, put the seeds into a gruel, feed them to your child and his life will be restored.'

The woman travelled from village to village, and from house to house, asking at each one if they had ever lost a loved one there. Everywhere she stopped she heard stories of heartbreak. Each one was different in its details, and all of them were the same. As she listened, the character of the woman's grief changed. It did not diminish. But in time it altered, from a black and suffocating mass to a form bright and crystalline, through which she was able to recognise death, not as the contradiction of life, but as the condition that makes it possible. She buried her child, and went back to thank the Buddha. 'By the time she returned to him,' Kaneta said, 'he didn't need to explain.'

There is no tidying away of loose ends to be done in a story about the deaths of young children, about the annihilation of a coast – only more stories to be told, and retold in different ways, and tested like radioactive material for the different kinds of meaning they give out. Stories alone show the way. 'This is consolation,' Kaneta said. 'This is understanding. We don't work simply by saying to people, "Accept." There's no point lecturing them about dogma. We stay with them, and walk with them until they find the answer on their own. We try to unthaw the frozen future. People feel as if they have staggered into a fantastic land of disaster and pain. But it is not a place of fantasy. It is the universe we inhabit, and the only life we have on these islands. Volcano, earthquake, tsunami and typhoon – they are our culture, they are as much a part of Japan as the rich crops in the fields. Everything that was built over a hundred years was destroyed by the tsunami. But in time it will be built again.'

Up and down I travelled between Tokyo and the disaster zone, for six years. My son – the small kicking creature on the scanner's screen – was born, and grew. His older sister grew up too, and before long she was entering Japanese primary school herself, as the single blonde-haired, blue-eyed child in the year's new intake. It was on a different scale from little Okawa – a big Tokyo school, reassuringly positioned on a hill and separated from the sea by miles of dense inner city. But, institutionally, the two were identical. Both had a head and deputy head, teachers of diverse ages and experience, a municipal education board, an emergency manual. Both had sports days, and graduation ceremonies, and disaster drills. Like the children in Okawa, my daughter wore a round hat and a badge bearing her name in Japanese, and carried one of the distinctive square rucksacks. The atmosphere at the school was warm and benign; the staff exuded assurance and professionalism. But there are some situations that cannot be tested or drilled for. It was impossible not to wonder how these teachers might react in the face of extremity; or to forget the image of the hats, badges and rucksacks of the Okawa children being hauled out of the mud.

I kept in touch with some of the people I had got to know in the north-east.

Tetsuya Tadano flourished at high school, and became captain of its judo team. He always kept with him a photograph of his lost classmates. 'If I carry it in my bag,' he said, 'I feel as if they are having lessons with me.'

His father, Hideaki, joined with Toshiro, the husband of the art teacher Katsura Sato, in conducting guided tours of the school. Toshiro had been a teacher too, an employee of the Ishinomaki board of education. Like his wife, he had walked away from his career after the death of their daughter, Mizuho. Now, he led groups of adults, and children from schools all over the country, around the school grounds. He showed them photographs of the children in the playground, now a patch of dried mud. He pointed to the path up the hill, which they could so easily have taken. He showed them Mizuho's name still there below the hook where she used to hang her coat, and on the black memorial stone erected at the back of the school. On the tour which I attended, many of the participants ended it in tears. "This," Hideaki said to me, "this is why we must preserve the school."

Naomi Hiratsuka continued to work at the school where Koharu would have gone. Her middle child, Koharu's brother, was autistic; sometimes Naomi imagined herself giving up teaching and establishing a new career, helping families with similar children. Miho Suzuki and her husband, Yoshiaki, finally bought a new house and moved out of their metal hut. The sad chill that had established itself between Miho and Naomi lingered, but both went to the site of the school from time to time, where Masaru Naganuma, their comrade during long weeks searching the mud, was still looking for his seven-year-old boy, Koto. Naganuma took no part in the action against the city, and refused all requests to talk to journalists. But his determination was unquenchable. He still spent virtually every day searching, alone or with his elderly father, digging ground that had repeatedly been worked over before. With every month that passed, the chances of finding any trace of his son dwindled; and Masaru knew this. 'Five years, ten years – to him it's nothing,' Naomi said. 'Masaru will keep looking for the rest of his life. He says that he cannot die. Even when the moment for his death comes, he cannot go.'

Sayomi Shito's mother and father had been ailing before the disaster; after the loss of their granddaughter, their decline accelerated. They died in 2015, three months apart; their *ihai* and portraits were added to that of Chisato on the household shrine. The burden of caring for two infirm and confused parents compounded Sayomi's anguish and her grief. She was treated for depression. One day she was at the supermarket, where she overheard the conversation of two younger mothers. It was evident from the way they spoke that they lived inland and had been completely unscathed by the disaster; they were talking, Sayomi realised, about the parents of Okawa School.

'If that happened to *me*,' said the first woman, 'I couldn't go on living.'

'I *know* – me neither,' said the second. 'I would definitely kill myself.'

Sayomi said, 'I had prayed so often that I could die and Chisato could live. I knew that I should have gone to the school and taken her home. Or stayed there, and died with her. When I heard that conversation, I felt that they were saying to me, "Why are you alive?"'

She dropped her shopping basket and ran back to her car. She drove onto the straight road that ran along the river, heading in the direction of the sea. The car accelerated, until it was travelling much too fast for the narrow carriageway. Sayomi was looking at the river. She was imagining how small a movement of the steering wheel would be necessary to swerve across the bank and into the water.

Her son, Kenya, her oldest child, was sitting in the car next to her.

As she drove, in agony and shame, an awareness came to her of what it would mean to kill her son as well as herself. She pulled over suddenly and leaped out. She started to clamber over the bank and towards the water. 'I was thinking to myself that it was so strange, ridiculous really, that Chisato was dead and I was still alive,' she said. 'How could that be? Why was I still living? I was making for the river, because I wanted to be in the water, just like Chisato was.'

She became aware that Kenya was beside her, gripping her arm so tightly that it left a bruise. 'Mum,' he was saying to her. 'Mum, Mum. If you die, what will become of those of us left behind?'

One day Reverend Kaneta told me the story of his last exorcism, the experience that had robbed him of his peace of mind. We sat in the room where the sun struck the screens. Lined up on the tatami were dozens of small clay statues, which would be handed out to the patrons of Café de Monku. They were representations of Jizo, the bodhisattva associated with kindness and mercy, who consoles the living and the dead.

It was in this room, Kaneta told me, that he had first met Rumiko Takahashi, the twenty-five-year-old woman who had telephoned him in a frenzy of suicidal despair. Late that evening, a car pulled up at the temple with her mother, sister, fiancé and, limp with exhaustion, Rumiko herself.

She was a nurse from the city of Sendai – 'a very gentle person,' Kaneta said, 'nothing peculiar or unusual about her at all'. Neither she nor her family had been hurt by the tsunami. But for weeks, her fiancé said, she had been assailed by the presence of the dead. She complained of someone, or something, pushing into her from a place deep below, of dead presences 'pouring out' invisibly around her.

Rumiko herself was slumped over the table. She stirred as Kaneta addressed the creature within her. 'I asked, "Who are you, and what do you want?"' he said. 'When it spoke, it didn't sound like her at all. It talked for three hours.'

It was the spirit of a young woman, whose mother had divorced and remarried, and who found herself unloved and unwanted by her new family. She ran away and found work in the *mizu shobai*, or 'water trade', the night-time world of clubs, bars and prostitution. There she became more and more isolated and depressed, and fell under the influence of a morbid and manipulative man. Unknown to her family, unmourned by anyone, she had killed herself. Since then, not a stick of incense had been lit in her memory.

Kaneta asked the spirit, 'Will you come with me? Do you want me to bring you to the light?' He led her to the main hall of the temple, where he recited the sutra and sprinkled holy water. By the time the prayers were done, Rumiko had returned to herself. It was half past one in the morning when she and her family left.

Three days later, she was back. She complained of great pain in her left leg; and, once again, she had the sensation of being stalked by an alien presence. The effort of keeping out the intruder exhausted her. 'That was the strain, the feeling that made her suicidal,' Kaneta said. 'I told her, "Don't worry – just let it in."' Rumiko's posture and voice immediately stiffened and deepened; Kaneta found himself talking to a gruff man with a barking, peremptory manner of speech. He was a sailor of the old Imperial Navy who had died in action during the Second World War after his left leg had been gravely injured by a shell.

The priest spoke soothingly to the old veteran; after he had prayed and chanted, the man departed, and Rumiko was at peace. But all this was just a prologue. 'All the people who came,' Kaneta said, 'and each one of the stories they told, had some connection with water.'

Over the course of a few weeks, Reverend Kaneta exorcised twenty-five spirits from Rumiko Takahashi. They came and went at the rate of several a week. All of them, after the wartime sailor, were ghosts of the tsunami.

For Kaneta, the days followed a relentless routine. The telephone call from Rumiko would come in the early evening; at nine o'clock her fiancé would pull up in front of the temple and carry her out of the car. As many as three spirits would appear in a single session. Kaneta talked to each personality in turn, sometimes over several hours. He established their circumstances, calmed their fears, and politely but firmly enjoined them to follow him towards the light. Kaneta's wife would sit with Rumiko; sometimes other priests were present to join in the prayers. 'Each time she would feel better, and go back to Sendai and go to work,' Kaneta told me. 'But then, after a few days, she'd be overwhelmed again.' Out among the living, surrounded by the city, she would become conscious of the dead, a thousand importunate spirits pressing in on her and trying to get inside.

One of the first was a middle-aged man who, speaking through Rumiko, despairingly called the name of his daughter.

'Kaori!' said the voice. 'Kaori! I have to get to Kaori. Where are you, Kaori? I have to get to the school, there's a tsunami coming.'

The man's daughter had been at a school by the sea when the earthquake struck. He had hurried out of work and driven along the coast road to pick her up, when the water had overtaken him. His agitation was intense; he was impatient and suspicious of Kaneta.

The voice asked, 'Am I alive or not?'

'No,' said Kaneta. 'You are dead.'

'And how many people died?' asked the voice.

'Twenty thousand people died.'

'Twenty thousand? So many?'

Later, Kaneta asked him where he was.

'I'm at the bottom of the sea. It is very cold.'

Kaneta said, 'Come up from the sea to the world of light.'

'But the light is so small,' the man replied. 'There are bodies all around me, and I can't reach it. And who are you anyway? Who are you to lead me to the world of light?'

The conversation went round and round for two hours. Eventually, Kaneta said, 'You are a father. You understand the anxieties of a parent. Consider this girl whose body you have used. She has a father and mother who are worried about her. Have you thought of that?'

There was a long pause, until finally the man said, 'You're right' and moaned deeply.

Kaneta chanted the sutra. He paused from time to time when the voice uttered choked sounds, but they faded to mumbles and finally the man was gone.

Day after day, week after week, the spirits kept coming – men and women, young people and old, with accents rough and polished. Rather than being angry or vengeful, they were confused and panicked at their sudden immersion in a world of darkness and cold. They told their stories at length, but there was never enough specific detail – surnames, place names, addresses – to verify any individual account, and Kaneta felt no urge to. One man had survived the tsunami, but killed himself after learning of the death of his two daughters. There was a young woman who had tried to escape the water, but could not run fast enough because she was heavily pregnant. There was an old man, who spoke in thick Tohoku dialect. He was desperately worried about his surviving widow, who lived alone and uncared for in one of the desolate tin huts. In a shoebox she kept a white rope, which she would contemplate and caress. He feared what she planned to use it for.

Kaneta reasoned and cajoled, prayed and chanted, and in the end each of the spirits gave way. But days or hours after one group of ghosts had been dismissed, more would stumble forward to take their place.

One night in the temple, Rumiko announced, 'There are dogs all around me – it's loud! They are barking so loudly I can't bear it.' Then she said, 'No! I don't want it. I don't want to be a dog.' Finally she said, 'Give it rice and water to eat. I'm going to let it in.'

'She seemed to think it would do something terrible,' Kaneta said. 'She told us to seize hold of her, and when the dog entered her, it had tremendous power. There were three men holding on to her, but they were not strong enough and she threw them off. She was scratching the floor, and roaring, a deep growl.' Later, after the chanting of the sutra, and the return to her peaceful self, Rumiko recounted the story of the dog. It had been the pet of an old couple who lived close to the Fukushima Dai-ichi nuclear power plant. When the radiation began to leak, its owners had fled in panic with all their neighbours. But they forgot to unchain the dog, which slowly died of thirst and hunger. Later, when it was much too late, the spirit of the animal observed men in white protective suits coming in and peering at its shrivelled corpse.

In time, Rumiko became able to exercise control over the spirits; she spoke of a container, which she could choose to open or close. A friend of Kaneta, who was present at one of the exorcisms, compared her to a chronically ill patient habituated to vomiting: what at first was painful and disgusting became, over time, familiar and bearable. Eventually Rumiko reported being able to brush the spirits away when they approached her. She was still conscious of their presence, but at a distance, no longer shoving and jostling her, but skulking at the room's edge. The evening telephone calls and late-night visits became less and less frequent. Rumiko and her fiancé married and moved away from Sendai; and, to his extreme relief, Kaneta stopped hearing from her.

The effort of the exorcisms was too much. This was the moment when his friends and family worried about him most. 'I was overwhelmed,' he said. 'Over the months, I'd become accustomed to hearing the stories of survivors. But all of a sudden, I found myself listening to the voices of the dead.'

Most difficult to bear were the occasions when Rumiko was possessed by the personalities of children. 'When a child appeared,' Kaneta said, 'my wife took her hand. She said, "It's Mummy – it's Mummy here. It's alright, it's all alright. Let's go together."' The first to appear was a tiny nameless boy, too young to understand what was being said to him, or to do more than call for his mother over and over again. The second was a girl of seven or eight years old. She kept repeating, 'I'm sorry, I'm sorry.' She had been with her even younger brother when the tsunami struck, and tried to run away with him. But in the water, as they were both drowning, she had let go of his hand; now she was afraid that her mother would be angry. She said, 'There's a black wave coming, Mummy. I'm scared, Mummy. Mummy, I'm sorry, I'm sorry.'

The voice of the girl was terrified and confused; her body was drifting helplessly in the cold water, and it was a long struggle to guide her upwards towards the light. 'She gripped my wife's hand tightly until she finally came to the gate of the world of light,' Kaneta recalled. 'Then she said, "Mum, I can go on my own now, you can let go."'

Afterwards, Mrs Kaneta tried to describe the moment when she released the hand of the young-woman-as-little-drowned-girl. The priest himself was weeping for pity at her lonely death, and for the twenty thousand other stories of terror and extinction. But his wife was aware only of a huge energy dissipating. It made her remember the experience of childbirth, and the sense of power discharging at the end of pain, as the newborn child finally enters the world.

An easing of walls,
A shuddering through soles:
A petal loosens, falls.

In the room, alone:
It begins, then it has gone.
Ripples outlast stone.

Rain-smell stirs the heart;
Nostrils flare. A breath. We wait
For something to start.

                              Anthony Thwaite

Acknowledgements

Many of the people who helped me most in the writing of this book are named in its pages: I thank all of those who agreed to talk to me, sometimes repeatedly and over the course of several years, and often at times of overwhelming grief. Among those who are not named, I am grateful to Kazuyoshi Abe, Yuko Kaneta, Akio Kumagai, Akemi Miura, Minoru Ota, Tsugio and Mayumi Nakamura, and Ken Sakashita.

For practical, professional, intellectual, and personal support of diverse kinds, I thank Lucy Alexander, Regis Arnaud, Lucy Birmingham, Peter Blakely, Azby Brown, Clare Bullock, Kyle Cleveland, Jamie Coleman, Margot and Bill Coles, Martin Colthorpe and the Japan Foundation, the Currie family, Alissa Descotes-Toyosaki, Toby Eady, Max Edwards, Natasha Fairweather and Rogers, Coleridge & White, the Foreign Correspondents' Club of Japan, Dan Franklin and Penguin Random House, Rob Gilhooly, Mandy Greenfield, Kuni Hatanaka, Jennifer Joel and ICM Partners, Chris Jue, Nagisa Kato, Angela Kubo, Leo Lewis, the Lloyd Parry family, Justin McCurry, Sean McDonald and Farrar, Straus and Giroux, Hamish Mackaskill and the English Agency Japan, Levi McLaughlin, David McNeill, Koichi Nakano, the staff of Oiwake Onsen, Kyoko Onoki, David Peace, Peter Popham, Roger Pulvers, Zaria Rich, Junzo Sawa, Shuji Shibuya, Iwayumi Suzuki, Jeremy Sutton-Hibbert, Hara Takahashi, Bunei Takayama, Chika Tonooka, Rick Wallace, and Fiona Wilson.

From the beginning, my employer, *The Times*, energetically sponsored my reporting of the disaster and graciously gave me time off for writing and research. I thank my colleagues there, past and present, especially the late Richard Beeston, James Harding, Anoushka Healy, Roland Watson, and John Witherow. Sections of this book first appeared in the *London Review of Books*. Among its editors, I thank especially Daniel Soar and Mary-Kay Wilmers.

There are numerous charitable organisations for victims of the tsunami. The Momo-Kaki Orphans Fund helps children who have lost their parents: http://www.momokaki.org.

Lines from 'Shock' from *Collected Poems* by Anthony Thwaite, published by Enitharmon, 2007. Reprinted by permission of Anthony Thwaite.

The excerpt from 'The Web' from *Le Citta Invisibili* (*Invisible Cities*) by Italo Calvino. Copyright © 2002, The Estate of Italo Calvino, used by permission of The Wylie Agency (UK) Limited.

The photograph facing page 1 is reproduced with the permission of the Tectonics Observatory at the California Institute of Techonology.

Photographs on page 48 provided by Tohoku Regional Development Association.

The photograph on page 118 was taken by a survivor of the tsunami, who wishes to remain anonymous.

Notes

This is a true story, based in large part on the accounts of the individuals named and quoted in its pages, and on my own observation. Other sources are recorded below.

Among the various authors I have consulted, I am indebted above all to Masaki Ikegami. Without his painstaking reporting, it would have been much more difficult to piece together events at Okawa Primary School, during and after the disaster.

Japanese names are given in the western order: given name first, family name last. Conversions of Japanese yen are approximate, and based on the exchange rate prevailing at the time. On 11 March 2011, one pound was worth about ¥131.

Page vii: *18,500 people had been crushed, burned to death or drowned* – The most commonly cited figures for casualties of the disaster are those published by Japan's National Police Agency, which counts separately the number of people killed and those officially regarded as missing. The former includes only those whose for whom a death certificate has been issued; but at this late stage, all those in the latter category can also be assumed to be dead. On 10 March 2017, there were 15,893 dead and 2,553 missing, a total of 18,446. See http://www.npa.go.jp/archive/keibi/biki/higaijokyo_e.pdf.

The separate count by the Fire and Disaster Management Agency records a significantly higher figure – 19,475 dead and 2,587 missing, a total of 22,062. This includes those who died after the disaster from causes related to it, such as sick people whose health deteriorated after they were forced to move precipitately from hospitals, and suicides. See http://www.fdma.go.jp/bn/higaihou/pdf/jishin/154.pdf.

Prologue: Solid Vapour

Page 9: *It knocked the Earth ten inches off its axis; it moved Japan* – Kenneth Chang, 'Quake Moves Japan Closer to U.S. and Alters Earth's Spin', *New York Times*, 14 March 2011.

Page 9: *The earthquake and tsunami caused more than $210 billion of damage* – Jeff Kingston, 'Introduction' in Jeff Kingston (ed), *Natural Disaster and Nuclear Crisis in Japan*, (Abingdon 2012).

Page 9: *Japan's remaining nuclear reactors – all fifty of them – were shut down* – On the morning of 11 March 2011, Japan had 54 functioning nuclear reactors. Four of the six at Fukushima Dai-ichi were rendered unusable by the tsunami; by May 2012, all of the others had been shut down due to public opposition. Ongoing efforts are being made to restart them, but the political and technical challenges are great. As of March 2017, only three were in operation.

Page 10: *Farmers, suddenly unable to sell their produce, committed suicide* – Richard Lloyd Parry, 'Suicide cases rise after triple disaster', *The Times*, 17 June 2011; and Richard Lloyd Parry, 'Tepco must pay damages over woman's suicide after Fukushima leak', *Times Online*, 26 August 2014, http://www.thetimes.co.uk/article/tepco-must-pay-damages-over-womans-suicide-after-fuku-shima-leak-vsm5tgbmh83.

Page 11: *'All at once ... something we could only have imagined was upon us'* – Philip Gourevitch, *We Wish to Inform You That Tomorrow We Will Be Killed with Our Families* (New York, 1998), p. 7.

Having Gone I Will Come

Page 16: *her son's graduation ceremony from middle school* – The Japanese school system is modelled on that of the United States. Children go to primary, or elementary, school from ages 6 to 12, middle school from 12 to 15, and to senior high school from 15 to 18.

Page 19: *connecting Okawa in the south with the Kitakami district on the northern bank* – The district on the south bank of the river, a sub-municipality of the city of Ishinomaki, is officially called Kahoku. Okawa is an older name for the area, but for ease of understanding, I have used it as a general term for the catchment area of Okawa Primary School. It is pronounced with a long 'O', close to English 'ore-cow-uh'.

Jigoku

Page 42: *She went on: 'He lifted up one of the blankets …'* – In this passage I have drawn on my own interviews with Sayomi Shito, and on Chris Heath's fine article, 'Graduation Day', *GQ* (US edition), 1 July 2011.

Abundant Nature

Page 50: *the meeting point, deep beneath the ocean, of the Pacific and North American tectonic plates* – For an accessible account of the workings of earthquakes and tsunamis, see Bruce Parker, *The Power of the Sea* (New York, 2010).

Page 54: *People cried and screamed, and could not stand.* – This is my adaptation of a translation from the *Nihon Sandai Jitsuroku* ['The True History of Three Reigns of Japan'] of 901A.D. which appears in Jeff Kingston (ed.), *Tsunami: Japan's Post-Fukushima Future* (Washington, 2011), p.10.

Page 54: *Geologists found layers of fine sand* – For the history of earthquakes and tsunamis on the Sanriku coast, see K. Minoura et al., 'The 869 Jogan tsunami deposit and recurrence interval of large-scale tsunami on the Pacific coast of northeast Japan', *Journal of Natural Disaster Science*, Volume 23, Number 2, 2001, pp. 83–88; and Masayuki Nakao, 'The Great Meiji Sanriku Tsunami', *Failure Knowledge Database*, Hatamura Institute for the Advancement of Technology, 2005, at http://www.sozogaku.com/fkd/en/hfen/HA1000616.pdf, accessed March 2017.

Page 55: *On 22 May 1960, a 9.5-magnitude earthquake* – Parker, op. cit., pp. 151–152.

Page 58: *the spiky-finned, bull-headed sculpions* – *Cottus pollux*, the Japanese fluvial sculpion or sculpin.

Page 58: *'We had so much from the river'* – quoted in Masaki Ikegami, *Ano toki, Okawa shogakko de nani ga okita noka* ['What happened that day at Okawa Primary School?'] (Tokyo, 2012), p.25.

Page 58: *Three hundred and ninety-three people lived in Kamaya* – Ikegami, op. cit., p.23.

The Old and the Young

Page 72: *one of the disaster's oldest victims* – Remarkably, Shimokawara was probably not the very oldest person to die in the tsunami. According to the Ministry of Health, Labour and Welfare, op. cit., twenty-five of those confirmed dead were 100 or over, three of them men, and 22 of them women.

Page 75: *Fifty-four per cent per cent of those who perished were 65 or older* – Ministry of Health, Labour and Welfare, 'Jinko dotai tokei kara mita Higashi Nihon daishinsai ni yoru shibo no jokyo ni tsuite' ['On mortality caused by the Great East Japan Disaster based on demographic statistics'] (Tokyo, 2011) at http://www.mhlw.go.jp/toukei/saikin/hw/jinkou/kakutei11/dl/14_x34.pdf, accessed March

2017. People of 75 and older made up a third of the dead; a man in his forties was more than twice as likely to have perished as one in his twenties.

Page 75: *In the Indian Ocean tsunami that struck Indonesia* – Richard Lloyd Parry, 'The town left without women', *The Times*, 12 January 2005.

Page 75: *Out of the 18,500 dead and missing, only 351 – fewer than one in fifty – were schoolchildren* – 'Over 110 schoolchildren die or go missing in tsunami after being picked up by parents', *Mainichi Daily News*, 12 August 2011.

Page 77: *a man named Teruyuki Kashiba* – I made repeated requests to speak to Mr Kashiba, but received no response.

Explanations

Page 80: 'Good evening to you all,' he croaked – Gakko Kyoiku-Ka, Ishinomaki-shi kyoiku iinkai jimukyoku, 'Kaigi-roku', Okawa shougakko hogosha setsumeikai [School Education Section, Secretariat of Ishinomaki City Board of Education, 'Proceedings of Meeting', in 'Explanatory Meeting for the Parents of Okawa Primary School'], 9 April 2011.

Page 83: *He rewrote the plan to require escape up a steep hill* – information from Katsura Sato.

Page 88: *Tricky old bastard.* – In Japanese, *Tanuki oyaji*: literally, 'father raccoon dog' – the raccoon dog being proverbially unreliable and deceitful.

Ghosts

Page 96: *There are no eyes, no ears, no nose, no tongue* – This is my adaptation of several translations of the Heart Sutra to be found on DharmaNet, at http://www.dharmanet.org/HeartSutra. htm, accessed March 2017.

Page 100: *academics at Tohoku University began to catalogue the stories* – see Hara Takahashi, 'The Ghosts of the Tsunami Dead and *Kokoro no kea* in Japan's Religious Landscape', *Journal of Religion in Japan* 5 (2016), pp. 176–198.

Page 101: *the true faith of Japan: the cult of the ancestors* – my account of the cult of the ancestors owes much to Robert J. Smith, *Ancestor Worship in Contemporary Japan* Stanford UP, (California, 1974).

Page 101: *'The dead are not as dead there as they are in our own society'* – Herbert Ooms, review of Smith, op.cit., *Japanese Journal of Religious Studies* 2/4 (1975).

What It's All About

Page 109: *The water had reached a height of thirty-five metres here* – Figures for the height of the tsunami are taken from Tsuyoshi Haraguchi and Akira Iwamatsu, *Higashi Nihon Daishinsai Tsunami Shosai Chizu/Detailed Maps of the Impacts of the 2011 Japan Tsunami* (bilingual, Tokyo, 2011).

Part 3: What Happened at Okawa

My account of the events at Okawa Primary School on 11 March draws on multiple sources, including Ikegami, op. cit.; author interviews with Toshinobu Oikawa, and Tetsuya and Hideaki Tadano; Japanese television interviews with Tetsuya Tadano, in the personal collection of Hideaki Tadano; official documents of Ishinomaki city; the final report of the Okawa Primary School Incident Verification Committee; summary documents supplied by Sayomi and Takahiro Shito; and documents submitted to Sendai District Court by Kazuhiro Yoshioka.

The Last Hour of the Old World

Page 119: *the Okawa school bus was waiting in the car park –* *Kahoku Shinpo* [newspaper], 'Gakko mae ni basu taiki' ['Bus was waiting in front of school'], 8 September 2011.

Page 119: *'It was shaking very slowly from side to side'–* BBC2, 'Children of the Tsunami', broadcast 1 March 2012.

Page 120: *the city authorities would compile a minute-by-minute log of the events of that afternoon –* Ishinomaki-shi kyoiku iinkai jimukyoku, 'Okawa shogakko tsuika kikitori chosa kiroku', Okawa shogakko kyoshokuin no goizoku-sama he no 3.11 ni kansuru kikitori-chosa no setsumeikai no kaisai ni tsuite, [Secretariat of Ishinomaki City Board of Education, 'Records of additional hearings concerning Okawa Primary School' in 'Concerning the holding of an explanatory meeting for the bereaved families of Okawa Primary School teachers on the hearing relating to 3.11'].

Page 123: *The Education Plan –* Ishinomaki-shi kyoiku iinkai jimukyoku, 'Heisei 22 nendo kyoiku keikaku Okawa shogakko (bassui)' [Secretariat of Ishinomaki City Board of Education, 'Fiscal Year 2010 Education Plan Okawa Primary School (Extracts)'], p. 81, pp. 145–146.

Page 125: *'I kept looking at the cars arriving and wondering, "Is Mum going to come?"'* – BBC2, 'Children of the Tsunami', broadcast 1 March 2012.

Page 131: *'Manno was right next to me'* – BBC2, 'Children of the Tsunami', broadcast 1 March 2012.

Page 131: *an elderly man named Kazuo Takahashi –* Takahashi's story is told in Ikegami, op. cit., pp. 187–193.

The River of Three Crossings

Page 147: *The 118-second film* – It can be viewed at https://www.youtube.com/watch?v=DW0dqWR4S7M, accessed March 2017.

In the Web

Page 155: *Tokyo will be shaken by an earthquake powerful enough to destroy large areas of the city* – for background on the coming Tokyo earthquake, see Peter Hadfield, *Sixty Seconds That Will Change the World* (London, 1991), and Peter Popham, *Tokyo: The City at the End of the World* (Tokyo, 1985).

Page 154: *Seismologists point out that it is not, in fact, as simple as this* – Rather than committing themselves to predictions, seismologists offer probabilities. A study by the Earthquake Research Institute of Tokyo University in 2012 calculated that there is a 70 per cent chance that Tokyo will be struck by an earthquake of magnitude 7 or higher by 2042. 'Researchers now predict 70 percent chance of major Tokyo quake within 30 years', *Mainichi Shimbun*, 25 May 2012.

Page 155: *an earthquake under Tokyo could kill as many as 13,000 people* – Richard Lloyd Parry, 'Quake experts shake Tokyo with forecast of 13,000 dead', *The Times*, 15 December 2004.

Page 155: *a tremor originating in one fault sets off earthquakes in two more* – Richard Lloyd Parry, 'Japanese make plans to survive overdue treble quake', *The Times*, 13 September 2010.

Page 155: *an earthquake and tsunami originating in the Nankai Trough* – Richard Lloyd Parry, 'Million victims from next tsunami, Japan disaster experts warn', *Times Online*, 31 August 2012, at http://www.thetimes.co.uk/article/million-victims-from-next-tsunami-japan-disaster-experts-warn-gc3tx7vpw8s.

Page 156: *only a tiny proportion of the victims was killed by the earthquake itself* – The *Kahoku Shinpo* newspaper tallied 90 people who were killed by the earthquake, rather than the tsunami. It is impossible to know exactly how many people died in collapsing houses, which were then inundated by the wave, but the overall number must be relatively low. 'Daishinsai – yure no gisei 90 nin cho' ['Great disaster – there were more than 90 victims from the earthquake'], *Kahoku Shinpo*, 17 May 2013.

Page 157: *'Why does it not upset people more ...?'* – Popham, op. cit., p. 28.

Page 158: *'Far from being dull to the dangers ...'* – Popham, op. cit., pp. 28–29 and p. 27.

Page 158: *'Now I will tell how Octavia, the spider-web city, is made ...'* – Italo Calvino, *Invisible Cities*, tr. William Weaver (London, 1974 [1972]), p.67.

What Use Is the Truth?

Page 164: *Kashiba claimed that immediately after the disaster* – Ikegami. op. cit., pp. 91–92.

Page 166: *'If it was such a big a quake that so many trees fell down ...'* – Ikegami, op. cit., p.89.

Page 167: *'He wore a check suit ...'* – Ikegami, op. cit., p. 211.

Page 167: *Endo wrote two letters* – Ishinomaki-shi kyoiku iinkai jimukyoku, '2011-nen 6-gatsu 3-nichi zuke, Endo Junji kyoyu kara no Kashiba kocho ate FAX', Okawa shogakko kyoshokuin no goizoku-sama he no 3.11 ni kansuru kikitori-chosa no setsumeikai no kaisai ni tsuite, [Secretariat of Ishinomaki City Board of Education, 'FAX from teacher Junji Endo to headmaster Kashiba dated 3 June 2011' in 'Concerning the holding of an explanatory meeting for the bereaved families of Okawa Primary School teachers on the hearing relating to 3.11'].

Page 168: *The men of the Ishinomaki city government were not villains* – this section draws on Ikegami, op. cit., pp. 113–127.

Page 170: *a signed statement of apology addressed to the parents* – Ishinomaki-shi kyoiku iinkai jimukyoku, 'Kashiba kocho shazai-bun', Okawa shogakko kyoshokuin no goizoku-sama he no 3.11 ni kansuru kikitori-chosa no setsumeikai no kaisai ni tsuite [Secretariat of Ishinomaki City Board of Education, 'Letter of Apology by Headmaster Kashiba' in 'Concerning the holding of an explanatory meeting for the bereaved families of Okawa Primary School teachers on the hearing relating to 3.11'].

Page 172: *Its findings were published in a 200-page report* – Okawa Primary School Incident Verification Committee, 'Okawa shogakko jiko kensho hokoku-sho' [Okawa Primary School Incident Verification Report], (Tokyo, 2014), at http://www.mext. go.jp/b_menu/shingi/chukyo/chukyo5/012/gijiroku/__icsFiles/ afieldfile/2014/08/07/1350542_01.pdf, accessed March 2017. See also *Mainichi Shinbun*, 'Report on tsunami-hit school should be used as disaster-prevention textbook', 28 February 2014.

Page 172: *The committee was funded by the city at a cost of ¥57 million (£390,000)* – 'Okawasho kensho-i saishu hokokushoan ni rakutan suru izoku' ['Bereaved families disappointed at the final report of the Okawa Primary Verification Committee'], *Shukan Diamondo* (Weekly Diamond), 22 January 2014.

Page 173: *Shigemi Kato … was promoted* – Ikegami, op. cit., p.112.

The Tsunami Is Not Water

Page 177: *'The Japanese people rose from the ashes …'* – Naoto Kan, 'Japan's road to recovery and rebirth', *International Herald Tribune*, 16 April 2011.

Page 184: *'The children were murdered by an invisible monster …* *It has no human warmth.'* – Ikegami, op. cit., p. 20. The rest of the quotations in this passage are from my interviews with Sayomi and Takahiro Shito.

Predestination

Page 195: *she was evolving into what Japanese call* hotoke-sama – for more on the *hotoke-sama*, see Smith, op. cit., pp. 50–56.

There May Be Gaps in Memory

Page 209: *the symbolic ruins* – Richard Lloyd Parry, 'Tsunami survivors face dilemma over its haunting ruins', *The Times*, 24 August 2012; Eugene Hoshiko, 'Legacies of a disaster dot Japan's tsunami coast', Associated Press, 10 March 2016; 'Residents divided over preservation of remains 5 years after disaster', Kyodo News, 10 March 2016.

Page 212: *'The Atomic Bomb Dome in Hiroshima was preserved …'* – 'Alumni of tsunami-devastated Miyagi school ask for support to preserve building', *Mainichi Shimbun*, 5 December 2014.

Page 212: *Tetsuya spoke at a symposium at Meiji University* – recording in the collection of Hideaki Tadano.

Consolation for the Spirits

Page 227: *the story of a man named Fukuji* – Kunio Yanagita, *The Legends of Tono*, tr. Ronald A. Morse (Lanham, 2008 [1910]), pp. 58–59.

Save Don't Fall to Sea

Page 234: *None of the towns destroyed by the wave had been rebuilt* – Zoning regulations were introduced which banned the construction of residential property in areas inundated by the wave. Businesses could still operate there, but homes were to be relocated inland, or to higher ground.

Page 236: *nothing that mattered would be significantly changed* – This is not to say that the actions of the education board are to be excused. Masaki Ikegami's trenchant conclusion is worth quoting at length: 'What the City Board of Education should have done from the beginning was to listen thoroughly and carefully to the parties involved, reliably document and record everything, disclose information obtained in the investigation to the bereaved families, ... verify the facts one by one, and investigate the truth.

'Furthermore, they should sincerely apologise for sacrificing the lives of children under the management of the school, and discuss punishment of officials who have been neglectful in their responses and oversight.

'On top of that, they should make public the lessons learned from the worst such accident in history to parties such as prefectural boards of education and the Ministry of Education, and create the opportunity to reconsider fundamentally disaster management in Japan. These actions should be performed with speed, and shared with the bereaved families to the greatest extent possible.

'By acting in such a lackadaisical and untransparent manner, the City Board of Education has made the problem worse.' Ikegami, op. cit., p.83.

Page 238: *But there could hardly have been less sense of triumph* – It was further undermined a few days later, when the defendants announced that they would appeal against the verdict in the High Court. The plaintiffs responded by making an appeal of their own, on the grounds that the damages awarded were inadequate. A verdict is expected in 2018.

Page 244: *Masaru knew this* – Masaru Naganuma declined to speak to me. This account is based on conversations with Naomi Hiratsuka and Miho Suzuki.

Page 249: *A friend of Kaneta, who was present at one of the exorcisms* – The religious studies scholar, Hara Takahashi, who corroborated Kaneta's account.

INDEX

Index